MW01193572

Americans and Queen Marie of Romania

A Selection of Documents

Americans and
Queen Marie of Romania

A Selection of Documents

Edited by Diana Fotescu

The Center for Romanian Studies
Iași ◆ Oxford ◆ Portland
1998

Published in Romania by

THE CENTER FOR ROMANIAN STUDIES
The Foundation for Romanian Culture and Studies
Oficiul Poştal I, Căsuţa Poştală 108
Str. Poligon nr. 11a
6600 Iaşi, Romania
www.romanianstudies.ro

Published in Great Britain by

THE CENTER FOR ROMANIAN STUDIES
c/o Drake International Services
Market House
Market Place
Deddington
Oxford OX15 0SE
Great Britain

Published in the United States of America by

THE CENTER FOR ROMANIAN STUDIES
c/o International Specialized Book Services
5804 N.E. Hassalo St.
Portland, Oregon 97213, USA
www.isbs.com

National Library of Romania Cataloging-in-Publication Data

MARIA, Queen of Romania
Americans and Queen Marie of Romania: A Selection of Documents / Edited
by Diana Fotescu. Iaşi, Oxford, Portland: The Center for Romanian Studies,
1998. 284 pp., illus., 22 cm.
Index
ISBN 973-98391-0-X

I. Huntington, George
II. Harris, Ray Baker
III. Fotescu, Diana (ed.)

859.0-6=20

Table of Contents

Introduction

This selection of documents, illustrating contacts between Americans and Queen Marie of Romania, helps to reveal unique aspects of the life and personality of this remarkable monarch, admired not only in Romania, but throughout the world. This collection is comprised of three parts. The first selection is the diary of George Huntington, an American professor who visited Queen Marie, together with his family, in 1925. The second is a text compiled by the British writer Hector Bolitho, presenting the correspondence between Queen Marie and an American admirer, Ray Baker Harris. This text contains extensive quotes from the Queen's letters to the young American. The final section is a collection of letters written by Ray Baker Harris to the Queen.

Dr. George Huntington was born on 12 April 1878 in Gorham, Maine, in the United States, and was 3 years younger than Queen Marie. A New Englander of modest means, he was the son of a Congregational minister, dedicated to a life of service. Huntington earned degrees in Education and Divinity at William College and Union Theological Seminary and spent the next thirty-eight years (1900-1937) teaching at Robert College — America's oldest such school outside the United States — in Istanbul.

During his tenure at Robert College, he held posts of professor, principal of the College, and vice-president. In 1916 he married Elizabeth W. Dodge, daughter of C.H. Dodge, vice-president of Phepls Dodge and President of the Board of Trustees of Robert College. Her grandfather was a major benefactor of Robert College and her great-grandfather was a founder of the American University in Beirut. The Huntingtons were continual anonymous benefactors of the college and often supplemented scholarship funds with their own financial resources. He continued his work on behalf of the college even after a polio attack in 1934, before retiring in 1938. He died 2 August 1953 in Portland, Maine.

George Huntington kept a special diary during his visit to Cotroceni Palace in Bucharest in 1925. This diary is found in the archives of Kent State University, in the special collection "Queen Marie," donated to the University archives by Ray Baker Harris. It discusses Professor Huntington's visit to Romania between 29 January-10 February 1925. Huntington described Bucharest, but principally the Cotroceni Palace, the official residence of King Ferdinand and Queen Marie, where the guests were received. Touched by the beauty of the palace, George Huntington, "the man with the notebook," as Queen's Marie lady-in-waiting, Adela Cantemir, referred to him,[1] described each and every room — the hall, the dining room with King Arthur's round table, the library of King Ferdinand, the Norwegian room, the bedroom of the Queen, the royal suites on the second floor of the palace, etc.

Huntington's method for keeping his diary was to take notes, compile, and edit them each evening, and put it all together with additional material upon his return to Istanbul. As a result, his diary combines on-the-spot reactions and later reflections.

In the pages of his diary, notes regarding meetings with several prominent personalities (Prime Minister Ionel Brătianu, Minister of Finance Vintilă Brătianu — whose name is misspelled in the text, Vitella — King George of Greece and his wife Queen Elisabeth, Queen Marie's sister, the Grand Duchess Kyril, with the Princess Ileana and the Princes Carol and Mihai, and Jay, Palmer, and McAndrews, etc., from the American Legation in Bucharest) intermingle with observations about Queen Marie's family. The diary also recounts major historical events such as Romania's entry into the war on the side of the Entente on 14 August 1916, the difficult years of war, the circumstances in which the Romanian national treasure was lost in Moscow — where the Bolsheviks had taken over the power and the Romanovs had been overthrown. Following his conversation with King George of Greece, Huntington made notes on the political situation of Greece. Two residences of the Romanian sovereigns, Copăceni and Scoroviște, are also described in detail.

The hosts, King Ferdinand and Queen Marie, simply charmed the American guests; Huntington confessed in his diary "If you read between the lines, you will see that I have frankly lost my heart to the Queen, and I am not ashamed to say so."

---

[1] see Glee Wilson "The Diary of George Huntington's Visit with Queen Marie at Cotroceni" in *Colocviul Româno-American "Cotrocenii în Istorie, iulie, 1992,"* București, 1993.

Ray Baker Harris was born in the Philippine Islands in 1907, where his father was working to build the first railway in that country. Educated at Stanford University in California, he worked for a time as an editor in New York, and later as a librarian at the Library of Congress in Washington D.C.

Drawn by the personality of Queen Marie, known throughout the world especially for her political-diplomatic or charitable efforts during the First World War, Ray Baker Harris wrote an impressive number of letters to the Queen, beginning in 1933 until her death in the summer of 1938. His letters can be found in the National Central Archives of Romania (casa regală, regina Maria, corespondență). They round off the image of the special friendship between a Queen and a clerk at the Library of Congress who never met. The confessions, advice, appreciation of certain personalities, of European royal families, or even works published at the time form the subject of the letters. Despite the great distance, the Queen and Ray Baker Harris were very close in their ideas and thoughts. In December 1933, Ray Harris wrote to the Queen: "I have never written to any other sovereign, except the contacts I have had with several of the Presidents of my own country... The great distance between a Queen and an American boy could be, in a way, bridged by my respect and admiration." Harris was impressed by "the combination of Great Sorrow and Great Happiness which has been in your majesty's life experience." This kind of epistolary friendship, Ray Harris admitted, made him "less dependent upon my immediate material world." Because of his admiration for the Queen, Ray Baker Harris started to collect books or articles about Romania, which he mentioned even in his letters.

This selection of his letters to Queen Marie not only reveals personal aspects of their friendship, but also reconstitutes the atmosphere of the epoch and the changes taking place in the political and cultural fields. This is a unique way to compile the atmosphere of the time and the image of certain personalities.

The letters of Queen Marie to Ray Baker Harris throw additional light on the relationship between the sovereign and her American friend. The British writer Hector Bolitho, an admirer of Queen Marie, made a contribution to the archives donated by Ray Baker Harris to Kent State University in Ohio with a manuscript presenting the Queen's correspondence with Ray Baker Harris.

Aware of the remarkable qualities of the Queen, Bolitho joined Ray Harris in his efforts to make information about her available to the public. He studied the letters of the Queen to several of her friends, convinced that they could present a new dimension of her image. He found letters of the Queen to Leila Milne in Austria and sent them to Ray Harris to include in the archives. Among Bolitho's most important published works are *Roumania under King Carol* (London, 1939), *Further Letter of Queen Victoria from the Archives of the House of Brandenburg-Prussia* (London, 1939), *Letters of Queen Victoria: From the Archives of the House of Brandenburg-Prussia* (Yale University Press, 1938).

These documents represent a significant source of information, helping to round off the image of Marie, Queen of Romania. They also emphasize the admiration of the contemporaries for a Queen who had, in her own lifetime, become a legend, a myth, and a symbol.

I would like to thank the archives of Kent State University in Ohio and the National Central Archives of Romania in Bucharest for facilitating my research and providing me with the materials to compile this collection.

Diana Fotescu

Americans and Queen Marie of Romania:
A Selection of Documents

The Diary of George Huntington's Visit with Queen Marie at Cotroceni Palace, Bucharest, 1925

Wednesday, January 28

We left the house at 9 a.m., getting a very comfortable start. Went on board the Roumanian steamer "Principessa Maria" before 10:00, having secured the aid of a very friendly young tout (Ahmet Hamdi, short and round, a Jew or Deurmeh (?), who put all our luggage through the Custom House with no trouble whatsoever.

The police control of passports took a long time and we did not get away from the quai until after 12 o'clock. It was a glorious day and we enjoyed the sail up the Bosphorus and out through the very picturesque mouth into the Black Sea. He had said nothing to the College community about the goal of our journey to Bucharest, although of course I had explained to Dr. Gates as soon as we accepted Her Majesty's invitation, and had told Elsie when I wrote to the family about it. We had a very quiet sea and enjoyed sitting and walking on the upper deck.

Thursday, January 29

The boat reached Constanţa at 5 a.m., when the steward roused us in order to be ready for the train at 6:40. There was a very minute examination of our luggage at the Customs, and they took our passports from us, saying we should receive them in Bucharest, by which we understood that the conductor on the train would give them to us when we reached the station, a method common in these days in Europe.

I may add here that later it turned out that the passports were not on the train with us and were not sent to Bucharest for some days. We had to appeal to the Marshall of the Palace who evidently had some difficulty in finding them in the hands of the police. Mr. Palmer, the American Consul at Bucharest tells me this in a constant occurrence although the Roumanian police rules may be that the passports must be put on to the train by which the passengers leave Constanţa for Bucharest. People passing through the country have been held up for several days because of the carelessness of the police.

This is simply one illustration, which could be multiplied 100-fold, of the present-day slipshod methods existing in Roumania. The rules on paper may be all right, but there is an endless amount of red tape and of utter neglect of duty among the common officials, and this makes life for the foreigner in Roumania, be he tourist or resident, a series of petty vexations which finally become very trying to the resident. It shows how utterly oriental the average Roumanian is beneath the skin, in spite of Western, and specially Parisian, veneer which has been spread over the life of the larger towns and cities.

Our train did not actually leave Constanţa until 7:40, an hour late. We crossed the huge bridges over the two branches of the Danube at Cernavodă, some two hours later. The river with its cakes of floating ice was more blue and beautiful than I ever saw it, for usually the Danube is the acme of brown mud. As we got away from the warning effect of the Black Sea the amount of snow on the ground increased until the wide bare fields were practically covered with six or eight inches. It was a bright clear day, and I may say here that absolutely every one of our days of our whole trip was similar, — and our friends at Constantinople gave the same report for that region. At Bucharest each night there was a heavy frost, and sometimes the thermometer must have dropped to at least 20 deg. as the ground stayed frozen in the shadows all day long.

Our train was held up by a derailment ahead of us so that we did not reach Bucharest until after three. Fortunately there was a dining car so we had a good luncheon.

We had wondered a good deal how we would be met at Bucharest. As I stepped off the train, in the station, a young man in a blue uniform trimmed with gold embroidery in which a crown was woven, stepped up to me and said in Roumanian, "Are you for the Palace?" I said we were and he ran off, coming back with a very gracious lady dressed in black, who introduced herself as a lady-in-waiting of Her Majesty Queen Marie. She had various attendants with her in whose hands we left everything.

It did not taken us long to discover that the presence of that blue uniform with gold trimming embroidered with a crown was a magic open sesame wherever we went. As Theron and I drove in the palace car, with a crown on it in place of a number, we were constantly saluted in the streets of Bucharest until it was positively embarrassing. We could not draw up in front of a shop without crowds stopping around the car. When we were with Her Majesty, the Queen, hundreds of people would gather on the sidewalk, and the two footmen who always accompanied her car and ours, always had to clear the way for the party to pass through. The people were always good natured and ready to fall back, but they were also curious to see Her Majesty, and perhaps her guests. I learned to march along without looking to right to left, as though it were all the customary thing. I learned also to expect and to demand every consideration and it was always given cheerfully and politely. Her Majesty said that if ever people showed any disposition to the rude — and that was rare — she took special pains to smile and bow in the most affable and friendly fashion, upon which the rudeness would melt away and smiles and politeness take its place. She is a clever person to handle a crowd.

It was really great fun, and vastly interesting, to be able to watch all the ways of royalty, and of the people with royalty from the standpoint of a person wholly detached, and caring nothing for their attitude toward himself.

Our lady-in-waiting turned out to be Mme. Procopiu, a lady of perhaps 55, speaking excellent English, very charming and gracious and well-read and thoroughly conversant with the best that Europe has to offer. The name will appear frequently later. Those who know Greek will recognize in her name a vestige of the old days when more than half of the leading families of Roumania were Greeks from Constantinople, possessing wealth and influence with the Turkish rulers, and therefore having been given great estates in the outlying provinces. There were two types of landed gentry in Roumania in bygone centuries, one being the boyards, many of whom were of Roumanian blood but having intermarried with Byzantine Greeks and claiming in many cases direct descent from Byzantine emperors; and the second class being pure Greek land holders who had come into power under the Turks because of their clever wits. Today both classes most haughtily claim to be pure Roumanian, and have very little to say about the Greek blood in their veins, although very proud of the ancient Byzantine connections.

Mme. Procopiu, Cornelia, and Elizabeth went in one car, and Theron and I followed. We discovered that Her Majesty had assigned to us four a motor of our own with a footman always ready to serve us.

King Ferdinand and Queen Marie now live in the Cotroceni Palace, which is on outskirts of the city toward the west and at least three or four miles from the business center. The palace is built on a little hill, a very rare article in the vicinity of Bucharest which is as flat as a floor, so that one wonders why the whole town is not flooded in any heavy rain. Two hundred years ago this whole hill and the land about it was a dense forest. One day a certain Prince Cantacuzino (this is one of the most famous ancient Roumanian-Byzantine families) was pursued by his enemies and hid in a cave in this forest. After he had escaped, in memory of his deliverance, he founded a monastery on this knoll in the forest and built a very attractive church of modest size upon the site of the old cave, giving it the name of Cotroceni, which is a word derived from a root meaning "having been hidden."

A cluster of buildings grew up about the church. After the coming of King Charles and Queen Elizabeth (Carmen Sylva), they were in search of a location for a palace near Bucharest but not cramped in the midst of the noise of the city like the original royal palace. They were charmed by the old monastery and the beautiful forest about it, and the government and church allowed them to have the property provided that the church were kept up. The result has been that bit by bit a really beautiful and extensive palace has been constructed in the form of a quadrangle, having the pretty old church in its center. Fine old trees are scattered about the inner courtyard around the church, and of course in summer time there are beautiful flowers everywhere. The forest surrounds the palace on three sides to the north, east, and south, and long drives wind in form the main entrance which is a quarter of a mile from the palace itself. It must be an enchanting place in summer, and we enjoyed wandering about it on the snow.

The more recent parts of the palace have been built in the Roumanian style, the chief feature of which is arcades with low, broad round arches (Romanesque in style), resting on short thick stone pillars sometimes smooth and sometimes fluted. The effect is very pretty. Queen Marie has made a special study of old Roumanian buildings, and since she became Queen in 1914 has introduced several features within and without in the Byzantine style as it grew up in Roumania, with local modifications. For instance, a wing has been thrown out to the north of the main quadrangle, the lower floor of which is built in style of a Roumanian monastery church, with broad round arches, low domes and stems copings about windows carved with Byzantine tracery. All the decorations in this dining room, with its ante-room, are genuine old Byzantine objects. For example, across the north end of the dining room is a genuine old iconostasis, that is, the screen between the nave and the apse of an orthodox church on

Cotroceni Palace — wing built in the neo-Romanian style.

which icons are hung or pictures of the saints painted. The interior walls are color-washed a cream white over rough plaster just as in a primitive church, so that the old crosses, icons, carved screens etc., stand out in beautiful simplicity. The whole thing is beautifully worked out and is an admirable illustration of the restrained artistic taste of Queen Marie. She has done a great deal in Roumania to introduce the old Roumanian-Byzantine style and they are beginning to replace their ugly florid villas and palaces, which were based on the ugly French ideas of fifty to one hundred years ago, by delightful houses with plain surfaces and carved stone in the Byzantine style. The house of a certain lawyer, just outside the main entrance to Cotroceni is a good example.

Our apartments were in the northwest wing. Theron and Cornelia happened to be on the main floor, and Elizabeth and I above them. Each of us four had for himself a large sitting room, bedroom, dressing room and bath, — each being a full apartment quite good enough for two persons. Mme. Procopiu took us first to Cornelia's apartment, and then came upstairs to ours. As we walked down the corridor with her toward our apartment she said, "Her Majesty hopes to see you as soon as you can come conveniently to her." It was then about half past three and we expressed some surprise, as we supposed the Queen would not see us until perhaps tea time, but Mme. Procopiu went on, "Do not trouble to change your clothes; just freshen yourselves and come with me now," and hardly had she uttered these words when a tall, gracious English lady came out of the door of Elizabeth's apartment, and we instantly recognized, from her pictures, the Queen.

We were in our street clothes, and dirty from a dusty train ride, and certainly never dreamed of meeting Her Majesty for the first time in a corridor! She came directly to us and greeted us as simply and warmly as though we had been old and intimate friends. I shall have to own that I was really embarrassed and did not know what to do. We managed to get through it, and realized afterward that it was wholly the unaffected simplicity of Her Majesty which made the situation so natural and so easy. She asked about our journey and then said, "I have been putting the finishing touches to your rooms, as I always do for all my guests, arranging the flowers etc." She walked back with Elizabeth into Elizabeth's apartment, and Mme. Procopiu came with me to show me mine, the two apartments being adjacent. As Her Majesty came out of Elizabeth's apartment she stopped at the door of my sitting room. I went to her and said, "Your Majesty took us by surprise. I never dreamed of meeting you for the first time in the corridor." She laughed and said, "I like to do things that way, and I love to welcome my guests personally as soon as they arrive." Then she walked into the sitting room and looked about and said, "I hope you will find everything comfortable here. You and Mrs. Huntington have the apartments which the King and Queen of Serbia occupy when they visit me, so you will be writing at the King and Queen's desk." Then she added, "We will have tea in the Studio together at five o'clock, and Mme. Procopiu will come to bring you to me then."

A pleasant young fellow, of Roumanian origin but born in Transylvania under Hungarian rule, was assigned to Elizabeth and me as valet. He spoke enough German so we could get along with him, and we found later he was one of the many footmen who serve at luncheon, dinner, etc. Cornelia and Theron had as their valet the footman who always accompanied our car. He spoke nothing but Roumanian so that we had much fun with him making him understand. Our chauffeur knew a little German, but generally Mlle. Cantemir, one of the lesser ladies-in-waiting, who resided in the palace, served as our interpreter. In fact her room was on our corridor, and she told us at the beginning she was at our service all the time. She appeared to be the only active lady-in-waiting who lived at the palace; the others are all fashionable ladies of the town who have their own homes and give one or two fixed days per week to Her Majesty. It is their business to arrange interviews, plan for luncheons and dinners, concerts and all sorts of social engagements, and act as hostesses to Her Majesty's guests. They were all unfailing in their kind attentions to us, and never once was their the remotest suggestion that we were any less welcome guests, or to be any less politely treated than, for example, the King and Queen of Serbia.

The other ladies-in-waiting of whom we saw much were Mme. Lahovary, who went about with us a good deal, Mme. Mavrodis, who was quite elderly and had been lady-in-waiting to Queen Carmen Sylva, and Mme. Perdicari. The latter was to me, intellectually, the most interesting of the group. She was of the type whom Father would have greatly enjoyed, with keen literary appreciation, broad human sympathies, and active in all sorts of philanthropies. Her father was a Frenchman named Charles Davila, who had to leave France in the middle of the 10th century on account of his liberal tendencies. He was educated as a physician, and began to practice in Roumania when it was nothing but a part of old Turkey. He soon came into prominence as a man of extraordinary ability both as a physician and as an organizer, and also as a man of unusual human sympathies. He devoted his life to unselfish philanthropy and scientific work, and the position he came to occupy in Roumania is well illustrated by the fact that in front of the new building of the Medical Faculty his statue has been erected, with a long inscription which Elizabeth and I read one day, describing the wonderfully varied work which he did. Evidently this daughter was a true chip off the old block, and has found joy throughout her life in following her beloved father.

It was she who took Elizabeth to visit the orphanage founded by her father. I went to see it later with the Mayor of Bucharest, as will appear in the diary of Monday, February 9th. It is an interesting side light on the Queen that she has chosen for her ladies-in-waiting women not only of social position but of real culture and character.

George Sirbo of Timişoara, our valet, unpacked and put away our things with precise care. I was much amused at his modest question as soon as we were left alone in our apartments, viz. "Are you only four persons? Is there not a fifth person?" Then hesitatingly, "Is there any femme de chambre?" by which he meant lady's maid. I laughed and told him we were not of the kind who travel with ladies' maids, at which he very politely said "What can I do to help you?" and I replied, "You can unpack my trunk and box and put the things away," which he did most admirably. He was always most polite and attentive and friendly. I should like to import him as head butler for my own home.

We went to Tea at five in the Studio, which is a beautiful large room in the style of a better class Norwegian peasant house, occupying the area above the Byzantine dining room which I described above. It is very high and opens directly to the roof. All the woodwork is very plain pine, stained almost black as in a smoke-stained peasant's home, and the plaster between the criss-cross beams is rough and color-washed in a soft cream. A dark wooden stairway rises on the south side opposite the huge fireplace and leads into a gallery which looks

The Queen's Norwegian Studio

down upon the room, where writing tables and bookshelves are gathered in attractive nooks. Heavy chairs in beautiful tapestry of soft old blues, pinks, and grays — characteristic colors of Her Majesty — are drawn up artistically on the left and in front of the huge fireplace, on the right being a large divan covered with two magnificent tiger skins, the heads serving as footstools. In the center of this group of chairs in front of the fireplace is a beautiful old Spanish wooden tabouret, not more than 18 in. high, but at least 7ft. in diameter, 8-sided, studded with polished brass nails, and carved ornaments; in the center is an opening over 2 ft. in diameter into which a brass bowl fits. The bowl was always filled with the choicest of flowers, these being for several days a mass of beautiful primroses planted in a low earthen jar that fitted the brass bowl. For tea a special low table has been made in two sections, which fits directly over this Spanish tabouret, but high enough so as not to disturb anything on the tabouret, and nine or ten feet wide. Her Majesty's special chair is at the left of the fireplace as one faces it, and she pours tea with her own hand.

King George of Greece, eldest son of King Constantine, and Queen Elizabeth, his wife, the eldest daughter of Queen Marie, were present at Tea. I happened to sit beside Queen Elizabeth on the tiger skin couch. She was a little girl of nine, with flowing golden hair, when I used to see riding her pony with her Uncle, King Charles, in the park at Sinaia in 1903. She used to wear a delightful little red jacket which quite marked her in any company of riders. As I sat beside her at Tea I told her about it and she warmed up over her childhood life in Sinaia. In fact all my various visits at Sinaia proved a capital starting point for many conversations, for most people were surprised that an American should know it so well, and should have tramped over the mountains there even more extensively than the vast majority of Roumanians.

Queen Elizabeth is naturally shy, and her unhappy experience in Greece has darkened the face of the world for her so that she is the least easy to approach of all the family group at Bucharest. In the end, however, she warmed to us very graciously. On our last day, after saying good-bye to the Queen, we scampered over to the apartments of George and Elizabeth and said good-by like old chums. Queen Elizabeth brought out two photographs of herself for Cornelia and Elizabeth.

I liked King George from the start. He is about 34 years old, and married Elizabeth of Roumania three or four years ago. He has never abdicated from the Greek throne. He merely retired at the request of the revolutionary military government on the ground that they claimed they could settle the future government of the country more satisfactorily if he were not present in the country. It is perfectly clear from all his conversations that he hopes and expects to go back as king. (I am giving his opinion, not my own, in all this question.) He talked with me very frankly about the situation in Greece, and one night in his apartment he brought me the *New York Times Current History* for December, 1924, open at an article by Mr. Polyzoides, editor of the Greek newspaper *Atlantis*, published in New York City, asking me if I had read it, and saying that he considered it a very good statement of the facts of the last two years in Greece. I sat at his desk that very evening, and in the intervals of music and talk skipped through it.

The point of it is that the revolutionary government which came into existence after the Smyrna disaster represents the usurpation of authority by a military oligarchy which has never done anything in a constitutional way, and still holds the country in control by force and by fear. Some day, King George is convinced, the Greek people will return to genuine constitutional forms, and he believes that they will then want a limited constitutional monarchy of the type of England rather than a republic.

He warmed to the subject of Robert College from our first meeting, praising its work and its students, and expressing again and again his desire for a similar institution in Athens. In fact, we often reverted to this subject, and it was generally introduced by him rather than by me, as of course I did not wish to worry him with it. Elizabeth spent a long time one day showing him our pictures of the College and its activities, and he asked many questions.

One morning I happened to go out to walk, and ran across him in the park. He proposed that we walk together, and brought up the subject of the religious life at Robert College, asking what our attitude was toward Protestant propaganda, and discussing the needs of religious character in the teachers if the moral influences are to be right. He is short and thickset, with a smooth face, and, according to his wife, "a beaver's profile." He is quite shortsighted and uses a monocle in his right eye for reading. He speaks English perfectly with a marked English accent, and would be taken for a pure blooded Englishman wherever he might be. He laughs heartily and loudly in a friendly, jovial way which disarms hostility. He loves dogs and the outdoor world, and played badminton at the country club almost every afternoon.

Of course, the last year has been a tremendously trying one for his wife and himself, but Queen Marie said that King George was much quieter and more self-contained and less nervous than during the first few months of his stay with her. She evidently thinks a great deal of him, and it was clear that he and his wife were given every possible consideration at the Roumanian court, although the exigencies of international relationships demand that the Roumanian government should recognize the present Greek regime and its diplomatic representative at Bucharest.

This first Tea disarmed all our anxieties, and any dread we might have had as to how our visit at the court would be received by the Queen and by all others. Our little gathering around the fireplace was as spontaneous and natural as though we were in our own home. After tea, conversation turned on the objects of art in the room with every one of which Her Majesty is perfectly familiar. This proved an endless topic of conversation and introduced a vast number of other subjects as many objects are gifts from persons to whose story we would turn in the conversation. All came from countries about which there were all sorts of things to talk.

Her Majesty's taste runs toward pottery. Practically every room in the house has one or more of the beautiful Persian jars decorated in soft blues or greys or dull pinks. Many of these were scattered about the Studio often with flowers, especially the prevailing primroses in shades that suited the colors of each jar. Her Majesty's eye for color is wonderful, and she has schooled herself to take in effects at a glance.

Let me record here something of her family. Her father was Prince Alfred, second son of Queen Victoria. He became Duke of Edinburgh, although he never lived there, and served for many years as Admiral in the British Navy. Marie's little girlhood was in England, but when she was nine or ten her family took up residence in Malta as her father was the Admiral in command of the Mediterranean fleet. She loves Malta, and persuaded her government to allow her to revisit it some three years ago. More than once she said that she was going to persuade her government to allow her to came to Constantinople, in which she has only spent a few hours when her yacht passed through on the way to Malta. Of course such visits as these have to be timed to suit the exigencies of diplomacy, and she frankly acknowledges that as Queen she is not a free agent, for even the most unostentatious visit which should mean for her nothing except her personal pleasure as a tourist, might be interpreted by the government of the country visited, or by some other government as a diplomatic or international move.

When she was 13 or 14 the family went back to England where she lived until she was married to Prince Ferdinand at the age of 17.

Princess Marie

Her Majesty talked to us with the most amasing confidence. In fact, I shall never put into writing many of the things she said nor repeat them to any-one until they appear some day in some published autobiography of her own. It was almost incomprehensible to us all that she could trust us suffi-ciently to talk so confidentially, and among ourselves we agreed to keep mum.

Time after time we sat down with her either to hear her read out loud from her books or from her private journal, read exactly as it was written in bygone years (she rises at 7 every morning and writes the doings and thoughts of the previous day), or talk together about her life and doings. She spent a long time one day telling us about her marriage and her transfer, at the age of 17, from the English environment, the only one she had known, to the life of Crown Princess in a little eastern country utterly unknown and undeveloped, surrounded by utter strangers. She is a woman capable of stormy passion, and she must have gone through a ter-rible experience in the first ten years of her married life. The marvel of it is that she came out so wonderfully refined and purified.

Mr. Frank Buchman said to us of her, "She is a released personality," and he was absolutely right. She has known every form of suffering and sorrow that can come to a woman. She lost her sixth child, a little boy named Mirtcho, at the age of four, in 1916, so she knows the sorrows of motherhood. Her eldest son, Crown Prince Carol, just when his country was in a state of utter humiliation at the hands of the Austrians and Ger-mans in the summer of 1918, ran away with a Roumanian girl (happily a girl of perfectly good character), without the consent of his parents or of the government, and was married to her. I can refer to the story, since it is public property and everyone talks of it. They have one child but the mar-riage has been annulled by the State, as the constitutional agreement with which the Hohenzollern line in King Charles came to the Roumanian throne was that no prince of the house should marry any Roumanian on account of the bitter family jealousies in the country. Prince Carol knew this fact perfectly when he ran away with this girl, and he did it at a time when his parents were living in exile in Iași, and nine-tenths of the country was in the hands of the Germans, and a pro-German Roumanian govern-ment was signing a most humiliating treaty of peace with their conquer-ors. Her Majesty talked with us very frankly about it, and called it a piece of young man's folly of which she said he had hardly repented. He was actually shut up for some length of time under strict confinement until the affair was tided over. I would not mention it if it were not easily to be found in many a book, but it is well known that King Ferdinand in his young manhood was far from morally straight, and had many an affair with women of every type. What a heartbreaking experience it must have been for a pure English girl of 17 to be pulled up from surroundings in which she herself had been absolutely shielded from the world, in order to be dumped down in Bucharest, one of the rottenest cities of Europe, as the wife of a man who could laught at, and participate in, the follies around him.

They were married January 10, 1893, and Carol was born October 15, 1895. As Queen Marie says now very frankly, that prompt presentation to her adopted country of an heir to the throne did a vast deal to win her public sympathy and admiration. Elizabeth was born October 11, 1894, Marie, now the Queen of Serbia, January 8, 1900; Nicholas, August 18, 1903, Ileana, (Roumanian for Helen) January 5, 1909, and Mirtcho in 1912. Queen Marie herself was born October 29, 1875, and Ferdinand and she succeeded to the throne on October 11, 1914. King Ferdinand was born August 24, 1865.

Crown Prince Carol was married to Princess Helen of Greece, March 10, 1921. If I remember rightly, King George of Greece was married to Elizabeth at the same time, or very nearly. How many queens of Europe have the daughters who themselves have become queens? Her Majesty laughs very frankly about Ileana, who is sweet sixteen in very truth, and wonders whether she is to become Queen of Bulgaria or France (!) or of England, — and who knows, for stranger things than any one of these have happened.

On Friday evening, February 6th, Prince Carol dined at the palace just after his return from London. He sat at the Queen's left and I sat at her right. In the course of the conversation he said, "I have been told that there is quite a Royalist party in France." Her Majesty looked up and called to Ileana at the opposite end of the table, "Ah, Ileana there is your chance, — Queen of France!" The whole table laughed. But again, who knows? Although of course everyone at the table knows perfectly well that the Royalist party in France is a mere handful, and probably never will be more.

Our conversation over tea with Her Majesty lasted until 7 o'clock, although the others left the Studio. No guest is free to withdraw until Her Majesty indicates that she herself is going, but of course we were only too delighted to see all that we could of her, and were only sorry when she felt obliged to go. Throughout our visit she gave us hours and hours of time with the most amazing generosity. She remembered little things that we said indicating our tastes and interests, and brought them up later in connection with books or her own stories or with objects of art about the palace or elsewhere. She is as finished and perfect a hostess as I ever met.

From left to right: Prince Carol, Mignon, Queen Marie with Nicolae, Elizabeth, and King Ferdinand in Cotroceni Palace

Watching her as I did later in large companies of people, she would move about the room, greeting each one in turn, always gracious and yet with queenly dignity and talking with each about some matter or interest which made each person feel her personal interest in him. Perhaps I might give her a little sentence which I ran across in her charming children's fairy story called *Peeping Pansy*, a mid-Victorian title, quite unworthy of a fascinating book. On page 186, someone, in speaking to Pansy, refers to an "imperial air." "What is an imperial air?" said little Pansy, aged seven. The person, probably some fairy bird in the story, and I am inclined to think Mrs. Grumps, the wise owl, replied, — "To look dignified, ladylike, and a little haughty, but at the same time, very gracious." The next day at dinner, at an opportune moment, I said to Her Majesty "I have discovered a beautiful description of Your Majesty's entrance into a reception room." She laughed, and said, "What is it?" I replied, "You will find it on page 186 of a certain book called *Peeping Pansy*," and gave her the quotation. She was immensely amused, and said, "It is not a bad description, is it?"

We dined that evening, as, in fact, every evening, in the Studio, a special table being prepared. Practically always I sat at Her Majesty's right and Theron at her left. Sometimes King George or Queen Elizabeth sat at my right, and occasionally Princess Ileana. Very rarely was there anyone outside of the royal group and we four at dinner in the evening. These were the delightful family parties which came to mean so much to us. The state luncheons were interesting and showy, but we never could have the jolly intimate group conversations that came with the cozy dinners in the Studio. It is merely the truth to say that they were just such happy family dinners as all the Dodge family might have when gathered at Riverdale, or all of us Huntingtons gathered in the old dining room at Hilton.

We spent the evening at the home of Mme. Procopiu, where some sixty society people of Bucharest were gathered to hear an excellent program of music. One player was a young Roumanian graduate of a Paris conservatory named Dumitrescu, who later came to the palace to play before Her Majesty. Of course every artist who wants to get before the public tries to secure a chance to play before royalty so as to be able to advertise the fact.

Strangely enough at Mme. Procopiu's house I met an old Robert College student, Tommy Bolton, whom I had been planning to look up. It seems that he made a very successful marriage about a year ago with a niece of Mr. Marghiloman, a well known politician and head of an old Roumanian family. Bolton was at Robert College some fifteen years ago. His father, an Englishman, physician, settled in Roumania and practiced for a while in Bucharest and later at Constanța. An older brother, Bourne, came to Robert College in the 90's, and a third brother has been settled in California for many years. We had a long and chummy talk. He seems to retain very happy and distinct memories of his R.C. life and likes to follow the course of things today. He visited Miss Hart in 1919 and dined with us one night.

This chance meeting set me in the way of getting in touch with some other students, among them his young half-brother Richard, who was at Robert College from 1910-1915. Dr. Bolton's second wife was an Italian lady who is still living in Bucharest with her own son Richard. I was Richard's guardian throughout his whole stay at Robert College, and had considerable correspondence with his mother. He is now a clerk in the accounting department of the Romano-Americana Company, Calea Victoriei 136, which is the Roumanian name of the Standard Oil Company.

Queen Marie did not attend the musical, but King George and Queen Elizabeth were there, and we got our first glimpse of what it means socially in a private home to have a king and queen present. To tell the truth the stiff and formal proceedings which seemed to be necessary in the actual room in which royalty was seated struck me as very stupid, and I was thankful that the palace atmosphere was so utterly different. Mrs. Jay, wife of Peter Augustus Jay, who has been Minister at Bucharest for four years, was present, and gave us all sorts of whispered instructions as to what was proper and what was not. I shall have to acknowledge that I lost patience with it all. Later I had quite a talk with Queen Elizabeth about such things, and realized that she desired that type of formality as much as anyone could. Perhaps it is necessary to hedge them in when they move about among ordinary people, as otherwise things would get "too familiar."

King George is very unconventional, and moved about the room chatting in a jolly way with everyone. Queen Elizabeth is more self-conscious, and told me herself she found it very difficult to talk easily with people. Absolutely no one was at liberty to leave the affair until Their Majesties departed, although I suppose if it were very urgent arrangements for quietly slipping out could be made.

Naturally, we four felt ourselves to be rather closely observed by all the guests, since we appeared as guests of Queen Marie. One could not help wondering what the people thought about these American interlopers, but all whom we met were certainly very agreeable and polite. So far as I know, Mrs. Jay was the only American present that evening. The music was long, and renewed after an interval for elaborate refreshments, so that I did not get to bed until two o'clock.

Friday, January 30th

Let me copy first what I wrote at 11.30 p.m. that evening. It is quite too late to start writing, but I must scribble a bit about today.

Again the sun has shone upon us from a radiant blue sky. Elizabeth and I had coffee in my sitting room at 9 a.m., then we settled down to read aloud a bit from Howard Walter's *Soul Surgery*, a book published in India in 1919 which I had never seen. This copy was sent to me just now from India by Frank Buchman, and chanced to arrive Tuesday evening just before we started for Bucharest. The inscription on the fly leaf is, "To George — from loyal team mates, in grateful memory of the author, our friend. (signed) Frank N.D. Buchman, (F.B.) 1924." On the opposite page, inside of the cover, each of the other three has signed his name, viz., Eustace H. Wade/ "Nick," Samuel M. Shoemaker Jr., A.S. Loudon Hamilton. A good deal of this book grew out of Howard's experience with Frank Buchman in India and during a tour of China with him in 1917, so that many of the ideas appear which Harold Bagbie presents in *More Twice Born Men*.

As we were reading we heard a most jolly rumpus in the corridor outside of our door, and went out to find young Prince Michael ("Mihai," the Roumanian for Michael), 3 years and 3 months old, the only child of Crown Prince Carol and Princess Helen (of Greece). He was riding a wonderful great automobile, really too big for him, and calling for more strength than his little legs could put into the pedals. He has been quite ill for some weeks, and is only now recovering, and looks very delicate. Just now his parents are both away, Prince Carol in London and his mother in Paris where she has gone for treatment of her eyes which are in very bad shape.

The discussion of her eyes with Queen Marie led us to describe Dr. Bates's treatment which helped Caroline Crane so much, and which Theron followed some years ago. Evidently the Paris physician got hold of the same principle.

Little Michael is a most winsome child, with fair hair and blue eyes, quite the image of his father's baby pictures. He loves to play and in later days he often came to visit us. When my bad ear developed he evinced great sympathy for "that poor man," and often came around to ask how I was. His elderly English nurse, Miss. St. John (pronounced Sinjin) was with him this morning and also Princess Ileana, the youngest daughter of Queen Marie, whom we just met for the first time as she was ill yesterday.

Ileana is of the family type — fair, blue eyes, very pretty and attractive. We fell to playing and talking, and finally it led to being taken around the palace by young Michael to see his nursery when he pulled open his "treasure drawer" and showed us the usual child's broken toys, bright colored boxes, etc. He seems to speak English all the time, and I never learned whether he knows Roumanian.

Our expedition with Michael led us by chance into the presence of Queen Marie who happened to be walking through the corridor near her own door. She had with her Prime Minister, Mr. Brătianu, the eldest of three brothers who seem to be the real power in the government of Roumania today. The second, generally called by his first name, Vitella, is Minister of Finance, and the youngest brother is a Senator, and chairman of the Finance Committee of the Senate. These three are the chief owners of one of the biggest banks of Roumania, the name of which I have forgotten. I am sorry to say that the "bank" (and hence themselves), is being vastly enriched through the favoritism of the present government which has been in power for about three years, and represents the so-called "Liberal" party. The testimony of most foreigners in Bucharest seems to be that the government is very corrupt. Will write more of this later.

Her Majesty presented me to Mr. Brătianu and I had a five-minute talk with him, especially with regard to Robert College and the attitude of the Turkish government toward us. His questions were rapid, very much to the point, clear cut, and clever. One could but feel instantly that he was a man of fine mind and quick penetration. Her Majesty carried him off in a few minutes, stopping to say, however, that she would be back in ten minutes and then would take us to see her own rooms.

We sat down in the nursery to play with Michael and she soon returned and drew us into her Boudoir, a charming room, again in the Norwegian style, with rough dark uneven wood like a peasant's cottage. It is filled with an endless array of pretty things, some simple and inexpensive, others rare and costly gifts, from dozens of famous people. We fell to talking about these numberless objects, among which were dozens of articles in every imaginable shape of jade, of which Her Majesty is specially fond, such as quaintly carved animals — elephants, tigers, frogs, fish, and unimaginable list.

Everywhere there were beautiful Persian jars filled with primroses which just now over run all the rooms of the palace in fascinating profusion, and mixed with them were jars of wonderful cyclamens. Lying on a table were several strings of wonderful Roumanian amber of very unusual shades quite different from any Persian or Turkish amber which we see in Constantinople.

She carried us on into her bedroom, a huge high room in the true Byzantine style of old Roumania, filled with art treasures which could

The Silver Bedroom of Queen Marie
Cotroceni Palace

absorb one for hours. She passed rapidly around the room, picking up this and that object, and telling about it in a fascinating way. She knows the inner history of each treasure, and evidently loves them all for their beauty as well as for their association. Her mind is ever agile and intense, and at the same time wonderfully appreciative of simple things.

The whole room was designed under her personal direction, and I will add, as I am writing this after our return to Constantinople, that I was truly sorry we did not have another opportunity to visit it and to linger about it. This morning she sat down by a bedroom window and fell to talking about her parents, her girlhood and her family. She drew Elizabeth down on to the couch beside her, and rather naturally I spread myself on the rug at her feet, and we had an extraordinary fifteen minutes as she told us about her girlhood in England, Malta, and again in England, her visits at the court of Queen Victoria, her father's tastes and life (she seems to have been very chummy with her father). He was Queen Victoria's second son, Prince Alfred, later Duke of Edinburgh, and still later Duke of Saxe-Coburg. She told us of her marriage at only 17, and then coming to "live with a husband she hardly knew in a land of which she literally knew nothing."

As I wrote in my diary at the moment, she must have had a bitter awakening for her girlhood was far too sheltered for her own good, and her discovery of an evil and false world proved a very painful and trying process. She evidently did not find life under King Charles and Queen Elizabeth any too easy, and she was far from being financially independent, which clearly irritated both her and her husband, Prince Ferdinand. She came to Roumania in 1893, and did not become Queen until 1914-21 long years of waiting, not always too patiently, as she said, but still years of wonderful inner growth and development. I shall never forget that conversation as I sat at her feet in that beautiful Byzantine bedroom. She is a woman of rarely disciplined character, as I said before truly a "released personality."

We did not leave Her Majesty until 12:30, — of course it is always for her to indicate when she wishes people to go, which she is very clever at doing. Then we found Theron and Cornelia and had a beautiful walk on the snow in the park around the palace grounds. They are not extensive, but are filled with fine old trees. There are terraces, ponds, many splendid old Roumanian jars five or six feet high, pergolas, and every indication of what must be fascinating beauty in the spring and early summer before the intense heat of the Roumanian plain has burned things brown.

At 1:30 we had our first "State luncheon," at the round table in the Byzantine dining room which I described yesterday. We were 13 present, — a good indication that Her Majesty has no troublesome superstitions. I counted the number as we sat there, and searched my memory for a time when I had sat at a table with 13, and I could not remember ever having done any although I could recall several instances when people have hustled around at the last minute to raise the number to 14. How absurd these superstitions are! King George of Greece sat at Her Majesty's right and I was at her left, while Queen Elizabeth of Greece sat directly opposite her mother in the place where King Ferdinand of Roumania would ordinarily be sitting. He is still in bed after a slight operation for hernia on Sunday, January 25th. We have not yet met him. Theron sat at Queen Elizabeth's right and Cornelia at my left with some officers beyond her who only spoke Roumanian. Elizabeth was beyond King George at his right with another aide at her right.

Writing later, as I do, I can say that I came to enjoy those rather formal lunches very thoroughly, and to be glad to try to do my part in contributing to the conversation. Some of the officers and aides who were there were decidedly dummy. On the other hand the ladies-in-waiting were always gracious, and generally successful in conversation. Her Majesty is clever indeed at drawing different persons into the conversation addressing directly first one and then another at the huge round table.

When one is not in conversation he can always enjoy the beautiful Byzantine capitals, the plain round arches, the jolly short stone columns, very plain and sturdy, the beautiful lines of the low dome which rises above the center of the round table with its hidden electric illumination, and the Byzantine pictures, screens, carved gilded chairs etc. There is no end of treasures in that dining room and its lovely anteroom and charming odd corners partitioned off where two or three could sit down for a cozy chat. Looking back at it now, the whole place seems to be redolent of Queen Marie, — her taste, her culture, and her appreciation of the real amenities of life. I generally sat with my back to the beautiful old Roman church screen, or iconostasis, of which I wrote above, so I slipped back one day after royalty had withdrawn to have a good look at it.

It was at lunch here one day that Queen Elizabeth told me the story of the founding of the monastery of Cotroceni which I wrote above. Over the door of the church are the arms of the Cantacuzino family — an eagle with one head — and above this an inscription in old Roumanian, written in Slavic characters which they formerly used.

Writing of this date on February 14th, I find that I cannot remember just what our afternoon program was. I know that we had tea in the Studio with Her Majesty, and then an hour of most delightful piano music by Mr. George Boskoff, a Roumanian artist about 40 years old, who must be one of their very best. He is short, simple, modest and quiet, intensely absorbed in his beloved music. He evidently found great pleasure in playing to so appreciative an audience as Her Majesty always is, and one could not wonder that she liked to have him come to the palace. Never in my life have I heard music under such favorable conditions, — nine or ten of us sitting about that charming Studio with the afternoon light filtering through the stained glass windows, harmony of color everywhere; a piano of beautiful tone, absolutely no applause, nor any need for applause. Imagine hearing Schumann's "12 Children's Pieces" played with delicious naiveté and a wonderful rippling touch under such ideal circumstances as those. Mr. Boskoff had preceded the Schumann by a charming group of five sketches, called "Années de Pèlerinage," written by Liszt during a tour of Switzerland who named them "The Chapel of William Tell," "The Obermann Valley," "Homesickness," "An Eclogue," and "The Storm." Schumann was followed by two selections of Roumanian music, and then he played a caprice "In the Spirit of Vienna," and finished off with a Nocturne of Chopin and the magnificent thing by Liszt called "La Campanella" which I have often heard Mr. Hegel play at Constantinople and here at Robert College.

How much we at Robert College owe to the musical taste of Professor Charles Anderson which set the pace for our music twenty and thirty years ago. It turned out that we were to hear the very same program at Mr. Boskoff's public concert the following Sunday morning.

Our dinner was the usual family party at the table at one end of the Studio. Her Majesty brought to the table her longest fairy story, a volume called *Peeping Pansy*, published by Hodder & Stoughton, London, 1919, and delightfully illustrated by Mabel B. Atwell. This particular copy proved to be the one given by the Queen to Ileana. In the front was written "For Ileana, this book that was written for her during the war when no books reached us any more, — Mame (Mama), Christmas, 1919." Ileana let us take this copy, the only one in the whole palace, and we kept it in our rooms until the day we came away, dipping into it now and then.

After dinner we drew away from the table and Queen Marie read aloud chapter three introducing the old witch, Dame Dannydimmydoo., who appears again and again in the story as the sometimes stern and severe, sometimes grumpy, and often good-humored and kindly adviser to little Fancy who is but seven years old and has all of life before her to discover. Knowing Queen Marie as I do I now see in the old witch more of the philosophy and life experience of the Queen than even she with all her frankness would be willing to admit. I told her that one day and she acknowledged that probably she had shown herself up only too well in the old dame. As I have read many different chapters of *Peeping Pansy* I have come to think it is not only a clever story to be read aloud to a little girl, but also a most wholesome book — unconsciously so to the child — as a real teacher of many a needed life lesson.

She also read chapter 32, where Mrs. Grumps, the owl, appears, and then led us on into Pansy's experience with the three tiny owlets, Rumpy, Bumpy, and Flampy. Then she slipped along over the pages, picking out a sentence here and there, and finally reading aloud the verses on pages 227, 235, and 6, and 237. It was a most charming, amusing, and gracious evening.

Saturday, January 31

We left at 10 a.m. with Her Majesty to hear the symphony rehearsal. There were only 9 of us in the theater besides the orchestra, namely, Her Majesty, King George, Queen Elizabeth, one of the ladies-in-waiting, the Queen's Aide de Camp, Rădescu, whose special business seemed to be to go about with Her Majesty to see that everything went smoothly, — and we four.

The first selection was the Overture to "Egmont" by Beethoven, my first hearing of it, — a magnificent thing. This was followed by a modern Roumanian selection filled with the latest type of dissonances which did not so much shock and offend us as amuse us, so that when it came to an end with a dissonant crash the whole orchestra and all nine of us burst out into a hearty laugh. Her Majesty has trained herself to the most careful attention to music, and is very appreciative of all its aspects. She would often whisper a comment to me on some chord or phrase as I sat beside her at her left, and clearly liked to talk things over after each selection.

The third piece was Richard Strauss' Overture to "Salomé", a tremendous work in its varied emotions, its sudden changes from anger to tears, and from tears to laughter, and with plenty of fire and a magnificent climax. I enjoyed it especially as the orchestra got lost two or three times and had to stop and start again, so that we had a sense of belonging to the affair which cannot come in a straight out concert.

King George sat at my left, and after the Strauss Overture there was quite an interval during which we fell to talking about Mt. Athos which he has visited. He spoke of the plans he had for encouraging a really new era of intellectual development among the monks there. I told him of my happy two weeks among the monasteries in 1901, and about the touching little prayer of the monk Zacharia as he sat in the sunshine on Easter Monday morning counting over his black woolen beads and whispering to himself with each bead, "Lord Jesus Christ help me."

King George is so frank and naive and friendly, and shows so distinct an interest in any religious topic that one can introduce, that I took pains after to turn the conversation to questions of religious experience and he always responded most sympathetically. I think we all came to feel that the opportunity of friendly fellowship with him which this visit to Roumania has afforded was one of its most valuable features. He has a certain simplicity of manner that makes him wear well as a companion. He told me how the French abused the hospitality of the monks during the war, stealing icons and other sacred objects, and, to cover their consciences, pinning five-franc pieces on the wall in place of the objects.

The last number of the program was a grand Symphony of Brahms, broad, smooth, mature, wise, and yet moving. I am sorry I cannot tell which number it was. The second movement, an adagio, was best.

As the theater door we parted from Her Majesty and went to the American Legation for a forty minute call on Mr. and Mrs. Jay. Mr. Jay was First Secretary in Constantinople many years ago, and later went to Japan and Egypt. He made a beautiful collection of Bokhara embroideries while living here which now cover the walls of their huge dining room, and make it most attractive. They have been fortunate in securing a very large, well built house which offers plenty of space and dignity for public functions. They had a good many stories to tell of Mr. Vopeka, their predecessor as American Minister to Roumania. I met him once in the station at Belgrade in July, 1914, and I shall never forget his tobacco-stained lips and teeth, and his conversation stained with every available profane interjection.

Mrs. Jay said that it took her three months to clean up the Legation, for they had taken over the house from him, and Mr. Jay added that it had taken him four years to clean up American relations with Roumania, which at the beginning were "very, very low," and now he thought might fairly be called at least good. The government of Roumania has put on all sorts of restrictions up on foreign societies and foreign capital, so that America as well as some of the European powers almost reached the point of breaking off the diplomatic relations. Our government summoned Mr. Jay to America last summer, but happily, since his return in November, relations have been a bit smoother. It is largely the fault of Vitella Brătianu, the Minister of Finance, of whom I wrote above. The older brother, John, the Prime Minister, could keep things more smooth externally if his two younger brothers would not mess them up.

I talked with Mr. Jay about the question of recognition of the Robert College diploma by the Roumanian government so that graduates from here could enter a Roumanian university. The question has been raised by Kuneff, who graduated last June. He is a Roumanian citizen, having always lived in Roumania, and the government has thus far refused to give him any credit for work done here. The matter was taken up some months ago through Mr. Jay. He urged me this morning to ask Queen Marie to arrange for an interview with Mr. Angelescu, the Minister of Education. Mr. Jay, like everyone else, says that outside of the cabinet itself the real power in the country is the Queen, and not King Ferdinand who is good-natured and easygoing, but not very effective.

We returned in time for our second lunch in the State dining room. We were not very numerous. In addition to Col. Rădescu and three Aides, Mme. Mavrodis, the oldest of the ladies-in-waiting, appeared. She is rather on the shelf so far as active duties go, having served her active career under Queen Elizabeth. The Queen of Greece was absent, — "Fasting," her mother said, "as she is too stout." I could not help observing, as I often sat beside Queen Elizabeth, that when she was not technically "fasting" she was eating a more abundant dinner than I ever thought of doing, and I doubt whether one day of fasting per week will ever balance the six others of pretty good living.

On the whole, I was surprised at the simplicity of the palace food. Such a society lady as Mrs. Arthur James would have far more appearance of elaborate preparation, and so would many a rich New York house, where they would employ some fabulously expensive French chef. The food was invariably delicious in quality, but clearly there was no extravagant spending of money upon it. The china and silver and glass were all good but in no sense extravagant. One day Her Majesty asked the butler to bring some silver-gilt plates which she uses for state dinners. She took special pains to tell us they were not solid gold, and I recalled the really solid gold plates on which two courses were served to us when we dined with Mrs. Arthur James in New York.

This noon, at lunch, Princess Ileana came in and out of the dinning room in a most informal way, talking with her mother about arrangements for a moving picture party at the palace for that afternoon, and consulting about the final list of guests, etc. She is certainly very capable, and in many ways has the energy and vivacity and directness of her mother. Evidently her mother relies upon her, and is training her early to organize little affairs with careful attention to every detail.

This noon I talked with Queen Marie about her grandmother, Queen Victoria, and she brought up Strachey's account of her, and quoted from various of Victoria's letters. I regret to think that I have never read Strachey's book, although I put it on my own bookshelves nearly a year ago. She told how Victoria was very sensitive, and at the age of 18, when her Prime Minister left an evening function without saying good-bye was very much hurt, and wrote him a little note in the third person, as she always did, saying, "The Queen deeply regrets that her Prime Minister should have left the gathering last night without bidding her good-night, and assumes that some very urgent business must have called him away in this unseemly haste."

Victoria was both queen and girl, and mixed the two in ways that sometimes amuses people.

After lunch we four sat down alone and read for about an hour from *Peeping Pansy*, going on from Pansy's visit to the witch, reading the story of the door through the hearth to the garden with the golden mosaics, where old Dame Dannydimmydoo, the witch, played for the lizards to dance until they stood straight up on the tips of their tails, and their green skins fell off and were gathered up by Gregrub the gardener, who saved them to make costumes for the tiny imps who did the witch's gardening. It is delightful to read the story aloud here in the palace, and we often stop to discuss Her Majesty, whose personality constantly shines out of the story when one knows her. Query: Would all books be as much enriched to the reader if he knew the writer well? It was in our reading this afternoon that I discovered the delightful definition of "an imperial air" on page 186, viz., "Look dignified, ladylike and a little haughty, but at the same time very gracious."

We started at 4:30 with Princess Ileana to visit the Y.M.C.A. where Miss Galitza and Miss Georgescu showed us their tiny beehive with 60 girls dancing on the top floor and the tiny cafeteria on the ground floor serving from three to four hundred meals every day. She said they reach about 1500 girls through their different activities at the building and in schools, and receive subventions from the Ministry of Labor, the Ministry of Education, and the Ministry of Finance on the ground that they are making contributions to the public good which belong in each one of those departments. I like both secretaries very much. Miss Calitza was a year in America and Miss. Georgescu spent a while in England, so they talk English fairly well. The Y.M.C.A. can get more use out of inadequate rooms than almost any organization I know.

We went from there to tea with Colonel and Mrs. Foy, where quite a group of Americans were gathered to meet us, among them Mr. Palmer, the American Consul and his wife, Mr. McAndrews, American Vice Consul, and his sister (she has been visiting him there for five months and came out on the "Braga" with the Wileys, spending three days on shipboard in the Bosphorus doing quarantine), Dr. Van Norman, Commercial Attaché of our Legation, and his wife, Colonel Crebel of the Baldwin Locomotive Works, and his wife (Florence Colgate, cousin of Mrs. Cleveland Mather), and Mr. Morgan of the Y.M.C.A.

We had the usual family dinner in the Studio, and adjourned from that to the beautiful blue tile reception room where people were gathering for the cinema party. Her Majesty wore a wonderful blue gown at dinner, and when she entered the brilliant blue and gold reception room she was as regal as heart could desire. She loves her beautiful jewels and very frankly likes to talk about them and show them. She took off a wonderful huge pearl from her necklace and let us pass it about the table, and one night she sent out for various precious stones, among them a tremendous sapphire not less than 1½ in. long, with one side cut to an infinite number of faces.

The moving picture was *The Moon of Israel*, for which I frankly did not care. There were some very striking Egyptian scenes, but in general I should call the play a monstrosity. Of course I am too hard perhaps on moving pictures. I consider most of them an awful waste of time, and would any day rather go to a good play or a good concert. The psychology of the "Moon of Israel" is absurdly unhuman.

Of course the text of all our cinema shown was printed in Roumanian so that we could not understand the stories except for kind interpreters. Young Mr. Mavrodis, whose mother is the eldest lady-in-waiting, sat beside me and put all the explanations into French. Others did the same for the various people in the party who did not know Roumanian. This includes King George of Greece, but he at least is studying Roumanian and beginning to use it.

Sunday, February 1st

Elizabeth and I got out at 9:30 for a good tramp of an hour. We ride in our automobile and sit on easy chairs, and we miss the exercise we get at Hissar.

Another perfect day. In the morning we went with Her Majesty to a concert by George Boskoff where he gave the same program as we heard in the Studio Friday afternoon. The concert hall was crowded with people. Her Majesty sat on a sofa at the very front of the hall with Cornelia and Elizabeth beside her, while Queen Elizabeth and the other satellites sat on easy chairs and front row seats. The concert was as good as on Friday, although I vastly prefer the atmosphere of the Studio and the piano there as well. Boskoff played a Berceuse by a young Roumanian named Brăiloiu, a cousin of Mme. Procopiu, who sat directly behind us, and when the audience applauded Mr. Boskoff made young Brăiloiu stand up and share the applause, — very gracefully done. I was interested in studying the faces of the people in the audience whom of course one could easily see by turning around. A great many seemed quite refined and thoughtful. It does one good to see such a group of the better classes together in a country whose morals and general character one cannot admire.

We were sorry to miss church. Her Majesty goes regularly to the chapel of the British Legation, and explained to us that on this particular Sunday she felt obliged to attend Boskoff's concert, which came at 11 a.m., as she had been largely responsible for his returning to Roumania and she felt that she must show herself publicly. Princess Ileana is a very devout Roumanian Orthodox, and goes to the service at 10 o'clock in the palace church. Had we known beforehand we would have asked to go with her, as we did the following Sunday. She seemed much pleased that we cared, and warned up about the meaning of the church service. King Ferdinand is a Roman Catholic but all the children are expected to belong to the Roumanian Church.

There was the usual lunch in the dining room during which I proposed to Queen Marie that she should arrange for me to have an interview with Dr. Angelescu, the Minister of Education. She promptly proposed to ask him to lunch at the palace. At 3 p.m. we four settled down again to read aloud one of Queen Marie's manuscripts, a most remarkable account of the death of her cousin Czar Nicholas II and his wife Alexandra. They were assassinated by the Bolsheviks in 1918, and this article was written in the heat and emotion which the news of their death produced in Queen Marie. It is really powerfully done and shows her best.

She has wonderfully clear insight into the meaning of such a hateful tyranny as that of the Czar's in Russia, and also into the wonderful scope and opportunity for helpful service to a great country which was theirs when they were crowned in 1894. The article is an extraordinary picture of the sinister and baleful influence of the Czarina Alexandra over her husband, and its terrible effect throughout the Russian Empire. This article was published in the *Revue de Deux Mondes* in 1918 or 1919. It is well worth reading. Of course Rasputine and his mysterious influence runs through it all. Nicholas II was Queen Marie's first cousin, and she was not only present at the coronation in 1894, but had visited "Cousin Nick," as she called him, several times. The last time she saw him was in the early summer of 1914 when he and the Czarina came to pay a visit to Roumania, stopping in their yacht at Constanța. Queen Marie evidently found the Russian court an oppressive place to visit, and she describes her relief in being hostess rather than guest, when the Czar and his wife came to Constanța. While at the palace we took pains to read as much of Queen Marie's work as we could and as wide a variety of it as possible, for talking about these articles led to endless interesting reminiscences.

This afternoon Her Majesty had a group of about fifteen social workers at tea for us to meet. Among them I had interesting conversations with the doctor who manages all of Queen Marie's private Benefactions, the president of the Red Cross, Mme. Pedicari, the daughter of Charles Davila, famous physician, and several other interesting women. I have mentioned before that Mme. Pedicari attracted me most of all that group. There was plenty of time for general conversation before we settled down to hear a young Pole play the piano most delightfully for about an hour. Those teas and hours of music in the late afternoon sunshine, and all the happy and amusing tête-à-têtes with Her Majesty have made that Studio a place we shall never forget.

We were all the guests of King George and Queen Elizabeth for dinner that evening in their own apartment on the south side of the palace court and joined to the main palace only by an open colonnade, so that one has to go outdoors to reach them. They have a tiny dining room where we eight had to sit very close in order to be served conveniently. It made it all the more cozy and homelike, and was another one of the family parties we love to remember.

From the dining room one climbs a creaky stairway and finds two modest rooms and a large hallway, which make up their public living quarters. All the furnishings are their own property. There are a good many nice Bokhara embroideries and some beautiful hand work from Greece, one being a very ancient piece of embroidery representing a chalice with two doves drinking from it while several of Noah's doves, each provided with a bit of olive branch, fly above. There are some fine old brasses and a very few ancient Greek jars, the most wonderful being a stone vase of black marble which dates from 1000 B.C., a beautiful archaic figure which may represent Mercury with wings and winged feet. It is carved in low relief on one side. It is really a museum piece, and King George acknowledged that he had to smuggle it out of Greece very quietly. Princess Ileana was there at dinner also, though she by no means always dined with us.

After dinner Elizabeth showed the Robert College photographs to King George and then I explained them to Queen Marie, while Queen Elizabeth showed her own drawings, etc., to Theron and Cornelia. Queen Elizabeth is really gifted with her pencil and brush, and has illustrated a book of Roumanian songs, the illustrations being wholly original with her. Some of them suggested the type of delicate handwork with which I became familiar in India, which is, of course, Persian in origin. I asked her about the source of her inspiration, but she did not seem to realize that her pictures had anything of the Persian or Indian atmosphere about them. She also showed us a complete book which is all her own work, including binding, pictures, poems, and writing, — a very clever production. She has been growing on us steadily. Her brilliant mother overshadows her in Roumania so that she needs calling out, and the friendly fellowship of people who will help her to show her best side. We had a most charming evening, with much variety. It was brought to a close by an hour's reading out loud by Queen Marie who spread herself comfortably on a couch and read to us *Loulaloo*, a story published in *Pearson's Magazine* of a mermaid (Loulaoo), a hermit, and a brave knight. It is good, but not one of her best.

Then she convulsed us with several delightful short ones which have not been published, among them being *The Imp and the Baby*, the story of a mischievous imp who carried off a baby while its grandmother was asleep, and of a friendly crow who kindly dropped it back into its own cradle on earth. Another clever bit was *The Fisherman who Smoked*, a description of peasant life among the Turkish population in the Dobrudja, which is the region bordering the Black Sea south of the mouths of the Danube, and reaching to the Bulgarian frontier, — a peasant who burned up his house, his possessions, and himself, leaving only his black boat.

Monday, February 2nd

Another fine day, although the clouds spread over the sky in the afternoon and looked a bit like rain. Princess Ileana took us to a service at the church for a few minutes after 10 a.m. It was a special feast day. Happily, they have steam heat with modern radiators in the church so it was not the usual cold tomb which one experiences in the East in winter. The nave was full of simple country people, a great many of them boys and girls in their mid-teens with shy quiet faces.

They have an excellent choir of boys and girls. On Sunday a group of men's voices is added. Fortunately the Roumanian church has been much influenced by its proximity to Russia, for their chorus, sung in four parts as in the Russian church is a great advance on the tiresome intoning of the old Greek church of Turkey. We noticed in the service a special prayer for Princess Ileana, and she told us afterwards that the priest said to her at the end that he was sorry she had not told him she was coming so that he might have arranged the service to be more interesting to her and her guests.

Theron went to town on business for the Chamber of Commerce, as he did two other mornings, and Elizabeth and Cornelia went with him to do some shopping. I stayed at home to write letters to Dr. Gates, Dr. Banninger of Madura, etc. Our five minutes in the church had interested me, and as we had to leave with the Princess I went out at 12:30 to have a look over it while it was still warm. The door was locked, and as I stood studying the inscription over it King George came along and proposed that we have a walk. He always goes out of his way to be friendly so we strolled about the palace grounds and talked.

He brought up the modern ideas of spiritual healing by faith, such as Dr. Worcester's in Boston, and cited some English clergyman in London with whom he had talked, who practices in his parish in this way. As I have perhaps indicated, it was interesting to see how often King George would introduce subjects along religious lines. He spoke of the work of the Near East Relief and its relation to Roman Catholics and to Protestants, and of his interest in it because it combined all denominations; he regretted that religious sects, including his own Orthodox Church, had to quarrel with each other.

He got into the subject of Mr. Morgenthau, who evidently is a very distasteful personality to him. He told of a very foolish speech Mr. Morgenthau made in Athens a year or more ago, of which I had never heard, in which Mr. Morgenthau directly favored the idea of a republic. This was before the Greek government sent the King and Queen away from Greece, and King George said there was much resentment among the foreign diplomats at Athens over Mr. Morgenthau's unwarranted expressions. They felt that he was in Greece on a purely private matter, that is, in the interests of the refugees, and that he should have refrained from all meddling in politics. Indeed King George went so far as to say that many people in Greece feared the influence of the United States as exerted through the Near East Relief, Mr. Morgenthau's committee, etc., because Americans consciously and unconsciously talk in favor of a republic form of government, and make people discontented, or stirred up the idea of a change in the form of government for which the ordinary Greek people are quite unprepared. Of course it is natural that King George should look at it from this point of view, but I imagine he is quite right in feeling that the quarrelsome Greeks are not yet ready for a republican type of government.

We lunched, as usual, at half past one in the main dining room. I sat at the right of Queen Elizabeth for the first time, and had Mme. Procopiu at my right. Colonel Rădescu, the Queen's chief Aide, was there as usual. He is a most solemn individual whom we all came to take delight in poking to stir him up in order to make him smile and get animated. Clearly he has produced the same effect on the royal family as upon us four, for one night at dinner someone mentioned him and Princess Ileana expressed the real girl's desire to wake him up and make him naughty. Queen Elizabeth, who is often silent, but who can be clever, remarked quietly, "Rădescu is the Ten Commandments in uniform," so apt a description that we all roared together. However, it is better to be the Ten Commandments in uniform than to be the reverse, and I fear there are altogether too many officers in Roumania who pay little attention to any one of the Ten Commandments.

The dinning table is a perfect circle so that it can easily accommodate from twelve to twenty people. Once there were thirteen of us. I happened to count up, but of course did not mention it, and not a soul ever spoke of it, not even anyone of us four to each other. I have described the Byzantine architecture and decorations of the dinning room.

We noticed that Queen Marie, in her story of the death of Czar Nicholas II, described the famous crypt built by Czar and Czarina at Moscow in preparation for their own burial. She visited it some years ago and I could not help wondering whether it had given her ideas for the dinning room, for her description of its Byzantine sculpture in stone and wood, its gilded screen, the Byzantine crosses and religious pictures on the walls certainly suggest this luncheon room at Cotroceni. Do not think that it has anything of the air of a crypt, however, for it is light and airy and cheerful and beautiful and dignified in every way. The state dinning room, where one can serve one hundred people, is a huge old-fashioned barn to the east of this Byzantine room, in the style of European palaces of fifty to eighty years ago, very grand, of course, but not at all attractive.

Today after luncheon Queen Marie took us into King Ferdinand's "cabinet" and "den," a series of three relatively small rooms lighted by warm southern sunshine, lined with bookshelves filled with beautiful sets of literature of all countries, with niches everywhere for artistic pieces of pottery from the Persian period of 500 years ago to the most beautiful and wonderful modern French glassware. She showed us many of these modern pieces of which the King is very fond. They are amazing things. Standing in their niches with a soft dark wood background, the colors seem to be grey or dull pearl, but when held out toward the light they become brilliant and flash violet, purple, and mauve. I will note the name of the French maker at the end of my diary.

The floors of the King's rooms were covered with fascinating Roumanian kelims. Never in Constantinople have I seen so many beautiful and unique kelims. Speaking of kelims reminds me of our visit with the Queen to a most entertaining open air bazaar where dozens of kelims were spread out in the sunshine on a broad sidewalk, a neighboring fence, the long ends of many dropping down from the fence and covering a long steep embankment leading down to the waters of a little river which flows through the city. This street is called The Quai, and is a favorite promenade on sunny afternoons, hence the peasant merchants, who bring in kelims from the outlying provinces, congregate here to sell their wares. Of course, many of the kelims are gaudy modern productions, but occasionally really artistic old ones can be found.

I have neglected to state on some previous day, — which day I have forgotten — that Queen Marie drove with us to the most important Roumanian embroidery shop called Țăranca, Calea Victoriei 120. We then had our first taste of what it means to go about shopping with the Queen. When her car drew up in front of Țăranca's, the footman went in first to warn the proprietor that the Queen was coming. He then had his clerks show everybody else out of the shop, and when it was clear the footman came back to open the door for Her Majesty. In the meantime a crowd of fifty or more persons had gathered on the side walk outside of the door, so that the footman from the two cars had to clear a passage-way for the Queen and her friends. Then the shop door was shut and nobody was admitted until we had finished our inspection, which took us over half an hour. All the while the crowd outside was growing until there were three or four hundred people spreading out into the street, and interfering with traffic. Again and again I glanced toward the shop door, and saw every inch of its glass panes occupied by peering faces and flattened noses. Of course Her Majesty ignored the whole thing, and her minions are accustomed to clearing the way for her.

The embroideries at Ţăranca's are fascinating, the choicest I have ever seen in Roumania. They bear corresponding prices and I do not wonder for the work is very fine. Her Majesty very sensibly said that we could not decide there, and asked the proprietor to send a box of his goods to the palace where we later made selections. Then we drove to the very outskirts of the city over horrible roads to a most fascinating pottery shop where a Transylvanian "Saxon" (the German population of Transylvania are called Saxons) has established one of the most entertaining and fascinating pottery shops I ever visited. He is really very artistic and clever, and under the Queen's patronage has unearthed hundreds of medieval designs for tiles, plates, and pots of every description.

Her Majesty loves all these things and Theron and she found a vast amount in common in their discussions on ceramics. Writing this later, I am able to say we concluded no present from us four would give Her Majesty more pleasure than a nice piece of the Chinese celedon ware, of which she has almost none, so yesterday (February 18) Theron found a large shallow bowl in the typical soft grey, green, pearly shades, and we are sending it off to be added to the collection at Cotroceni. There is a famous collection of celedon ware in the old Treasury on the Seraglio grounds in Constantinople, and fifteen or twenty pieces have somehow crept into the Bazaars of Stamboul.

At the pottery — Ruffer by name — they have copied old German tiles, and have designed most wonderful tile stoves of the sort that are still used in most German and Roumanian houses. This man made all the stoves for Her Majesty's house at The Farm, Copăceni, which we visited later.

This afternoon we also visited for five or ten minutes each five exhibitions of Roumanian paintings, each exhibit representing the work of one man. There was very little that any of us cared for, most of it was flat, hard, and in heavily lined modern style which bores me to extinction. We had to pass through a large book store in going to one exhibit which led us to inquire for the Queen's books. We could not discover a single one of them on sale anywhere in Bucharest. Is not that amazing? Possibly we might have found them in Roumanian, but certainly no original editions in English or French.

We had tea with King George and Queen Elizabeth alone, a very cozy familiar time, with a considerable talk about modern poetry, during which the story of Alice Neynell and Francis Thompson was told by Cornelia, which they heard for the first time. Thompson's essay on Shelley is one of the indestructible gems in the English literature. Queen Elizabeth brought out a good many of her Greek costumes. Among them was an exquisite robe which belonged to the wife of the famous Ali Pasha of Yan-ina, an island in the Lake of Yanina, who was murdered by her own hus-band on the island. King George visited the family and they presented him with this robe. One morning he found them on the point of chopping up a delightfully carved old family chest. He protested and offered to buy it, whereat they of course gave it to him, remarking that it was a shame to insult a King by such a poor gift. It is there in their bedroom at Cotroceni, and is a most quaint and delightful souvenir of Albanian peasantry.

Ali Pasha is famous in art because in any known picture he is repre-sented as wearing a certain cap, the like of which never appeared in any other painting or engraving of that era. An American dealer actually sent an antiquity hunter on a special trip to Europe to search for it, for many people believe it must be preserved somewhere as it was so unique a cap. Thus far it has not been discovered.

We handled the old Minoan jar of heavy green stone with its raised figures with wings and winged feet, which King George says wise masons claim to be masonic symbols. It is supposed to date from 4000 B.C., and is not from Crete but from the Peloponnesus. I must look up Evans's fasci-nating account of the Minoan finds in Crete.

This afternoon Queen Elizabeth brought out some of her own embroidery, so fine that she says her eyes will not permit her to work on it for more than half an hour at a time. It will take her years to complete it. She does pretty carved work in ivory, and showed us a dear little relief of the Virgin and Child, on which she is now at work. We feel about Queen Elizabeth that although she is quiet, and sometimes difficult to meet, and is of course unhappy in her present situation, she is a really strong woman who could be of much real service to any country in such a position as queen. This morning she spent three hours with the conductor of the Bucharest Symphony, who was testing her voice to see whether it was worth her while to go on with vocal lessons.

We had dinner in the Studio, Princess Ileana being present. Then the family went off to a private play given in Roumanian which would of course have meant nothing to us. Queen Marie kept us roaring with laughter during dinner by the tales of her peasant friends in Iaşi and else-where, especially old man and women who came to her wishing cures for all their ills, and pathetically filled with faith in her power to heal them; or else filled with amusing and petty jealousies and pouring them all out in her ears. At Iaşi she got acquainted with a strange old man who often came to see her and begged to be allowed to come to Bucharest and visit her, when she was restored after the Germans left the country. He did come two or three times for brief stays, and finally spent a week in a very comfortable room provided by Her Majesty. One morning the servants came in consternation to tell her that he had disappeared, and begged her to come and see his room. When she entered it she found that the whole contents of the room were gone, even his bathtub and bed! Of course the servants were horrified, but Her Majesty laughed until she cried, and said if he needed those things so much he would better keep them. So, much to the disgust of the footmen, the police were not informed, and probably he is still sleeping in one or both of those articles.

The Queen said that she gave him a new suit of clothes each time he came so that he could go about the palace looking like a gentleman. She added that no matter how much she might give these old peasants, they always asked for more, — a very familiar story to my Elizabeth and to any of us who live in the Orient.

Her Majesty was full of reminiscences about the life of Iaşi. How cordially she and her country do hate the Germans! She described the German ministry headed by Mr. Marghiloman which His Majesty had to accept during the latter part of their stay in Iaşi, after the Bolshevik revolution left them helpless in the hands of the Germans. The Roumanian state treasury and many of the Queen's own jewels were sent to Moscow when the Germans overran Bucharest, and consequently fell into the hands of the Bolsheviks who absolutely refused to give them back except in exchange for Bessarabia, and have probably sold them long ago.

We have picked up many direct and indirect words that Queen Marie as Princess Marie, and wife of the Crown Prince Ferdinand, did not find it easy to get along with Carmen Sylva of Roumania. Queen Marie speaks with great respect for many of her abilities, but makes it clear also that she was not easy for the family to get along with. Most books about Carmen Sylva represent her as a saint on earth. I imagine no *German* saint, whether on earth or in heaven, would be very easy for anyone to get along with.

We four sat down in our much beloved Studio together and read aloud one of the Queen's tales called *The Legend of Mount Athos*. It describes a visit of the Virgin Mary to Mount Athos. Owing to the fact that all the women are excluded from the sacred precincts of that peninsular, everything became so dirty that even the easy-going monks could no longer stand it, and declared their absolute need of the help of a woman. One of them prayed in such faith to the Virgin that she could not resist and came down from her enthronement in Heaven and spent a month with the monks of Athos. The description of the changes brought by her presence is quite too delightful. As she stayed on, the monks noticed that she began to be sad, and finally was clearly so unhappy that they were in dire fear that she would leave them for the happier life in Heaven. Finally the faithful one whose prayers had brought her there came and begged to know what the trouble was, and she told him that the presence of crucifixes everywhere portraying the suffering of her Son wounded her soul, and said that pictures of the Virgin and her Baby were far more human and sympathetic. Upon hearing this, the monks in solemn conclave decreed that all the Crucifixes which had formerly been scattered about in their churches in full view should be put far up on high, above the highest point of iconostasis, or screen, where no person could see them unless he rest his eyes far up. On the other hand, they decreed that there should always be a picture of the Madonna and her Child immediately over the door of the screen, hung low before the eyes of all the people. If you do not believe this story go to Mount Athos, or indeed to any Greek church, and study the relative positions of the Crucifix and the Madonna.

The description in the story of the monks' joy in the presence of a woman is both amusing and pathetic. They justified their happiness in her presence by saying "This is no earthly woman, hence it is no sin for us to sit at her feet." I could not help applying these words in a little different sense to our astonishing intimacy with Queen Marie, for she has been so placed in earthly society that men and women alike may give her a certain type of intimacy which would not be possible to give were she nearer to them in social station.

Tuesday, February 3rd

Another beautiful day with blue sky and floating clouds and some slush below as the streets thaw. We spent some time selecting purchases from a box of embroideries sent to the palace by Țaranca.

Theron and I went to town at half past ten and had an hour's talk with Mr. Hughes, Manager of the Romano-Americana Company, Calea Victoriei 126. He talked at length with regard to business conditions, the treatment of foreign capital and the proposed new labor law which gives 15% of the net profits of every concern back to the workers. This law, he says, is proposed by the present so-called Liberal government to check the demands of the Țărăniști, or Peasant Party who are growing in strength, and while not at present Communistic or Bolshevik might become a very dangerous party if their demands were thwarted and they should ally themselves with the Bolsheviks. In fact, the constant threat of trouble with Bolshevik Russia seems to be the darkest cloud on the Roumanian horizon, and it was growing more menacing during our stay at Bucharest.

Mr. Hughes told us about his dealings with the Minister of Finance, Mr. Vitella Brătianu, who has just been to Europe to secure a loan, but in vain. Mr. Hughes had nothing but evil to say of the Roumanians and their government, and one heard very much the same story from other American business men. This point of view needs to be checked up by many other contacts.

Mr. Hughes called in one of his American assistants, Mr. Martin, who is president of the little American Men's Luncheon Club, a genial fellow with unusually attractive eyes. They insisted that we must be present next Thursday at the weekly luncheon. I also asked to see Richard Bolton who was a student at Robert College between 1910-1915, who is a clerk in this office, and had five minutes' talk with him. His dress and manners savor strongly of Roumania.

From the Standard Oil we went to call on Colonel Foy, military attaché and after a pleasant half hour with him we stopped at the Legation to inquire after Mr. Jay who is still suffering severely from his broken bones. Last Sunday morning his horse slipped on the frosty pavements and gave him a bad throw, breaking his right collarbone and two upper ribs, so that he will be in bed for three weeks. He was suffering from a bronchial cold, and the constant coughing against the broken ribs has proved very painful. Naturally this caused the postponement of our dinner at the Legation.

We got back to the palace barely in time for luncheon at one. I sat, as generally, at the left of Her Majesty, and this noon I told her my famous experience at the Restaurant Capşa in September, 1903, when I only had ten francs left to my name, plus my ticket to Constantinople, and ordered what was supposed to be a modest 3½ franc lunch at this famous and rather expensive Bucharest restaurant. I innocently supposed that the delicious *hors-d'oeuvre* which were brought in addition to my order were included in the luncheon, as in those days they were included at Tokatlian's restaurant in Constantinople, so I partook amply of them, and found to my horror when the bill came that it was 7½ francs! I was ashamed then not to give a good tip of one franc, and spent the next 24 hours with 1½ francs in my pocket, eating nothing but an apple until 11 p.m. when I boarded the boat at Constanţa and found late tea being served and included in the ticket. Her Majesty seemed to enjoy the tale as much as I still enjoy its recollection.

We all left at 2:30 for the "Farm" called "Copăceni". Theron and I went and returned in Her Majesty's car, and had the jolliest time imaginable during the fifty-minute drive. The Farm House is about fifty kilometers to the south, on the highroad to Giurgiu, which is the river port on the Danube where one ferries across to Rustchuk in Bulgaria and strikes the railroad to Serbia and Constantinople. Her Majesty gave us an animated account of how the farm came into her possession. It was owned by a very disagreeable old man who had a very lovely wife, and was so afraid to have her go out alone, lest when he was out someone should come to see her secretly, that before leaving the house he would shut her hair into a bureau drawer, and lock the drawer, taking the key with

Copăceni

him! That sounds like a fairy tale, but is positively true. He took a great fancy to the Queen, and as his farm had a beautiful forest with wild flowers she occasionally went out to it. I think she even went so far as to propose to buy the place, but he refused to sell. To her surprise, when he died, just before the great war, she found that he had willed the old house and forest to her, although the agricultural part of the huge estate was entailed and could not pass out of his family. In 1919 she began to rebuild the old house which was already in the charming country Roumanian style, with pretty balconies with low round arches resting on short thick round pillars. My photographs show the place well.

We made a hasty survey of the house itself which is only one story high, and then took a real tramp around the farm, visiting the barn filled with fine cows, fat pigs (several with most amusing litters of tiny piglets), a group of sturdy work horses, jolly calves, ducks, and geese, a big flock of sheep with a number of little lambs, one which was brought to us being only three hours old, and a furry donkey of the most fascinating sort. There is a picturesque gardener's house with a tower for a water tank which my photographs show, and a long, long rose alley where Her Majesty has brought every kind of rose she can lay her hands on from all over the world.

Far down the alley, and most picturesque in the distance, rises a typical peasant hut, very low, with widespreading caves and very steep thatched roof rising like a slender pyramid to a height of certainly 26 ft. above the low hanging caves. Typical Roumanian wooden peasant crosses, from eight to twelve feet high, capped with a little roof, are scattered about the hut, and inside on the walls hang a series of primitive holy pictures, done by a peasant, and exhibiting all their simple naiveté. There is a picturesque wall with a long tree trunk with the roots attached for its sweep.

The snow was soft, and in a good many places quite deep, so we had a really jolly rambled an hour, and came in to tea by one Ruffer's tile stoves. A huge hamper had been brought along in one of the cars, and every stove in the house had been set to roaring so that the huge white domed rooms had become quite comfortably warm.

The Queen went again around all the rooms and showed us her treasures, — kelims in extraordinary blacks and greens, jars of every imaginable description, a huge divan from the Sultan's palace of the type I have often seen in pictures of a century ago, delightful peasant brasses and wrought iron, yellow silk curtains woven by the peasants out of the coarser left-over silk which no one had thought of using until Her Majesty had it prepared; black carved shelves set in the walls making jolly odd recessed for pottery; some new paintings still unhung, one of them done by her sister, the Duchess Kyril, of blue corn flowers in a garden, and another, still more charming, of a peasant cottage hidden under beech trees in full blossom in Transylvania. The whole farm in a creation of the Queen, and bears her artistic impress everywhere.

As Theron and I motored back with her she told us one of her own fairy tales, a story of Christmas which I believe appeared in the Christmas edition of the *London Evening News* last December, — about a chimney sweep and his "smuts," and how his dreams came true. Her Majesty was in her gayest and most talkative and springhtly mood. One feels with her at such times as though he were a little boy sitting on the floor to hear his mother tell fairy stories. Her children must have worshiped her, and they are certainly very devoted to her now.

We found our crockery from Ruffer waiting for us when we reached home. Her Majesty gave a lamp to Theron and another to me and also two peasant jugs, and to Elizabeth and Cornelia each a jar.

Our dinner was in the Studio, and after it Her Majesty and we four sat down around the fire while she read aloud from her diary, written in Iași in December and January, 1916-1917. She read it exactly as it was written, as I could not help seeing for I sat beside her, and she often held the book in such a way that it was perfectly easy to read over her shoulder, which I did not do. It was not only intensely interesting, but at times really thrilling, and full of emotion. Remember that the whole royal family had had to run away from Bucharest with the army, that the Germans occupied 90% of Roumania, and that the Roumanian system of transport and supplies had broken down completely.

On every hand there was discouragement, disorganization, and despair, everyone complaining and laying the blame on others. One can imagine that the endless courage of Her Majesty must have been a great source of inspiration to her officers and soldiers. She always wore a plain nurse's garb, and spent hours every day in visiting hospitals and arranging with a group of her ladies packets for sick soldiers. Typhus had begun to spread, and her physicians tried to keep her out of the hospitals but she refused to obey them and went everywhere, and escaped from it unscathed.

In those months she was trying with King Ferdinand to arrange a new Ministry, and it was then that the Brătianu brothers took up the leadership where others had failed. I hardly dare put down her comments on her own family and country and on the Roumanian people. It was amazing that she should read it to us just as it was, but she said that only thus could we really get the spirit of the period. She understands her husband as clearly as anyone in the world could, and sees his good-nature, his kind heart, his modesty, his timidity, and often his failure as King to take the lead which he might have. He could see, as we heard on all sides, that the real power in the family is Queen Marie, and not King Ferdinand.

Her sister, the Grand Duchess Kyril, was with her a good deal, and was evidently a great comfort to her during those months. A great many people at that time constantly tormented her, trying to persuade her to go to Russia to her cousin the Czar, to plead with him for more effective Russian aid. She was perfectly willing to do this, but the Ministry under Brătianu, and the King were absolutely opposed to what they called a crazy idea. The debate over it appeared again and again in the journal until one wonders that Her Majesty was not driven crazy.

There was finally a government decision to send Crown Prince Carol and Mr. Brătianu, but before they had reached Petrograd the revolutionary break-up had begun, and of course after that there was not only no aid from Russia, but the presence of the disorganized Russian army became a terrific menace. In January, 1917, her sister, who had gone to Petrograd, was able to send her a whole car full of supplies for sick soldiers, and her joy in the privilege of distributing these things appeared on every page. She has the real English ability to organize and the appreciation of precision, and the sense of time. "My people," as she always referred to Roumanians, "are never on time," she writes, and her recognition of their inability to "run things" and of their dreadful neglect of the sick and wounded constantly appears.

She gave an amusing picture of her growing displeasure with her chief Aide, who fell under the influence of one of the ladies-in-waiting, and began to take orders from this lady rather than from the Queen. The Queen watched this for some time and concluded that she must make it clear that he was to do her bidding or leave her service, and she described her scene with him, his anger, and then his abject confession.

She was constantly overdoing, and clearly growing ill. She finally came down with bronchitis which ran into pneumonia, but made an astonishingly rapid recovery, which is characteristic of her indomitable will.

There is much talk in the diary of Russia and Rasputine and the follies of the Czar and Czarina, who brought the end of Imperial Russia upon themselves. "What blind obstinacy and corruption," she exclaims. Her Majesty read to us until midnight, and was evidently quite worked up over the rereading of her diary.

Princess Ileana was at dinner this evening, and we saw more of her than at any previous time. She is "sweet 16" with a vengeance, and kept us in gales of laughter telling about her visit to London last summer, where a room had been prepared for her at the Roumanian Legation. Her train was late, and she reached the Legation about 5:30 in the morning. They were astonished to see her, and she was still more astonished to find Prince Paul, the youngest brother of the King of Greece, occupying the bedroom prepared for her.

It seems that Prince Paul and Crown Prince Carol had been out at a dance, and as Paul had come up from the country he had no place to go when the dance was over, so Carol brought him back to the Legation, looked around for a room, found the one prepared for Princess Ileana and told Paul he could have it. Princess Ileana was rather indignant, but naturally did not wish to disturb Paul, but found Carol in bed in his room, and gave him a piece of her mind which was specially sharp as there was absolutely no place for the poor Princess to sit down except in the hallway and she was fatigued beyond measure. According to Ileana, Carol refused to get out of bed, but finally woke up sufficiently to ring his bell and summon a valet and have some tea brought for them. He then went and pulled Paul out of bed and the three had a morning meal at six o'clock, during which Ileana's room was hastily arranged, and she then retired to bed. The lively narration of this tale made me think of Constance and Carol, who would find Ileana a most jolly comrade I am sure. She works hard at her lessons, her drawing, her music etc., and evidently has a very keenly developed sense of responsibilities laid upon her by her birth and position. She has much of the energy and vitality of Queen Marie, and I judge also a good deal of her organizing power. She gave us a lesson in Roumanian. I discovered that "ul" is the article "the," and is put after the word, hence "palatul Cotroceni" means "the palace of Cotroceni."

Wednesday, February 4th

Still another beautiful day with a blue sky. My left ear, alas, gave me a bad turn yesterday afternoon, and ached so during the evening that it made it hard to listen to the Queen's reading of her journal. The left side of my throat is badly swollen, and I feel like a rather miserable specimen this morning. Cornelia loaned me her hot water bottle which I put under my ear as I went to sleep. I awoke at five to discover that most of its contents had leaked through a tiny pinhole in the rubber, and royalty's pillow was thoroughly soaked, to say nothing of sheets and blankets. Such a mess! Happily the palace is steam heated, so I opened the radiator and shut my windows, and got dried out before long.

Theron went off to town at 9 a.m., and Cornelia and Elizabeth with Mme. Perdicari visited an orphanage. I was sorry not to go, but was better off at home, and spent the morning writing, reading some of the Queen's articles, and sleeping. We get to bed so late that even breakfast at 9 does not give one very long nights.

I enjoyed this morning's study of the beautiful "Portrait of a Girl," by Joshua Reynolds, 1729-1792, which hangs over the fireplace in my sitting room. The Queen tells me it was bought by King Carol some thirty years ago. A young girl with a sweet face and fascinating golden hair is crouching under the dark, half invisible branches of a tree, with her left arm thrown around a bird-cage, from which she has released a pet bird which is alighting on her right shoulder in order to feet from her right hand which is bent up to throw a bit of bread to his bill.

The bay window is hung with golden silk curtains embroidered in olive green. On the wall close by is a charming Egyptian Nile scene — purple pyramids with the sunset gold behind them, and palms in the foreground reflected in the river just as I saw it in Cairo, all in a deep gold frame, in beautiful harmony with the golden curtains.

I love the view upon the park from this window, including the balcony outside the Studio windows, which Elizabeth and I have named "The Jasmine Tower," a memory of Shah Jehan and his queen's jasmine tower on the walls of the fort at Agra. One of my photographs shows it beautifully.

I amused myself this morning copying from a towel the details of the national arms of Roumania. It is a shield in four sections, with a tiny Hohenzollern shield occupying the center showing the addition of a Hohenzollern dynasty to the four provinces of Roumania, the arms of which appear in the four quarters.

The upper left quarter is an eagle looking up towards a tiny sun in the corner of the shield. The upper right quarter is the ox head of Moldavia with its huge spreading horns such as one sees on hundreds of oxen plodding along the country roads, with a star and crescent between the horns. Is this reminiscent of relationship with Turkey? I have pumped everyone I could meet as to the details of this shield and not a soul has yet been able to answer half my questions. The lower left quarter is a lion rampant standing on a crown with a star between his two front paws, and the lower right corner is two dolphins on their heads, the arms of the Dobrudja, which is the province along the Black Sea coast, south and east of the huge bend and the delta of the Danube.

In the autumn of 1916, after Roumania's declaration of war (August 27, 1916), the Russian armies chose the Dobrudja as the path for their advance on Bulgaria and Constantinople. The main Roumanian army at that time advanced across the Carpathians into Transylvania, but one or two divisions supplemented the Russian army in the Dobrudja. A combined German-Bulgarian-Turkish army under Mackensen opposed the Russo-Roumanian advance, and within two months Mackensen's army had cleared the Russians and Roumanians out of almost all the Dobrudja, captured Constanța and the railroad line to Bucharest, with the huge bridge and causeway, over nine miles long, across the two branches and the marshes of the Danube river at Cernavodă. The Roumanians blew up this bridge in their retreat, the only bridge across the Danube between the Iron Gates and the Black Sea.

Among other articles this morning I read Queen Marie's story *Baragladin's Treasure*, a fascinating legend of a gypsy boy of seven who played the violin with extraordinary beauty. Like every boy, he had dreamed of the box at the end of the rainbow, and one day after a summer shower he ran hard enough actually to find the rainbow's end before it vanished, and sure enough there was the box. Unhappily, he could not force the little treasure open, and for fear that his gypsy comrades would discover it, he hid it in a certain willow tree by a river in Roumania. In his exuberant joy over his success he composed a wonderful hymn to the rainbow, but kept this hymn secret, never playing it on his violin except when he was entirely alone. When he awoke the next morning he found himself jolting along in the family gypsy cart far from the river, the willow tree and his hidden box. No protests or tears would persuade the family to return, and he would not tell why he wanted to go back. The little fellow lost his way completely, and although he never forgot the willow tree he was never able to find its location.

He spent years of wandering, hunting for it in vain, and so absorbed was he in his search that he never thought of marrying. His violin charmed everyone but otherwise he was considered a poor crazy boy. One day, on a holiday in town, he meets a painted beauty. She hears his violin and asks him to play for the dancing at her wild parties. He falls in love with her, but at one of the dances when all had been drinking, she insults and taunts him before them all. He becomes furiously angry, and in his rage boasts that he can give her what no one else can, namely, a wonderful box found at the end of the rainbow. The crowd gather around him jeering and thinking him mad. Beside himself he seizes his violin, and for the first time plays in public the wonderful rainbow hymn. They listen in amazement and grow quiet and stupid at the marvelous beauty. As he finishes the sublime hymn he realizes that in his folly he has paraded his life secret and life treasure before a vulgar crowd, and rushes out of the hall vainly repenting his madness.

His father has died, his mother grows old, they wander for years, and she finally dies, but as he sits beside her at the end she says that she knows he has had a life secret, and begs him to let her hear it. He takes his violin and plays to her the rainbow hymn for the first time, and tells her of the box hidden in the willow. His own life draws on into old age, and, ready to die he wanders with his clan on a spring day into a lovely meadow. A spring shower passes over the sky followed by a wonderful rainbow, the end of which discloses to his old eyes a rotting willow tree, and he suddenly realizes that he is back in the scene of his boyhood experience at the age of seven. He rushes to the old willow, takes out the rotten stump, finds the treasure box, opens it and finds concealed all his own youth with its joy and strength, and he dies happy in the thought that he will wake up in the next life with the purity, strength, and happy health of his lost boyhood, — rather a pretty tale and very well told.

Cornelia and Elizabeth were enthusiastic about their trip to the orphanage. Mme. Perdicari had told them of her own girlhood when her father, the famous French doctor, Charles Davila, who started the orphanage had put his own daughter into it as a boarding pupil in order to prove to the world at large that the school was worthy of public confidence and respect, although nominally an orphanage.

As generally, I sat at Queen Marie's left at luncheon. She got out samples of her beautiful silver-gilt plates for state dinners, and also three sizes of beautiful Bohemian glass, designed to go with the gilt plates, and three wonderful Russian silks which she uses for the center of the table on those occasions. One is embroidered in gold tulips with tiny red tips on the stamens; another is embroidered in small round figures of various soft shades of blue on a gold background, and the third is a gorgeous tapestry cross in gold and a soft rusty brown. Her Majesty took as much joy in showing these treasures as any child might take, and said laughingly "Aren't they sumptuous?" which she shortened into "sumpchus," with a jolly arching of her eyebrows and a sparkle in her blue eyes. It is a wonderful thing for a woman of fifty to have retained all those girlish enthusiasms. She is fairly running over with energy and vitality, and one marvels that she can give out so constantly and yet seem to have plenty of reserve.

In the afternoon we read a little from *The need of knowledge*, which I later finished by myself. It is the story of a lonely old King, Demetrius by name, who is very wise but has never found the real seed of knowledge. He hears that a lonely hermit in the mountains possesses it, and as refuses to come to him he shakes his rheumatic old bones for three days on the back of a white donkey in order to visit him. He secures the seed and plants it and it grows into a hideous tree which spreads so rapidly that in a few days its roots and gnarled and powerful branches have broken down the palace, swept over the beautiful countryside, and destroyed all the happy peasants' homes and fields. In his despair, King Demetrius appeals again to the hermit who gives him a new seed (humility?), which he plants and which springs up to destroy the ugly old tree of all knowledge and to restore the land to happiness.

The Queen's theory of kings and queens and their lonely life and their desire to be let alone by their bothersome and far too numerous attendants, is cleverly brought out in the story.

Quite a company was invited in the city and a Polish pianist played charmingly.

We had the usual family dinner in the Studio and then went over to spend the evening with King George and Queen Elizabeth, who had a group of musicians and a very delightful company of guests. Among them were Mrs. Jay and the enormously tall Counselor of the Serbian Legation, and others whom we had met at Mme. Procopiu's. There was music on the cello and piano and singing by two of three persons.

It was this evening that King George showed me the article in the *December Current History* which led to our discussion of the prospects of his return to the throne. He and I also talked about the excavations at Ephesus, carried on by the Greeks while they were occupying the Smyrna, and he got out an interesting volume of pictures illustrating the finds. He also brought up the subject of Loeb's Classical Library, a series of translations from the Greek and Latin authors intended to give modern readers the treasures of classical literature in attractive form, and well translated, but at a modest expense.

King George told how he was smoking after dinner in the lobby of a hotel at Florence a few months ago when a man stepped up and said, "You are King George of Greece. I want to get acquainted. My name is Loeb. I am a Jew. I am publishing a Classical Library. Do you know about it? Let me show you a volume." The result was a very pleasant acquaintance, and Mr. Loeb promised to send him each volume as it appeared, and King George added that he was gathering the whole collection as a nucleus for the school library of the second Robert College to be built some day in Athens.

About 11 p.m. the music stopped, and there was a "sumpchus" tea served, as Her Majesty slyly remarked to me. Queen Elizabeth enjoys good living, and evidently likes to supplement the more modest teas in the Queen's Studio by wonderful fancy cakes sent up from the city. Then there was more music and we walked back across the open court with Her Majesty at 1 a.m. I was nearly dead and my ear was bad. The palace doctor had come to see me at 7 p.m., and had given some drops for my ear and a gargle to King Ferdinand's kind nurse, who sat up to care for me until that unearthly hour. I sat in a big chair in my bedroom while she fussed around for half an hour, making a gargle, preparing linden tea in which I took a tablet of aspirin, and finally doing my ear and head up until I closely resembled an Egyptian mummy. Happily, the cold compress did me good and my ear was less obnoxious on Thursday.

Thursday, February 5th

I slept as late as possible and breakfasted with Elisabeth dressed in my bathrobe, and still wearing my mummy bandages. George Sirbo, the valet, hovered around as usual, and I could not detect the slightest tendency to laugh up his sleeve at the strange appearance of his master.

While we were eating a copy of *My Country* reached us from Queen Marie, accompanied by two beautiful large photographs of herself, one marked for Elizabeth and one for me, and a third, of post card size, on which she had written, "I hope the earache is better." After getting dressed I wrote her a little note of thanks for the book and the photographs.

The trees this morning were all aglitter with ice formed from the heavy due. I did not go out with the others, but read in *My Country*, and enjoyed the beautiful photographs with which it is illustrated. Among others it contains the picture of a monastery balcony, from which the balcony forming the north-east entrance to the Byzantine dining room is copied.

I left at 12:30 for the city to join Mr. Martin of the Standard Oil Company, who is president of the American Men's Luncheon Club. The luncheon was held in a local restaurant and there were fifteen men present, including Messrs. Stevens, Morgan, and Brown of the Y.M.C.A., an American dentist, Dr. Costwald, Rev. Mr. Hurley, a Baptist missionary who has been eighteen months in Bucharest and has just received notice that his residence permit will not be renewed and that he must leave the country within two weeks, — Dr. VanNorman, commercial attaché, Mr. Hinckley, second secretary, Mr. Christie, a local business man, Mr. Redfern, formerly a private secretary with Charles R. Crane and now working in Dr. Van-Norman's office and is also acting correspondent for the Associated Press, Mr. Daly of the Standard Oil, Mr. Hollinger of Geneva and the Y.M.C.A., Theron, and another guest by the name of Schoenfeld.

Quite unlike our Constantinople Luncheon Club they do not begin at all on time, and we loitered around in conversation for over half an hour over the time set. Then they did not begin the speeches promptly, but gave me the first chance. I talked for seven or eight minutes, and was proposing to stop, but they said to go on, so, including their questions and my answers I was twenty-four minutes on my feet. Poor Mr. Hollinger, who was to have spoken, had no chance.

I got back to the palace about three, and did not go out again with Elizabeth and Cornelia who went to visit the asylum for the blind with Mme. Rahovary and Mme. Poienaru. I rested and read until tea time. At tea there was quite a company, including the Serbian minister, who was much interested in Robert College, a young Roumanian actress recently returned from considerable success in Paris, who later recited in French in an affected and meaningless way, utterly unattractive to Anglo-Saxons, and two artists, both elderly gentlemen, one named Verona, whose delightful painting which hangs in the palace, called "The Three Frontiers," we later went to study with one of the military attachés who explained that it represented a high bluff in Moldavia from which there is a view across the Pruth River, and from which is visible the un-redeemed land of Bessarabia (in possession of Russia when the picture was painted but now a part of Roumania), and also the province of Bucovina which was then in Austria but is now also a part of Roumania. A Roumanian peasant girl is stretched out in the sunshine on top of the bluff, shading her eyes with her hand as she looks across into the unredeemed territory. The fact that the dream has come true makes this picture very popular now among visitors at the palace. It is very well done as a matter of color and emotion. We had piano music after tea by Miss Dumitrescu, the young lady who had played at Mme. Procopiu's the week before.

We had a really wonderful and interesting dinner evening with Her Majesty. During dinner she talked very freely about predecessor, Queen

Elizabeth (Carmen Sylva). It is very clear that the Princess Marie found Queen Elizabeth a very difficult person to live with. Perhaps it was the natural difficulties which would arise between a high spirited English girl, bubbling over with physical energy, and possessed of very great ability, and a rather set elderly German *hausfrau*, who looked with great disfavor (and perhaps with good reason) upon the escapades of her husband's nephew, Prince Ferdinand, the heir to the throne, and, in her desire to repress him, repressed the Princess Marie more than was wise. Both King Carol and Queen Elizabeth held the purse strings very tightly. The younger members of the court had little to spend. Considering the finances of Roumania King Carol was very wise. The quote from Queen Marie: "Carmen Sylva was always strongly under the influence of her immediate surroundings. She was emotional and intense after the German style. She had many old dames among her ladies-in-waiting who often led her around by the nose. She would become emotionally intense over the needs of some new charity and would select a leader for it, often quite unfit, and unwisely chosen, whom she would keep with her morning, afternoon, and night, to the exclusion of all others and for the time being no other person would seem to the Queen of any use. Hence she stirred up jealousies in the court and there was considerable trouble."

Princess Marie came to Roumania in 1893. Carmen Sylva had wanted to marry young Ferdinand to Mme. Văcărescu, a very charming Roumanian lady "with absolutely nothing against her," as Queen Marie said, except that she was a Roumanian, and the agreement had been when Roumania invited Prince Carol to take the throne, that neither he nor his descendents should ever marry into any Roumanian family. Queen Carmen made her plans for this marriage secretly, and strange to say King Carol knew nothing of it until it was sprung upon him by Ferdinand coming, at the Queen's instigation, to ask permission for the marriage. King Carol was very clever in his answer, saying, "I am quite ready to give my consent if you can get the consent of my government, of my parliament, and of my people."

Of course this was utterly impossible, as there was violent opposition to a local alliance. Probably the Roumanians have been very wise in this as they realize that the elevation of any Roumanian family to such a position as that of furnishing a queen would create endless jealousies and complications. You remember that the present Crown Prince Carol secretly married a worthy Roumanian lady, but was compelled to give her up.

As these plans had failed King Carol looked about Europe for a suitable wife for the Crown Prince. Prince Albert, afterward Edward VII of England, was appealed to, and being a court social light he made out a list of eligible young ladies, and it was sent to Prince Ferdinand for him to examine. As Queen Marie told us, "My name appeared at the top of the list, and Ferdinand said, 'She looks promising, trot her out,' and rather took to me when he met me, and we were married. Carmen Sylva was 'banished' for two years and went to live with her Mamma in Germany. I came at once to Bucharest, and in nine months I made a present to the country of a young heir to the throne. Speedy work was it not? Between January 10, 1893 and October 15th. Dear Carmen Sylva had written me from Germany before the baby arrived, 'I hope it will be a girl.' What do you think of that for a nasty remark? She was furiously angry when she learned that it was a boy, the heir to the throne."

Earlier in the conversation Queen Marie had said, "When I came to Roumania in 1893 they were all afraid of the 'Young Light' as I was called. Imagine it. I certainly had no aspiring to shine at the age of seventeen. I was terribly homesick and lonely, and anxious only to be let alone. However, during those early years as a young crown princess *I made every mistake I could make* (her exact words emphatically repeated), and I had to get out of all sorts of messes as best I could."

Years later Mr. P.P. Carp, a famous statesman of Roumania said to Princess Marie, "I have entire confidence in your future." "Why?" she asked, and he replied, "I have watched the way you have gotten out of your mistakes, and have discovered that you could get yourself out without the help of others." Queen Marie told that remark with much relish, and although it may sound rather egotistic as I write it here, it did not seem at all so as she talked. In fact, I never met a woman who could talk so much about herself and so frankly, and yet with such freedom from any disagreeable egotism. She is always so clever and amusing in her accounts of herself that one forgets that it is the first person of whom she is talking, and, furthermore, she is really clever and so abounding in vital energy that one cannot help feeling that all of what she says is really true.

During dinner she had the footman bring some of her papers and she read to us *A Queen's Prayer*, and *A Prayer of Thanksgiving*, both written by her. They were so striking that I later asked her for a copy of each. I give them here.

A Queen's Prayer

Oh! God, I lift up my heart unto Thee, listen I pray Thee to my humble prayer.

Thou hast exalted me oh! God, Thou hast set me up in high places; Thou hast laid into my hands a power not given to many.

Thou hast shown me a road that must be my road, upon which I must walk without faltering, to others it may appear to run through nothing but sunshine, but I have felt its stones, and the thorns also oh! Lord which grow beneath the roses in my garden.

Thou hast made my face to shine before the lowly ones of this world oh! Lord. Thou hast placed purple on my shoulders and a crown on my head and Thou didst bid me bear it as though it were not a burden.

Thou hast said unto me: "Thou art chosen amongst many, be worthy of the honour done unto Thee; let thy hand be gentle, thy word full of comfort, thy heart a resting place for the weary and sad. Be up early at dawn, and at night sleep not too soundly so as to hear any cry that may be cried unto Thee. For Thou art the mother of a people chosen so as to be able to lead them towards light and to carry the weight of their joys and their pains."

Therefore I cry unto Thee, O Lord, to give me strength to breast any storm, to face any fate, to live down any fear, to crush all impatience, to stand up through never matter what adversity.

O Lord, give me a heart brave enough to bear the sorrow of all I hear and of all I see, strong enough not to be discouraged when the long day is over, large enough to love even him whom no man loveth and just enough never to condemn in a hurry.

Give me the gift of words, O Lord, of sympathy, mercy, and forgiveness.

Let me hold my head high, not in pride, O Lord, but because my conscience is clear and so that I can look each man in the eyes.

And when cometh my hour of rest, O Lord, let those whom I lived for remember me with a smile on my lips, a gift in my hand, and a heart brimfull of love and understanding.

Prayer of Thanksgiving

Enough petitions, enough complaints, enough cries for forgiveness and help mount towards Thy throne, O God. Today the cry I send up to Thee is a cry of thanksgiving which rises as a song of sunshine out of the centre of my heart.

Blessed be Thou, O Lord, for all the wonders, for all the beauties that so boundlessly Thou hast scattered over the earth.

For the green freshness of spring I thank Thee, O Lord, for summer's ripe abundance and for the gorgeous farewell which autumn says to the year.

For the winter do I thank Thee, dear Lord, for its peace; for the tranquillity of deep shining snows beneath which our weary Mother Earth can slumber restfully.

For the forests and plains, for high mighty mountains whose topmost peaks touch the clouds, for the song of a bird, for the smell of fresh hay, for the sound of deep bells of an evening, O dear Lord, I thank Thee!

For dawn's rosy red, for sunset's flaming fires, for rain after drought, for hope after fear, for smiles after tears, for peace after strife, for silence after turmoil, for wide wild worlds where eagles dwell in solitude, O dear God, I thank Thee!

For all that is beautiful, for all that is good, for all that is sweet, for all that is rare, for the laughter of a child, for the scent of a rose, for the sound of grand music, for moonshine on water, for the rainbow in the sky, message of Thy mercy, O dear Lord, I thank Thee!

For the shadows of night, for gardens full of colour, for the cool breeze which awakes me at dawn, for the shine on a butterfly's wing, for the grasp of a hand in friendship, dear God, I thank Thee!

For my heart which can love, for my hand which can give, for my soul full of faith, for the feet that can lead me for cherished places, dear Lord, I thank Thee!

For the green of the fields, for the dows of the morning, for the honey the bees gather, for the water that runs, for the roof overhead, for the flame on the hearth, for sky, sea, and earth, for sun, stars, and moon, for light, sight, and smell, O dear God, I thank Thee!

For the joy of living which runs through my veins like a river, for eyes full of trust, for the voice that defends me, for the gratitude I feel towards others, for the face I love best, for the heart on which I can lean and for Thy ultimate Mercy, O Lord in which I joyfully believe.

Praise be unto Thee, O Lord, a hymn of thanksgiving; may each man lift up his voice singing to Thy glory, blessing the Almighty, for the beauteous, wondrous works of His Hand!

When one thinks of all the background of nearly fifty years of life out of which they have grown they become very significant. I was struck especially by the phrase, in the Prayer of Thanksgiving, — "For the grasp of a hand in friendship," for Queen Marie has an extraordinary handclasp with which she makes one feel that she is taking him right into her personality. I noticed in the very first time we were greeted by her in the corridor that memorable Thursday afternoon, and I felt it again and again, and growingly. She does not give you her hand, nor does shake hands in the usual sense. She gives a real clasp of friendship which seems to express a strong inner sense of goodwill.

Her reading of the two prayers to us turned the conversation very personal and religious, and she was evidently quite ready to have it move on in that way. I quoted to her the saying by La Bruyère, — "After a spirit of perception the rarest things in the world are diamonds and pearls." She did not quite catch in the first time, and I repeated it. She said it over to me slowly with shining eyes, and then repeated it two or three times. I shall trust her to remember it the rest of her life although I may forget it. I really believe that she herself does genuinely possess such a "spirit of perception."

She had said so many things about the burdens and difficulties and sorrows and trials that had come to her in the thirty years between 17 and 47 that I said to her "Perhaps Your Majesty has learned to love one of the hymns in your Anglican Church hymnbook which I discovered for the first time at a Sunday morning service held in the loungs of the Aquitania as I crossed the Atlantic on my way home to America in the summer of 1921. It begins, "And now, 'O Father mindful of the love,' do you remember it?" "Quote it to me," she said. Happily I know the whole hymn by heart, and I quoted the four stanzas, and added, "The words of which I was thinking especially in connection with Your Majesty are the words of the last line of the third stanza, — "And crown Thy gifts with strength to persevere." She repeated the line over two or three times, and said, "Yes, that is what one needs, — the gift of endless patience and faith."

It is worth recording here that King George who was sitting at my right and listening, came quietly to me alone after dinner, and said, "Are you willing to write out for me the words of that hymn?" He added, "I like especially the lines beginning, 'And then for those our dearest and our best.'" I did so later and he seemed very grateful. Poor fellow, I fear that no amount of persevering in the hope of an ultimate restoration to the Greek throne will bring him what his heart desires. I have talked with a good many Greeks in the weeks since our visit in Roumania, and before writing this diary, and I find almost none whose opinion is worth considering who thinks there is much possibility of a restoration of the monarchy in Greece.

Later at dinner we got to talking about little Prince Michael, the Queen's grandson, whom I have already described as living at the palace during our visit. I remarked on the delightful spirit of wonder which he carries around with him so naively, and said to Queen Marie, "I judge from your books and stories that Your Majesty has been happy enough to have lost spirit of wonder," which led my Elizabeth to quote the inscription on a stone, "He who wonders reigns, and he who reigns shall rest." Queen Marie, with her quick intuition, caught the implication and echoed the words two or three times in her characteristic manner. Perhaps she puts them away in her memory by that quick repetition as though she were settling the thoughts once for all into her mind.

We lingered over the dinner table until 9:50 p.m., when it was time for the party to leave for a musical at Mme. Procopiu's. As I had a real headache, and my ear was still very troublesome it seemed better to stay at home and go to bed.

Early in the dinner, sitting at her right as I so often did, and around the corner of the table which was long and narrow, I had admired the superb pearl hanging from the end of her diamond necklace. In fact I had recognized the diamond necklace as the one which she wore at her coronation, which appears in the coronation pictures where she is wearing her gown. She unfastened the pearl from the flat diamond chain, and let us pass it from hand to hand about the table. It is a huge thing, almost round and even more velvety in quality than the beautiful pear shaped pearls she has worn in her ears and on another chain, and she said it was the best quality of all she had. It has never been pierced in any way but is most cleverly held by tiny platinum feet. Never in my life have I handled and examined so closely such superb things as she has let us play with quite like children. She enjoys them thoroughly herself and makes no concealment of her pleasure in them. We asked her whether she was never afraid of losing her jewels. She said that she left money and jewels about her boudoir and bedroom perfectly freely, expecting her maids to care for them properly, and that she had never lost a single thing.

As I had been reading *My Country* I spoke of the fact that she gave to an old peasant woman some money, and asked whether she had the habit of often giving money directly. She replied that before the war she had never done so, but that poverty became so great during the war that both she and King Ferdinand had concluded that they must make direct gifts of small amounts of money to large numbers of the poor. At one time, while in Iaşi in exile, King Ferdinand gave her a million lei out of his own funds, which she distributed in tiny sums to thousands of people as she went about the country. Now that conditions are becoming more normal she is ceasing to give money directly, and instead she maintains the charities of which I wrote above.

During this evening she also gave us a thrilling story of the ovation to herself after the death of King Charles in October, 1914. The funeral of King Charles was in the morning, and in the afternoon there was a solemn Te Deum for the new King at the Cathedral. The next day young King Ferdinand took the oath of Loyalty to the constitution before the parliament, and when the ceremony was over there was, of course, great applause. Queen Marie was dressed in black with a heavy veil in accordance with court etiquette, so that she could see but her face could not be seen. Suddenly there was a cry from the crowd, "Viva Regina Maria!" and everyone turned toward her. She raised her black veil, and one can imagine how striking her yellow hair and bright color would appear with such a background. Instantly there was a wild ovation, and (according to Her Majesty) "My people said afterward it was Her Day as well as His." Of course, it sounds rather egotistical to repeat such a story from her own lips, but one cannot wonder that she was pleased, and likes to remember it. Of course, the fact is that Queen Marie is more of the real power behind the throne than is King Ferdinand.

Although the others went to the musical and left me to go to bed, I sat up for a long time writing up this extraordinary evening.

Friday, February 6th

There was a dense fog last night. I awoke at five this morning with a very bad ear and throat, and thought I was really going to be thoroughly ill. I shut my windows to keep out the intensely damp night air, and went to bed again, waking up in time for breakfast at nine, when I felt somewhat better. I did not get dressed until eleven o'clock, and stayed inside all the morning.

Queen Marie sent to each of us at breakfast a copy of her book *Why?* Later we read aloud some thirty pages of it. It is in a very different style from any other thing of hers I have read, — more of the romantic novel about it. This time I did not acknowledge the gift by any note as I had acknowledged *My Country*, and wondered afterward whether I made a mistake in not doing so, for Her Majesty likes to have one appreciative of the numberless little kindnesses which she seems to take constant pleasure in doing.

We started at one o'clock for luncheon with Colonel and Mrs. Greble. She was Florence Colgate, a cousin of Mrs. Father Cleveland of Riverdale, with whom Elizabeth and I had dined in 1922, and whom I had liked very much. I sat at Mrs. Greble 's right, and made the very foolish mistake of saying early in the meal that I had sat beside her cousin Mrs.

Cleveland and had found her immensely interesting. The result was that poor Mrs. Greble became terribly self-conscious, and conversation between us lagged desperately, so that by silent and mutual consent I left her to Theron, at her left, and chattered with Mrs. Foy, wife of one of the military attachés, at my right. She is very jolly and we are hoping that she and her husband may be transferred to Constantinople when Major and Mrs. Miles leave us in the spring.

Other guests were Mme. Filipescu, Col. Foy, Mr. and Mrs. Hollinger of the Y.M.C.A. at Geneva, and a French count who married a Pittsburgh girl possessed of some millions of sugar dollars. Not one of us four could bear the French count, and we discovered that Mrs. Greble shared our sentiment and only had him at lunch as a business necessity. We liked Col. Greble exceedingly. He gave us a long account of his efforts to start a country club in Bucharest, and showed us the original designs he made and the photograph of the accomplished reality. He got into endless rows over the matters, and showed how difficult it is to engineer anything like that amid the endless petty jealousies of the social world in a city like Bucharest. He has been the representative of the Baldwin Locomotive Works there for four years. Not long after his arrival at Bucharest he felt the need of some place for the best classes of young men where they could have healthy sport and amusement under worthy auspices.

As Mr. Greble and his wife are possessed of ample means he was in a position to help finance the country club and to secure influential backers. He still has some $5000 of his own money in it, and the club is not a financial success although the initiation is only 6000 lei ($16 at present rates of exchange), and the annual dues 2000 lei.

We did not get away from the Grebles until 4 p.m., then I had a forty minute call on Dr. Van Norman, the commercial attaché, and found him exceedingly interesting. He feels strongly that the present attempt of old Roumania to rule the whole country must cease. Transylvania, Bucovina, and Bessarabia are very large in area and population as compared with old Roumania, and much more advanced. They will not tamely submit to the present dictation from old Roumania, — especially Transylvania with its seven million people of fairly developed intelligence. The three Brătianu brothers are able men, he said, but their effort to keep everything in their own hands is hopeless.

He says Transylvania has begun to realize that it is her special mission to educate both old and new Roumania in what real Roumanianism is. He believes the country can ultimately accomplish a very vital unity and that it stands good chance of preserving Bessarabia in spite of the Russian Soviet attitude. Vitella Brătianu, the minister of finance, ablest of the three brothers, is a tremendously hard worker, he said, often spending eighteen hours a day at his office. He is blessed with health and can do what very few men can do, but, owing to his set and obstinate nature he keeps himself and his country in constant hot water.

We all went to the Y.M.C.A. for an hour between five and six o'clock, finding there Mr. Stevens, general secretary, Mr. Brown, the boys' worker, Mr. and Mrs. Morgan, Mr. and Mrs. Hollinger and an interesting clerical leader who speaks English well, and is an enthusiastic supporter of the Y.M.C.A. The Morgans have been married but for three months and have just established a little home of their own, so, before going back to the palace, we drove around with her to the tiny apartment which they have fixed up attractively, and she sat down at the piano in a most simple way and sang for us, first "A Song of the Rebrides," and second, "Fiddle and I," the old song for which I used to play the violin obligate as a small boy in Milton. I have not heard it in years. Mr. Morgan had worked directly with Queen Marie in Iași in 1917-1918.

At dinner this evening Crown Prince Carol appeared. He arrived today from London, leaving Princess Helen, his Greek wife, in Paris to continue the treatment for her eyes. Prince Carol sat at Queen Marie's left, directly opposite me so that I had a good chance to study him as well as to talk with him. His first appearance is not especially prepossessing. He is good natured and friendly but rather quiet, — perhaps overshadowed by his active and talkative mother, as I fear all her children are. He gives at first no sense of strength or virile manhood, or of any special degree of thoughtfulness. He was perfectly agreeable, but initiated almost no conversation. King George of Greece makes a far better first impression.

Prince Carol has inherited some of the weak facial features of his father but without his father's dignity and his mother's charm. However, I must add here that I liked him better the more I saw of him. Queen Elizabeth was absent from dinner, in bed with a cold, but Princess Ileana was there in one of her jolliest moods. She brought her sketchbook and showed us the head of Miss Marr, her governess, which she made this morning, very cleverly done. This lead Queen Marie to bring out some of her own sketches and also her plans for her new Turkish cottage to be built on the shores of the Black Sea, south of Constanța, in the region known as Dobrudja, where there are still several hundred thousand Turks. They are a simple peasant people, talking Turkish, among whom she likes to visit.

Queen Marie clearly has very sharp eyes, and must have visited a large number of Turkish villages, for her conversation and sketches showed that she was perfectly familiar with the kind of life which I know so well from my horseback tours through Asia Minor. Little did I ever dream that those months on horseback with Ellsworth in the summer heat of Anatolia would some day furnish me with a social and artistic background and fund of knowledge which would enable me to bring some real contribution to the thinking and plans of the Queen of Roumania! She also brought out some superb photographs of the monasteries of Metora, etc., in Thessaly which she visited some years ago, being drawn up in the traditional rope basket.

After dinner we four and Queen Marie established ourselves about the fireplace, and she read aloud from her diary of March, 1917. March third was the anniversary of the death of Carmen Sylva in 1916, and it was recalled in the diary. The Queen recalled a delightful story of a pony, called *Tangolitsa*, upon whom some of her children had learned to ride, whose long bushy tail had to be trimmed to nothing because it got infected and they were afraid the children would pick up the infection. She did not explain in detail what the infection was, but one could guess that it was that form of small animal life well known in the Near East.

Those days in March, 1917, were among the most trying, as the absolute failure of her own army was perfectly clear, and the breaking up of Russia was also certain, so that every source of help for Roumania had been cut off. Queen Marie's loss of faith in her army and her people became apparent, and her intense struggle with the resulting disgust and disappointment. She had tried to maintain her faith all through the disasters of 1916 and the winter of 1917, but she had been compelled to acknowledge that the faith was ill-deserved.

Her constant struggles with her ministry in Iași appeared almost every day. "You cannot change your ministers as you can your clothes," she commented as she laid the diary down in her lap for a moment. We all laughed together over her frequent contacts with the good-natured Russian General Zacharoff, whose abominable French she loved to quote. With regard to the appeal to Czar Nicholas II he said "Ça honte pour Russie," meaning that it was a shame to Russia that such an appeal is necessary, and added "Roi parle — toi parle — moi parle — Carol parle — Czar dit 'ou-ee-aaa.'" The poor General could never say the French word for 'yes,' making it three distinct syllables, the 'a' being prolonged. I presume he found this pronunciation amused people, and as he did not mind furnishing entertainment in those dark days he had developed the practice of exaggerating this oo-ee-aa when he talked French. He would often say to Queen Marie "Russie aime beaucoup vous!"

Of one of her ministers she had written, "He is a man with the face of a well-kept family dog." Again she wrote, "In my country they detest the right man in the right place," and elsewhere she said "defeat, retreat, and invasion is an ugly cruel thing."

On March 13, 1917, came their first news of the real meaning of the revolution at Petrograd. Each day in the journal there appeared long comments on the character and failure of the Czarina — her lack of love, her evil influence both over her husband and over all around her, her absolute waste of the twenty years of possible help to Russia, and how generally cursed and widely hated she was. The diary summed it up at the end of one day in this way: "She had no love; she let hate dwell in her heart."

Prince Ştirbey appears constantly in the story. He was head of the King's household, and was evidently a man upon whose quiet judgement Queen Marie greatly relied. He resigned from office two years ago. As he was closely related to the Brātianus, having married their sister, it was better for the head of the King's household to be wholly apart from politics. Queen Marie still keeps in close touch with him by correspondence, and evidently has great respect for his judgment in the solution of the present problems of Roumania. She read to us at dinner from his recent letters to her.

The diary of Queen Marie also gives a pitiful account of the treachery of General Sturza, a Roumanian general who proved a traitor to the country, having succumbed to the bribes of the Germans. There is a striking account of the ceremony of public degradation of this general who ran away in battle with his whole battalion.

Lady Barclay, a well-known character at the British Embassy at Constantinople, whose husband was minister in Roumania, often appears in the diary, and there are frequent comments upon her "riotous ways." Baliff, a sort of private helper to Queen Marie in her charities, and work with the soldiers, also appears frequently. Other people gave us a less attractive account of Col. Baliff than Her Majesty's, and one wonders whether he was not one of those favorites of whom other people often become jealous and sometimes perhaps with good reason?

Saturday, February 7th

I felt better this morning, although my ear still growls a bit, and my throat will not stand abuse.

We got off promptly at ten o'clock with Her Majesty to the Symphony rehearsal. Her reading the night before had tired her, and we had more than once tried to indicate that she ought to stop, but this morning she was as fresh and pretty as ever in her hat with pink trimmings, which the natural color of her pink cheeks perfectly matched.

**Visit of the Huntington Family to Romania in 1925 (from left to right):
King George of Greece, a member of the Huntington family, Queen Marie,
Ileana, Mrs. Huntington, Prince Carol, and George Huntington**

The concert began with a Weber Symphony, pretty and bright as usual. Then there was a superb Spanish suite by Lalo with a violin solo by a young Roumanian hopeful with tremendously long straight black hair and shaven face and neck, who nevertheless played the violin remarkably well. He is a local prodigy whom Queen Marie had helped with her own money to get an education in Paris, so he was full of animated gratitude to his beloved Majesty.

I had to leave at 11, in the middle of the concert, to keep my appointment for an interview with Mr. Angelescu, the minister of education. I realized again what magic effect a footman with a crown on his collar can have. The gates of the Ministry swung open to my royal car, and every door flew open before us as the footman led the way toward the Minister's private office. When I entered the waiting room there were some fifteen people there, and others came during the two or three minutes which he kept me waiting while he finished his previous interview. He then passed over the whole crowd and drew me off into his private room behind.

He is a man of fifty-five, with a heavy moustache, and quite a bit gray, — younger than I expected from what people had told me, and far more animated than Mr. Jay had led me to expect. Several people had called him "a nice old codger." I had between twenty and twenty-five minutes with him, which was far more than I or my cause was entitled to considering the ante-room which was still fuller when I passed out and which gave me some very pointed looks, evidently wondering what right this stranger had to delay them all. I showed him the College catalog and some of our pictures, to which he gave fair attention but no very great interest. He evidently thought that I was boasting a bit about the American schools at Constantinople, and there is scarcely a Roumanian alive who does not look with scorn and contempt upon Constantinople and the Turks as the epitome of the uncivilized. He suddenly jumped up and broke into what I was saying with the exclamation "Do you know what *we* are doing?" with the emphasis of the "we," and plunged into a sea of figures and descriptions and photographs showing changes in the system of education in Roumania since the war. It is really a remarkable story and I was only too glad to hear it.

He had a huge pile of pictures through which he rapidly ran, showing simple village schools and very fine city high schools, etc. He rang his bell furiously and demanded the immediate presence of the Director of Elementary Education who appeared at once and flooded me with more statistics. The Minister grew more and more enthusiastic as he talked, raising his voice at the same time in a typical Roumanian manner such as I have often seen in their restaurants, hotels, and railroad trains, finally blowing off steam gesturing and lecturing with the most intense volubility.

I could hardly keep my face straight. From the standpoint of my personal interest and a typical Roumanian show, it was thoroughly worth while, but far from what I had expected. I finally indicated that I had kept him for too long, and brought him down to earth by insisting that we must have another word about Robert College, whereupon he promised with great unction "that the Roumanian government will recognize whatever Robert College is doing," and I withdrew, followed by him through the ante-room to the outer door, after having made a date for the following Monday to visit schools with the Director of Elementary Education.

The footman was patiently waiting outside the door and led me back down the huge corridors, so typical of Eastern office buildings, — dingy and dusty with occasional dirty smoky stoves whose ashtrays are always littered with cigar stubs and burnt matches.

I drove directly to the American Legation to report my interview to Mr. Benjamin Riggs who is first secretary, as Mr. Jay was still suffering in bed. Mr. Riggs had that morning received an answer to his first letter which was weeks old, in regard to Robert College, and said they asked certain further information which he supplied. I learned there, to my great regret, of the sudden death early this morning of the little four-year-old son of the Caffreys. The American colony was utterly upset over it, and all the ladies were busy helping at the Caffrey's home. Hence our tea with Mrs. Palmer, the Consul's wife, planned for that afternoon was called off. I also met Mrs. Riggs at the Embassy, and Mr. Minckley, the second secretary. Then I slipped off to find Richard Bolton of the Standard Oil, and to plan for the afternoon with him.

There was the usual formal luncheon at 1:30 in the Byzantine dining room. Both King George and Prince Carol were there at the right and left of Queen Marie, as would be proper at a formal dinner, while I sat further around the board and had a chance to study Prince Carol by daylight.

He has long light wavy hair, quite the color of his mother's, rather fishy blue eyes, bulging a bit, a short yellow moustache, pretty cheeks with considerable pink and white color, a weak mouth over a weak retreating chin, a pleasant affable smile, a marked English accent, and many mannerisms picked up from his mother which fit him less well than they do her. As at dinner the night before, he made no special endeavor to talk or to be entertaining or agreeable, and I wondered whether he is really rather self-centered or whether it is because it is the proper thing to leave the King and Queen to take the lead in everything.

Prince Carol has the same peculiar pronounciation of the word 'pretty,' which his mother has. It is impossible to repeat it in letters, but one might write it "peuty," pronouncing the *eu* in the French manner. Queen Marie has the most fetching way of suddenly saying about something one is looking at, "Isn't it peuty?" Or even rather slyly, "Ain't it peuty?" Prince Carol in the first five minutes that I saw him at dinner the first time, had repeated the same expression in almost the same tone, "Ain't it peuty?" One wonders whether he consciously imitates his mother, or began it in joking mimicry.

I went to town at three and spent over two hours with Richard Bolton and seeing Robert College students. D.G. Inglessis came to see me at the Standard Oil office, looking like the small boy I knew ten years ago, still short with a round face and intensely black sparkling eyes and straight black hair, — decidedly attractive. He is much interested in a Greek club which he has been instrumental in organizing. It includes whole families, old and young alike, and is an endeavor to bring into the Greek colony in Bucharest some of the interests to which he had grown accustomed at Robert College. Indeed, as he described it to me, I said to myself that, unconsciously, he was taking our College and American community life as his model and was trying to introduce the music, lectures, sports, and social events which he had experienced there. I did not even mention it to him, fearing that it would make him self-conscious or might diminish his enthusiasm for the project on the ground that some of his colleagues would say he was simply imitating foreigners. It shows how big an impression a few years residence at Robert College does make on our students.

Richard Bolton spent an hour with me trying to find various Robert College students. We failed to find Leonidas Metaxas, John Garbis, and Troyanos but discovered Henry Presente, 1914, in the office of his wholesale grocery, looking very stout and prosperous and Jewish, and effusively friendly. He went with us to another large retail and wholesale grocery store kept by a Greek student who called himself Mainoff while at school, but now uses the name Mainoff Antoniades.

I got back to the palace in time to dress for the afternoon cinema party which lasted from six to eight o'clock. Tea was served again in the beautiful blue and gold Byzantine reception room where some forty or fifty people gathered, among whom we found enough acquaintances to make it very pleasant.

For the first time in our visit King Ferdinand himself appeared. The Queen had told us in the morning that the doctor had consented to his walking for the first time, and that he would probably come to the cinema. After all the guests had been served there was a sudden expectant hush, such as I had learned to realize meant the coming of some great dignitary, and King Ferdinand and Queen Marie appeared in the doorway.

The King was resting a little heavily on the arm of his wife, who looked very proud to be privileged thus to bring him in. He was dressed very simply, with less "nicety" than any other man in the room. He is a trifle stout, tall, and well-built, a great hand with a broad square forehand, which reappears in the fine head of his daughter Elizabeth; thick gray hair and a heavy beard, jolly twinkling blue eyes with a very kindly expression, and a most attractive smile, and a hearty, jolly laugh...

After such an affair no one leaves the room until after the King and Queen have retired; then the guests rapidly melted away, and we four made the most of the chance to wander around the reception room to study its furnishings more fully.

A Miss Beckley had been invited to the party and she stayed with us to talk it over. She has been sent to Europe by some newspaper syndicate especially to get acquainted with Queen Marie and to write her up. I am dictating this on April 17th, and will say here that Miss Beckley turned up at Constantinople some two weeks ago, after many weeks in Roumania, full of enthusiasm for Her Majesty, and also clearly realizing her limitations.

The more I see and hear of articles about Queen Marie the more I realize what a clever, self-advertising person she is. I wish she would not let her name and photograph be used with Pond's Vanishing Cream, but certainly the picture of her in the full page advertisement of Pond's cream in the New York *Times* was very well done. After all, one must remember that she is thoroughly human even though she may compel herself to believe in the divine right of kings.

There was the usual delightful family dinner in the Studio. As we gathered about the dining table the Queen looked over the eight persons with her, evidently studying anew the question of seating, and then said, "Let me have my guests beside me and my family in the middle." She then took her usual place at the end of the mather narrow long table, seating me as usual at her right, and Theron at her left. Next to me at my right she put Princess Ileana, then King George of Greece, then Elizabeth. Next to Theron, who was opposite me, at his left, she put Queen Elizabeth of Greece, then Prince Carol, and then Cornelia. She always settled such a little question as that with grace and graciousness, and with instant precision. I never saw a woman who hesitated less over which course to follow. I think she has schooled herself never to appear to hesitate even though internally she is meditating many possibilities.

This seating arrangement proved exceedingly pleasant, and we had one of the happiest dinners of our visit. The royal family all left at ten after nine as there was some grand ball going on in which we four were not interested, and Queen Marie had the mercy and good sense to spare us. We went off to bed early, though after I was undressed I tried to write up my diary, and fall asleep with my head on the precious desk of the King of Serbia. I wonder whether he was ever done likewise?

Sunday, February 8th

A beautiful fair day. We have been getting a lofty idea of the beauty of the winter weather in Bucharest, although they all tell us it can be as nasty as anywhere when it pleases.

Princess Ileana came to take us with her to church at 10 o'clock. She again enjoyed the beautiful choir of boys and men, and I enjoyed watching the large group of peasant people and palace retainers, with the few more tony persons. It was evident that they made the most of every opportunity to fasten their eyes on "Sweet Sixteen," in the person of Princess Ileana, and I do not wonder.

The service was only half an hour, and we left soon after to hear another delightful piano recital by Mr. Boskoff. I liked especially a Bach

Fugue, a Rondo by Beethoven, and a Lizst Ballade. But with his encores it was too long. The hall was crowded to the doors with hundreds of people standing in the aisles, — a fearfully dangerous situation in case of fire. Boskoff ought to make a success in America.

We did not leave the theater until ten to one, and went directly to the residence of Crown Prince Carol where we divided up into two groups, — one was Her Majesty, Cornelia, Theron, and myself in her Lincoln limousine, and the other group was Crown Prince Carol, who drown his own car, King George, Princess Ileana, and Elizabeth. We had a long and beautiful drive through the country to the north, finally entering some beautiful forests where the roads were snowy and icy, causing us to skid so often that more than once I feared we were to be landed upside down in a ditch. Queen Marie takes every such incident with absolute equanimity, and we three did have an exceedingly jolly hour in that car with her. How she can keep up that endless sense of vitality with spicy and interesting and worth while conversation, is a real marvel. Nothing ever flags when she is present.

We wound up at the King's hunting lodge, called "Soroviste," which is pronounced "Soro-vish-tée." It is situated at the edge of a lovely little lake, rather long and narrow, which was so solidly frozen that we want out for a walk on the ice. At least six inches of snow covered the ground everywhere, having lain there since the previous November when a tremendous storm deposited over three feet of snow. Since that time, no more snow had fallen. As we drove through the woods, Her Majesty described some of her many horseback rides among them. There are many miles of forests with all sorts of intricate roads intercepting them which she knows so well that she never loses her way. She hinted that she rather enjoyed getting Mr. Jay out there to ride with her, and then, pretending she did not know the road, upon which he would be very much alarmed, as one might ride there for days without coming out at the right spot.

Queen Marie has been much amused at the perfectly open adoration of Her Majesty exhibited by the Mon. Peter Augustus Jay, — an adoration which has aroused considerable indignation in his very *proper* wife, who was born Susan McCook of a haughty and very old New York family, who would be scandalized if they knew one of their adopted sons was paying too gallant attentions to a queen. Evidently the Queen rather likes him, and clearly she finds him very amusing as many people do, with his huge body and embarrassed stammering accent. She had remarked early in our visit, "Jay cannot stand the direct rays of the sun," a remark which can be interpreted as one pleases. He keeps some twelve riding horses as he is so heavy we would kill an animal if he were to ride him more than once or twice a week, and he also likes to have an occasional horse to loan to Her Majesty.

Writing at this late date, I must record that he has just been promoted to be ambassador to Argentina, and Mrs. Jay has written that she and he are very sorry to leave Bucharest.

Soroviste is a group of simple attractive cottages surrounded by fine trees, with an open lawn stretching down to the lake. The King's lodge has five good rooms, besides a big dining room where there is a large chimney and jolly great fireplace, with old fashioned solid iron doors.

Evidently a car full of food and servants had been sent ahead, for fires had been built in the tile stoves of every room in the King's lodge including the huge bathrooms. And the most delicious country luncheon had been prepared, which was served to us soon after our arrival. We were both cold and hungry and quite ready to make the most of it.

All the dishes in the King's dining room were made in a Greek porcelain factory, and there are delightful pieces of Roumanian and German pottery everywhere. His own special den has been done in hangings and finish of black and red brick, planned especially by Her Majesty to please her husband, after he had said to her, on seeing the rooms in her own hunting lodge which was built much later, "Why can't mine be as pretty as yours?" Up to that moment he had planned everything in his own lodge himself, and the Queen had let him alone, supposing he preferred to do it that way.

In the meantime, she had built her pretty little house of two stories, where we found a perfectly enchanting dinning room thickly hung with rows and rows of Roumanian peasant pottery collected by herself, and furnished with hand painted chairs in imitation of an old piece of furniture she had found in a peasant's home. She took us into every nook and cranny of it. It speaks of her in a marvelous way and yet there has been no lavish expenditure of money on it. In fact, I presume that six or seven thousand dollars would do the whole thing. It is simply that she "knows how."

She took down from the walls of the dining room two peasant jugs and gave one to Theron and one to me. Mine appears in my hand in one of the photographs. A cute little sight-sided guest house has been built on a pretty knoll overlooking the lake, two minutes away from the Queen's cottage, where "a guest can be quiet and not too much bothered by other people," as Her Majesty said.

We spent an hour strolling about the grounds, over the ice on the lake and taking pictures. After the gaiety of the drive out our lunch had been rather silent at first, perhaps because we were all hungry and had had enough talking. Before the end of it, however, people got to telling stories and we had some of the jolliest laughter of all our visit. I raked up my old tale about the American who insisted upon smoking in non-smoking first-class compartment on an English railroad, although he had only a third-class ticket. King George and Prince Carol had never heard the story and got the point instantly, and Prince Carol laughed more heartily than at any other time. King George sees and enjoys a good joke better than Prince Carol.

We got back to the city about half past four and Theron and I stopped to have tea at the home of Prince Carol which is in the city some three miles away from Cotroceni. He has a modern house with bloane furniture, fitted up much more like an American home than anything else that I saw in Bucharest. There were some splendid portraits of King George and Queen Olga of Greece by Lazlo, the famous London painter who did the beautiful portrait of Queen Marie which hangs on the Studio wall in the little recess at the west end of the room, beyond the grand piano, where the afternoon light makes it glow.

Prince Carol is an ardent stamp collector and has made with his own hands a complete stamp album consisting of loose leaves of heavy paper, with places for stamps of every issue of all countries, ruled, dated, and described with his own pen. It must have been months of work. He showed it to us with great pride and interest, and I do not wonder that he is pleased with it. Queen Marie had told us of the collection and I was curious to see whether the Prince had spent much money on it. Clearly he had not, for it was the sort of collection any intelligent young man might make by gradual acquirement and exchange with friends. Of course, he had the issues of his own country much more complete than most people could gather unless they paid large sums of money.

After tea he took us to his Foundation which is located in a rather handsome private house recently bought by the government, and presented to the Foundation. There we found the Director and several other intelligent young men who formed the nucleus of an office staff being trained to carry out the ideas of the Foundation.

The Foundation was started only two years ago. Prince Carol says its purpose is to spread "culture" and to supplement the work being done by public schools or existing private organizations. For example, several trained men are employed to go about among Roumanian villages introducing new books and encouraging the people to establish some center where reading matter can be found out of which a village library might develop. The Foundation provides at very moderate cost paper bound copies of standard Roumanian books including many translations of French and English literature.

Another group of men goes about the village lecturing on public hygiene, the history of Roumania, the meaning of democratic government, etc., and Prince Carol plans to have another group of trained men who will go about lecturing on improved methods of agriculture and household economics.

Still another activity of the Foundation is the extension of music. The Roumanian people are natural music lovers, with something of the gypsy instinct in them. The fine symphony orchestra in Bucharest had great difficulty in meeting its expenses and a year ago the Foundation took over the management of it, guaranteeing its expenses — a work somewhat similar to that done by Colonel Higginson for the Boston Symphony. The result has been that three other symphony orchestras which had been trying to get started in Iași and the smaller cities of Roumania have applied for similar assistance, and negotiations are under way for similar cooperation.

The Foundation possesses a four-story building fully equipped as a printing establishment. We went all through it and were astonished at the modern equipment. For example, there were eight linotype machines. He said it was valued at 80,000$, but the whole affair would cost much more than that in America. He plans that this press shall put out good literature at minimum prices. It has only been going a few months and just now is doing some general printing business for the government. He is having men translate the best books from other countries, as such books are generally not available excepting at very high prices.

Prince Carol has a man to direct the Foundation but gives a large amount of his own time to its personal supervision. It is evidently an activity to which his indefatigable mother has stimulated him. She never told us a word about it except to mention "my son's Foundation," but after he arrived from London she had said to Theron and me, "I have told Carol to show you the whole Foundation with great care." He certainly did so, and his intelligent appreciation of its present meaning and future possibilities called out our real enthusiasm.

We found a special car waiting for us when we came out of the Foundation at 7:50, and so got back in time to dress for dinner.

Monday, February 9th

At ten o'clock the Director of Elementary Education in Roumania, whom I had met during my interview with Mr. Angelescu, the minister of public instruction, called for me at the palace to take me on a tour of some of the city schools. He brought with him the Mayor of the city Mr. Onescu, of whom Mrs. Jay later spoke very favorably.

They took me first to visit a girls' normal school, just a few minutes distant from the palace. The Directress, Mme. Sadoveanu, is quite an extraordinary woman — short, thickset, vigorous, energetic, and quite up to date. She talks English fluently, having studied for some time in England. I later heard from Miss Brown, an English Y.W.C.A. secretary from Iaşi, that Mme. Sadoveanu is considered the best normal school leader in Roumania. As is usual in Orient, the buildings are huge rambling affairs with high ceilings and plenty of air space — utilized to the utmost in every classroom into which I went by apparently hermetically ceiling the windows.

The smallest class I saw was over fifty, and many groups numbered seventy to eighty, and one had ninety students. What a handicap to successful work such huge groups must be. The building was plainly furnished but had the needful things, and everything was very clean and orderly.

There is evidently a tour planned for visitors, according to which we looked into various classrooms, saw an exhibition of beautiful sawing and drawing, visited several dormitories, and wound up in a large assembly hall, the whole floor of which was vacant even of chairs as we entered. To my surprise, I found at least three hundred girls gathered in the galleries which run around three sides of the assembly hall. They burst into a chorus as we four entered, and I was informed this was a song of welcome to a distinguished visitor. I applauded liberally when it was done, and threw kisses, metaphorically speaking, to the girls who looked very jolly and neat and smiling. It is clearly a staged affair to produce an impression. Then they sang several very pretty selections, including some folk songs.

The general impression one gets is of a happy and well run school, but I can say nothing as to the real quality of the training. These girls, some from all over the country, many of them being from peasant families, picked out for superior ability as indicated in the village schools. They have to promise to teach at least three years in the public schools before marrying or going into other work. I was told that there are nine special normal schools in Bucharest, more that half of them for girls, and that a tenth institution is being built. In fact, the Mayor said those buildings were quite old, as was evident, and that there were much modern schools further away in the city.

Then we hastened on to a large orphanage near by the one which Elizabeth and Cornelia visited as described in their letters. I went through much the same performance in this place. There are not so many girls, and they varied more in age as I found when they gathered in a large hall to sing to me. There we sat down, and different groups of girls sang all sorts of selections without any piano accompaniment. Finally, from behind three or four rows of tall girls who had been standing, appeared a most jolly company of sixteen picked little tots dressed quite enchantingly, who marched forward, bowed, took positions on the floor and did a jolly dance together, the piano being played for this. Other groups were produced of varying ages who went through folk dances very prettily. Certainly the girls appeared best and happy, although there was rather more sense or formality about this institution than about the girls' normal school. It was rather overwhelming to have all this done for me alone, although naturally the Mayor and the Director of Elementary Education were people of sufficient importance to be pleased.

Next we drove to a very interesting elementary school which has been in operation only about a year in a new building. It is in a section of the city not more than ten minutes from Cotroceni where the Tobacco Regie, a government monopoly in control of all the tobacco industry in Roumania has a large factory, and has built about two hundred small model working men's homes for its people. Of course it was winter and the streets were snowy and muddy, but for such a country as Roumania the houses looked very comfortable and attractive. Naturally this new community wanted an elementary school, and the government agreed to bear part of the expense if the tobacco company and the people themselves would also subscribe. 300,000 lei (2,500$ at present rates of exchange, although that sum seems vastly more in Roumania than in America) was subscribed by the working people themselves. The company, I believe, gave as much more and the government subscribed the remaining 600,000 lei, the cost of the building being 2,400,000 lei, that is, 20,000$ in American money. I have a fairly good photograph of the building, a plain rectangular two stories and a good basement, simply built but in good taste. In the basement are shower baths where hot and cold water can be utilized twice a week, not only by the children, but by the community householders. The classes in this building varied in size from forty to sixty.

Then, in order that I might see one of their better new elementary schools, they drove me ten minutes to a much more substantially built school of brick and stucco with stone trimmings, part of which was still under construction and the balance already utilized for classrooms. This building cost over 3,000,000 lei, that is, over 25,000$, and was very good looking. My photograph of it is rather poor as I could not get far enough away to show it up well.

We had to hasten back to Cotroceni in order that I might dress for luncheon with Mrs. Jay, we four being the only ones present. Mr. Jay was still suffering much from his broken ribs.

We then went to the picturesque home of the owner of the beautiful embroidery shop to which Queen Marie had taken us early in our visit. She and her daughter and two young friends were dressed in their best ancient Roumanian costumes and took us about the house which is a regular museum of Roumanian art. The Queen joined us there. We were finally brought to the dining room where elaborate refreshments, including champagne, had been arranged. The luncheon at Mrs. Jays had been quite too abundant, and it was only 5:30 then, so we were not very hungry. I fear the mistress of the house thought we were not appreciative of her elaborate goodies. If I were not a tea-totaler I would say that the champagne tasted very good, at least such of it I imbibed which was a tiny fraction of that provided, and more to please our friendly hostess than anything else. I noticed that Queen Marie barely touched hers, in fact, she never took any wines at all when I had a chance to observe, and the very simplest service of modest wines at her luncheons and dinners. Indeed, at the family dinners, when she found we did not take anything, no liqueurs at all were served, even for King George and Prince Carol. It was a marked contrast to Dr. Prew's winey dinners during the days of the English occupation of Constantinople, when he had a big dinner of twelve to fourteen persons every Friday evening, with at least four kinds of wine, cocktails beforehand and liqueurs afterward in the drawing room. The Queen's attitude in this is simply another indication of what I admire in her, namely, a certain deliberate self-restraint in the spending of money and in the use of her exalted position.

There was the usual quiet dinner, after which Queen Marie read to us again from her diary. We watched her put it away that night with real regret.

Tuesday, February 10th

The earlier part of the morning was taken up with packing, but Queen Marie sent word early that she would see us at eleven, and we had a delightful hour and a half with her in the Studio. King Ferdinand himself came to luncheon — Elizabeth and I to our horror arriving in the dining room late, after the King and Queen had entered. Queen Marie was most gracious about it, and showed me her wrist watch as I sat beside her at her left, which certainly indicated that we were amply on time for 1:30 luncheon, and that she and the King had arrived five minutes too early.

King Ferdinand took an active part in the conversation, a part of which turned on the treatment of Roumania by the great countries of Europe. He is evidently very cynical about professions of friendship from the great Powers, his position being this — "When they need your assistance they know how to take you, but as soon as the need has passed they throw you into the gutter." After luncheon he talked with various people and then sought me out and gave ten minutes of undivided attention to Robert College and its work. From that we passed on to the needs of Roumania, and he talked of his ideals for the education of the common people. He emphasized especially the need of religious tolerance, and recommended Robert College for the position it takes in that matter. He was very frank about recognizing the narrowness of the average Roumanian on that subject. He himself is a Roman Catholic.

I wish I could describe properly our farewell minutes with Queen Marie. I suppose Cornelia or Elizabeth have given it in better detail. She took each one of them by both hands and kissed them on each cheek, and spoke us warmly about her pleasure in our visit as any dear old friend whom we had known for years might have done. There was absolutely nothing affected or put on about it, and her friendly blue eyes looked one full in the face and spoke volumes.

Our mood in those moments was an amazing contrast to all the uncertainties with which we had approached Bucharest on the train only twelve days ago. It still amazes me to think that a woman with all her host of friends and commanding so much in the world, could have given to four strangers such an extraordinarily intimate and affectionate understanding of herself. I never finished any visit in my life with more real regret. Whatever criticisms you may read here of Queen Marie — and of course she is no more perfect than other very excellent human beings — we all found her to be a woman of extraordinary lovely character, a most attractive and delightful personality, and as perfect a hostess as the world can show. She is less than three years older than I, but she treated me in a distinctly motherly, as well as friendly and affectionate way, and I think I gave myself to her more in that attitude, as I might have to our own dear mother.

Perhaps it was that frank, friendly, and really affectionate comradeship which her attitude enabled us to give as well as to receive, which made our stay at the palace so endlessly delightful. I will not deny at all that I covet the chance to go back there, although my reason tells me it is folly even to think of it for she cannot expect to do such a thing again. At any rate a really great experience has entered our lives which will certainly prove unforgettable. Writing as I do, so long afterward, I realize more completely how true this is. The other day a copy of *Peeping Pansy* finally arrived from London. It is out of print but my agent there hunted up a copy. I turned to some of the chapters which Queen Marie had read aloud to us, and the mere running over of the pages brought back all the "atmosphere" which her reading it aloud to us has cast about the story.

If you read between the lines you will see that I have frankly lost my heart to the Queen, and I am not ashamed to say so. Some people talk of her colossal egotism, and complain of the way she talks about herself so constantly. I know intellectually that is a fact, but I am quite ready to overlook it. I found at the Palace that by forgetting that side of it entirely I could enter into her life with extraordinary intimacy. Of course, if one thought about that frequently, it would raise a barrier.

This morning she got out a lot of her wonderful Roumanian costumes. She had her men unpack dozens of delightful peasant kelims from all over Roumania so that we might see her really marvelous collection. She plans to use these partly in furnishing the farm house at Copăceni, and the Turkish cottage in Dobrudja on the coast of the Black Sea.

Everything was planned to make our departure easy and comfortable. Mme. Procopiu, who had met us on our arrival, was there to see us off. We had some pleasant farewell minutes in the apartment of King George and Queen Elizabeth, and left the palace at four, finding an apartment reserved on the train and all our luggage carefully attended to. You can imagine how we settled down

Queen Marie in Romanian folk costume

and looked at each other as the train drew out of the station at Bucharest, thinking that at last it was all over. The six hours to Constanța seemed very short as we talked over hundreds of delightful details, and even read aloud from *Why*, one of Queen Marie's books. The sail through the Black Sea and down the Bosphorus on Wednesday, February 11th was in glorious weather, and we enjoyed it to the full, and were back at home in the College before five o'clock.

Notes

Throughout all my visit at the palace, I carried in my pocket a tiny notebook, given to me by my faithful friend, Robert Seager last Christmas, — unutterably ugly on the outside, and noted in it all sorts of stray names and ideas. In fact, Mlle. Cantemir soon began to call me, "The man with the note book," and would often say, "Pull it out and jot that down." If I ever go again I shall have a better looking one and I shall write far more in it. I wish to gather here some stray jottings that have not appeared before.

1. In conversation one day Queen Marie referred to the French artist Jouvre, and described her joy in his beautiful drawings of Mount Athos which she saw in the Luxembourg in Paris. She has subscribed for a beautiful new book of his which is just coming out at a cost of two thousand francs. Although she has never visited Mount Athos, she has read about it, and her keen eye has studied pictures of it so well that she recalled to my mind many names and places and types connected it which I had entirely forgotten although I spent twelve days there in 1901.

2. List of Books of Short Stories by Queen Marie:

a) *Princess Kildine.* Published also in French by Marne et Pils, Paris, under the title, *Histoire d'une Princess Méchante*

b) *The Country That I Love*

c) *My Country,* (Hodder & Stoughton, 1916)

d) *Peeping Fansy,* (Hodder & Stoughton, 1919)

e) *The Lily of Life,* (Hodder & Stoughton)

f) *The Voice of the Mountain*

g) *The Stealers of Light* (Hodder & Stoughton 1916)

h) *King Codra's Message* (short story)

i) *Baragladin's Treasure* (short story)

j) *Lulaloo,* (short story)

k) *Dreamer of Dreams* (Hodder & Stoughton)

l) *The Sleeping Princess* (short story). Her Majesty planned for this story the title "Kara Bara Dela, the Witch," but the publishers insisted that no English child would read it. Imagine it!

3. Queen Marie loves to visit the castle called "Hled" in Croaţia which was once the summer chateau of the Prince of Windisgrat and now serves as the summer home for the King, and Queen of Serbia — "Mignon" as Queen Marie calls her daughter Marie, now Queen of Serbia. The Serbian family also enjoy their old family home, "Topolla," in old Serbia.

4. On the piano in the Studio is a striking portrait of the son of Richard Wagner, painted by Franz von Lenbach, the Munich artist who cooperated with Count Schack in creating the collection of paintings now included in the Schack gallery at Munich. This portrait is in von Lenbach's best style, and reminds me of the charming little picture, about the same size, of a little girl of nine who always seemed to me a curious combination of Cornelia and Theresa.

5. Among the amusing things in the Studio is a collection of frogs in every imaginable position and size, all made of different sorts of jade varying from an almost transparent greenish white to the darkest and most superb Chinese green.

Another jolly little object lying on the brick floor of the hugh fireplace was a tiny pair of bellows, evidently the loving handwork of some Norwegian carver. Queen Elizabeth once told me she liked to do carving, so one day I accused her of being the sculptress of these bellows, but she denied it completely.

Over the first landing of the stairs which rise directly out of the Studio to the gallery surrounding it, hangs a fascinating portrait, about one foot square, of little Marie (Mignon) at the age of five, wearing the most fascinating Russian cap of grey fur. The jolly child's eyes follow one all around the Studio. Above this portrait hang the excellent portraits of Queen Marie and King Ferdinand. Of course, the chef d'oeuvre in the Studio is the magnificent portrait of Her Majesty, done in 1924 by Lazlo. As an object of art and a true creation, it is the best thing we saw in the whole palace.

Her Majesty has any number of wonderfully bound books, several being collections of her own paintings. She and her sister in their middle and late teens were very fond of that sort of work and did it beautifully.

On the Spanish tea table, with its fascinating brass inlay, in front of the fireplace in the Studio, there lay a superbly bound copy of Charles Dichl's *History of Byzantine Art*, which Her Majesty says is a treasure house of information, to which she often referred in her study of the creations of old Byzantine days which she has tried to renew for Roumania.

One of my photographs shows the handsome house of a leading lawyer of Bucharest which was recently built in the new Roumanian adaptation of the Roumanian-Byzantine style. This house stands just outside of the lodge gate where one enters the park of Cotroceni. My photograph does not do it justice as it is really very attractive, the only trouble being that it is too near the street and has quite too limited grounds.

6. Her Majesty is very fond of goblets in the style of medieval Munich, such as one sees on the stage representations of Wagner's Meistersingers. One finds them in odd corners all over the palace, and the Queen herself always has two beautiful ones at her place at luncheon, — a larger one for plain water and a smaller one for some mineral water. I believe these were gifts of the King to her. In my sitting room was the beautiful one in hammered silver gilt, with Byzantine decorations and rather large semi-precious stones scattered over it. Many of hers were made to order by M. Stroble, Munich.

7. We heard a number of times about a certain Col. Băjulescu, who has started a school for physical education, intended to train gymnastic and athletic leaders for Roumanian village schools. His work was highly praised by the secretaries at the Y.W.C.A. It will be something to visit when we next go to Bucharest.

G.H.C. graduates, Students & ex-Students in Roumania:

Bucharest:

Tommy A. Bolton

Henry Presente, 1915

Richard Bolton, 1910-1915

Leonidas Metaxas

John Garbis

D.G. Inglesis, 1906-1915, through Sophomore; with British Consulate summer of 1910; for two years with Y.M.C.A. in army under Mr. Morgan, and for one year with Roumanian Red Cross.

John Mainoff Antoniades, 1908-1915

Leon Eatibian

The last two also with Mr. Morgan with Y.M.C.A. in the army)

Constanţa:

Theodoron, a lawyer

Constantine Bosi

Brăila:

Lasimakis, Engineer, having studied at Edinburgh and in Germany.

9. The Roumanians often refer to Mărăşeşti and with great pride. This is their name for a battle in the summer of 1917, in which, such as they had been able to gather of their army after the revolution in Russia had left them helpless, fought a most gallant fight with the Austrians, who were assisted by some German battalions and for some days more than held their own, although, of course, in the end they had to yield the superior numbers and supplies. They evidently take great comfort in the thought that this battle has retrieved somewhat the disgrace of their disaster in the autumn of 1916.

10. A figure which frequently appeared in the Queen's diary was Col. Bailiff, a rather mysterious character, to whom Her Majesty evidently took a great fancy, but said to be unsavory reputation by some people.

Another character who frequently comes in is Col. Boyle, an Irishman of rather extraordinary personality, of whom she saw a great deal.

She also speaks several times of "My great friend Col. Anderson of the American Red Cross."

In the diary she speaks more than once of Lady Barclay, wife of the British minister, as "that riotous person." Of Mr. Arthur Baker of Constantinople, who was in the British Red Cross service in Roumania, she wrote February 17, 1918, "I like old Baker," and in another place she wrote "Anderson and Baker are often hobnobbing together."

She referred sometimes to Mr. Mills of the Associated Press, who was with the American Red Cross in charge of a centeon in Iaşi, mentioned on February 25, 1918.

In a conversation with Averescu, her minister, reported in the diary relative to the peace with Germany which was being forced upon them in the spring of 1918, she listed as the three points upon which she as Queen insisted her government should demand: 1. The Germans are not to touch the royal family, 2. There is to be no reduction in the army, 3. There is to be no reduction of territory. Of course the Roumanians were powerless to insist upon the last two, and the so called Treaty of Bucharest, of July, 1918, cut Roumania entirely off the Black Sea and took away all her mountain frontier along the old Hungarian frontier, as well as the Iron Gates of the Danube. She called Averescu in her diary "That ambitious and discontented, civilized, and Germanized imp."

The diary of the days of 1918, when the Germans and Austrians were presenting their demands, is almost pitiful in its hopelessness and fever heat of resentment and hatred toward the Germans. The interview described by the Queen between Count Czernin of Austria and von Kuhlmann, the German representative, and King Ferdinand, when "they demanded everything with smiles and politeness and the iron hand;" "I prefer war a outrance," she writes, — although of course she knew in her heart this was an utter impossibility.

Prince Știrbey was with King Ferdinand during this interview, "ever loyal and unselfish, and ready with well-thought-out advice." The Germans and Austrians refused to treat except on the basis they themselves proposed, and demanded an answer before 12, noon, on March 1st.

Queen Marie describes the Crown council held that day to consider Vienna's terms, and told how the King came back at 2:30 a.m., simply saying "No hope." According to the diary the Queen still clung to some hope. She describes on March 2nd an interview with the Irishman, Col. Boyle, whom she saw and received for the first time that day.

On March 3rd she gives an amusing account of her own stormy interview with King Ferdinand and credits herself with winding up by saying, "I am ashamed to be the Queen of no one but cowards!" She looked up when she read those words, and was silent a minute, drumming with her fingers meditatively on the arm of her chair, and then said almost apologetically "Of course I was utterly unstrung, and was unreasonably hard upon the poor King and on them all. I suppose it was all inevitable."

11. The last day we were at the palace as we gathered for luncheon, Mme. Procopiu turned to Cornelia and said with real feeling, "Well the visit is done, and *she* does not want you to go. Do you want to go?" You can imagine Cornelia's reply.

12. On the last morning of our visit we had over an hour with the Queen in the Studio, from 11 until after 12. As we then separated to get ready for luncheon, we started to make some good-by expressions of our gratitude, and Queen Marie said exactly these words: "We *have* had a beautiful visit together haven't we?" and then added something to this effect, although I may not quote it exactly: "I am sure that I have enjoyed it as much as you have." Of course, all this might be merely polite nothings, but she certainly has a way of saying such things that makes her guests feel as though she meant them, — and to paraphrase Mr. Bakke in the last chapter of *Little Lord Fauntleroy*, — and who knows but what she *did* mean them?

Ray Baker Harris and Queen Marie

by Hector Bolitho

When he was a boy in grade school, at the end of the 1914-1918 war, he wrote an essay on Queen Marie; his choice among the celebrated figures of the war. He was at the age when many imaginative boys like to fix their eyes on some exalted person, with devotion. The American boy had some literary talent and the headmaster sent the essay to Queen Marie of Roumania. Within a few weeks she sent back a signed photograph of herself, and a letter of appreciation. The story might have closed with this generous gesture.

Eight years passed and Queen Marie made her fabulous journey through the United States, where she was the victim of toadies, and of blazing publicity. She was too spontaneous; too lacking in shrewd caution to repel these clutching forces. The American, who had the gift of fidelity, hoped he would be presented to her, but the tour was cut short by the illness of the King of Roumania and the Queen hurried home.

Nine more years passed, but the devotion did not fade. The gallant boy had grown to scholarship, responsibility, and manhood and among his friends was an American woman who had exchanged letters with Queen Marie for many years. At last the Queen was told of the boy's fidelity and one more reward came; a Christmas book, with a dedication in her broad, rich handwriting.

The friendship began and although they never met, Queen Marie wrote him hundreds of pages, from 1934 to 1938, when she died. She poured out her thoughts and loneliness with a wealth of heart and words that are astonishing when one recalls the busy curriculum of her life. But she had found a new kind of friend in the young American; she explained the need, and his fulfillment of it, in a letter written from Bran, on August 1, 1935.

> The friendship question will eternally remain difficult, but I have sadly realized there are few people one likes to *live* with. Few friends are tolerable under one's roof. They respect one's freedom too little. Personally I do not stand sentimental friendship. Love is naturally sentimental, but friendship must have another, harder quality.

> Lovers *must* encroach — friends must not, or finally one feels like murdering them. One stands a certain amount of jealousy from the one who is in love with you. But friendship must be based on mutual freedom. I have only been able to keep my unsentimental women friends — the others I had to put outside my life. But this does not mean that something does not still link them to me, especially the illusion I had when the friendship began. But no one understands the weakness of *not* putting them out of my life if they exasperate me and suck my vitality. I have two women in my life that I regret having ever met, because of the sentimental weight they today represent. But their need of me is so great that I have not the courage to put them quite aside. It would be like cutting into live flesh. They live by their adoration for me, but to try and get them to realize that they are not to me what I am to them is impossible. So, when together, I have to keep up to a certain degree this illusion. But if only they do not begin to what the school-boy calls "to paw" me, all is well. If they try this, it is only a question of minutes about how long I can stand it. And the dreadful thing is that, instead of being thanked for my patience, there are outbursts of reproaches because of my coldness — and ever again, that all overpowering pity obliges me to submit to their reproaches and scenes. But as a consequence, of course I avoid them more and more.

> I am interested to see that you too have pondered over this subject. I can be written to about every subject. Just because our material life does not come together, everything can be told and discussed...

> Nietzsche says somewhere: it is difficult to live with people because silence is so difficult. But you and I need not be silent. We are not going to be called upon to help each other materially, and therein lies the splendid freedom of our exchange of thought.

> ...Excuse the messiness of this letter, but occasionally a sort of irritation overtakes me about the physical part of writing! Then I smear!

The other side of the story of these letters is in a note written by the "American boy." He has written:

> We never met. The relationship was never weighted by any material considerations, and for that reason our correspondence became an extraordinary free exchange of friendly feelings, thoughts, ideas, and discussions. I discovered that it was possible to write to the Queen as unaffectedly as if I were merely writing down thoughts and feelings for my own satisfaction, and the Queen responded always with complete friendliness and freedom... There was never anything mean or small about her, she was ever honest, outspoken, forthright, full of good feeling, generous, and loyal. She wrote to me a few months before her death: "Your letters are a great pleasure to me. I read out of them such a breath of affection and appreciation of our rather unusual friendship that after reading them I felt each time refreshed...!"

The first letters from Queen Marie were from Cotroceni, the white palace on a far edge of Bucharest, where she usually lived during Christmas and the New Year. "Dear Mr......," she wrote, on February 14, 1934,

> You can imagine that I receive many letters, but there are very few I really care to answer... And today I have... an 'American Boy' who believes in me... I think I am very human and that my heart has remained very young. I am so pleased that you like *The Story of My Life*.[1] I think it will interest you more and as it goes I hope that, although having been often humourous, I have never allowed myself to descend to unkind irony or any form of spite, although I have seen humanity from all sides and not all of them pretty, alas!... As I had the courage to tell my own tale to the world, every word is important... The most minute change or omission can become betrayal, as it needs courage as Queen to step out into the open and become the prey of every criticism. I must be able to stand for every word I say, every expression I use, every criticism I make — 'C'est le ton qui fait la chanson.'

The next letter, written one month later, began "Dear Mr......" or shall I say: "Dear American Boy?" Then came the Queen's first move towards the refreshing intimacy that grew continuously, during the next four years.

> I am really a very unconventional Queen... There is something eternally rejuvenated in my nature which explains why the young find me stimulating, besides occasionally wise when they want a little

---

[1] Queen Marie's reminiscences, then being published in America.

advice as well as understanding... I do not think that I have ever allowed bitterness to deaden my sympathy for others. I have an irritating way of seeing all sides of a question, although this faculty does not prevent my being very energetic, but it does make me rather terribly forgiving. This is not always practical, though it enters Christ's creed.

I so well understand what you say about priests, clergymen, and the church. If you follow what I say in my book about religion you will see that the same feeling is expressed all through a necessity of finding God without human intervention... This dissatisfaction with every religious form made of me a great appreciator of the Bahai teachings, so that I have even been called a Bahai! But I am nothing except myself, though officially I am Anglican, but call myself a Protestant. When asked what sort of Protestant, I throw out my hands and smile a smile that might mean anything.

Nine days later the Queen wrote again, thanking her friend for his photograph which she had "carefully studied." "I like the intense look of your eyes," she told him, "but indeed you look quite a boy." In her next letter, written on April 19, one more step was made in the friendship. Queen Marie addressed her "American Boy" by his Christian name, and broke into criticism of her own character, and of her children.

I may be rash, sometimes even inconsiderate, but this is out of over-honesty, never with an intention to hurt. My fear of hurting has in fact been a shackle in my life and much of the trouble I have today with my children[2] is that I always respected over-much their personalities and never wanted to tyrannize or oppress... I was the thread upon which they were strung. My will, my faith, my ideal, my love, my sense of duty kept them straight and gave straight to the King. But at his death they all came into their separate fortune, and they cut the string and each rolled into his own little corner and did his or her worst, except Ileana and Mignon. This is the truth, and, being a sad truth, it will make the later story of my life difficult to tell.

...I am again struck by your extraordinary fairness of Judgment... especially I am grateful that you should sense that nothing in me

---

[2]At that time Queen Marie's eldest son, King Carol, had been on the throne since his return to Roumania. Her second son, Prince Nicholas was abroad and without useful occupation. Her eldest daughter, referred to in the letters as *Mignon,* was Queen of Yugoslavia. Princess Elizabeth was in retirement, having divorced her husband, King George of Greece, Queen Marie's youngest daughter, Princess Ileana, was married to the Archduke Anton of Habsburg.

was *acting*... The stage was always set, I was always the one who had to appear, who was expected, awaited. Why disappoint them when I came? Why not my most radiant smile? Why not my prettiest dress, my most becoming hat? Why not a gesture of appreciation towards the eager mother showing off her child; why not a kind word to the old Granny who was clapping her hands in wild excitement; why not a helpful word to a man with one leg; a look of appreciation for the young girl's new Spring gown? There was no acting in all this, only a real desire to spread joy around me, good understanding and a joyful atmosphere of good will, and kindly, human understanding... My so-called acting was in fact unselfishness, because one is no more self-conscious when one thinks of others instead of oneself.

Besides, I also had this feeling: the crowds are waiting for you in sunshine or rain... then do your best, do not disappoint them; look as well as you can, let it be worth while having you as a Princess, as Queen. Your position is special, *they* have set you in that position; many envy you, some spontaneously love you because you are their Queen, others are merely curious, a few are cynical, have dark thoughts, object to you, but they are all waiting — *you* are the only one they are waiting for, do not be an anti-climax!

My face which they always liked was of course my best ally, and even today, ṣalthough I am nearly 60, I am pleasant to look at;ʈ I wear my clothes well, I have taste; my eyes have become sad, but my smile is still humanly warm, spontaneous.

Am I ridiculous to write thus about myself? But it is the truth. You see my road has been long. I have learned much, felt much, loved much and have been loved... So today I know, not everything, but a good deal... I never want to teach or preach, but only to help — I have much to give...

In May, Queen Marie was staying with Princess Ileana in "a delightful old *schloss* with hugely thick walls and large light rooms," which she had recently bought, at Hollsbrunn, in Austria. "I have a whole wing of five rooms for myself" wrote the Queen. She had arranged them with her "own things" and had given them her "own imprint." But she was constantly alarmed by King Carol's flashes of unwise independence and she wrote to her American friend:

I do not care to remain too long away from Roumania just now, as there is constant trouble and the one who should be wise, unselfish, and an example to others makes mistake upon mistake, so that I am continually trembling for him. But when he is in danger, I feel I ought to be there. I am a sort of assurance, but alas I am more a moral than a real help, because I am never listened to. I have been set aside as one who understands nothing of modern ways, "vieux jeu" — and yet I know my people so well. I led them during the greatest crisis, and I know they need strong upholding and especially a good example. Being near the East, morality is lacking, but for all their laxness, they want to find morality in their rulers, having chosen foreigners, knowing they were not capable to rule themselves, they want those virtues they have not got!

...A Sovereign's share is austere and it needs a sunny nature like mine to make a sovereign's duty look pleasant and happy — but it *must* be self denial... Yes, I am living through a tragedy but I must not put it into words...

The rulers of Roumania, before King Carol II, had been colourless sovereigns, compared with their consorts. The first King, Carol I, had been overshadowed by his wife, "Carmen Sylva." Likewise, King Ferdinand I had been a pale figure beside the Byzantine luxuriousness of Queen Marie. In the letter written in May, 1934, Queen Marie wrote of "Carmen Sylva," "She was a tremendous personality, big, fine, and often absurd, and her books[3] and writings are difficult to read; they are over-crowded like a Victorian room, a bit confused in conception... She was an enthusiast, and the topic and interest of the moment was always preponderant and overthrew the interest, the enthusiasm, the theory of yesterday... She had little sense of values and no feeling for atmosphere... Nor did she ever sense the comic or absurdity of a situation. She was always deadly, dreadfully earnest, and took every one of her passing enthusiasms with the same earnestness, blissfully unaware of how changing they were. But, for all that, she was big, generous, loveable... As I say in my book, I love her memory more than I loved her when she was alive. She was too fatiguing. There was no repose about her and none of the serenity of old age..."

The Queen and the "American boy" seemed to agree in their letters that they should never meet. With this assurance, Queen Marie seemed to open her heart more lavishly than before, and she welcomed the thought that her friend would someday make a pilgrimage to Roumania, after she died. "I was touched," she wrote, "about what you said about coming once in your life, perhaps years after my disappearance from this world, to Balcic to look at the places I loved and beautified and to be in communion

---

[3]"Carmen Sylva", Queen Elizabeth of Roumania, was the author of many books of fairy stories and romances, fashionable in their time.

with my spirit. I shall therefore tell you something only Ileana and two others to whom I had to leave my "Will," know.

According to royal tradition, when I die I am supposed to be laid at rest in the beautiful church of Curtea de Argeş where my husband lies. My place is at his side; but in my Will I ask that my heart should be taken from my body, put in a precious casket (which I leave) and buried in the little Stella Maris in Balcic, the small rustic church overlooking the sea.

In olden days the hearts of Kings or Queens were often taken from their bodies and brought either back to their former homes, or to some special sanctuary, and though in life I hated all thought of a knife mutilating my exceedingly healthy body — I *do* wish to have my heart buried in the wee church I built myself. All through life so many people came to my heart for love or understanding that I would like them to come also when I am gone — walk up along the lily path, up to where my heart lies beneath the screened-in little altar of the little Orthodox church built by a Protestant... So if you really did carry out your plan, you would come to my heart... And if the church is still standing, you will find beside it a bell — and the bell was given to me by a man who loved and served me, but whose I could never be; because I was Queen. Pull that bell, and it will be like the echo of a great love which was all the greater because it had to be denied...

Sentimental? Perhaps. But, as you say, we are like two spirits talking to each other through space; a woman who kept her ideals alive and a young man looking out upon life, with all his years before him.

But... there is always a large 'but.' Balcic is very near to the Bulgarian frontier. If there were new convulsions the place of my heart might easily again fall into their hands, and then, oh dear, my poor heart!

I was very interested to hear about the Soviet Embassy! So fraudulous, so false, and also so ugly! I resent the deadly ugliness of their conceptions, the murdering of all beauty, personality, initiative... And it is all a vast delusion. Tzarism was also a delusion no doubt, but it had its beautiful and sacred sides... 'Das Land Ohne Sonntag,' 'Das Land Ohur Lachlen' as poor Russia has been called. Horror fills my very soul when I think of their sinister creed, the hideousness of the fear and destruction they have spread around them. To me their creed appears to be the very negation of life and all that makes life worthwhile!

Tena Yuvah, Balcic,
June 14, 1934

...In your last letter you say: 'You have the courage to reveal yourself as you honestly are'... Yes, I do... I suppose it needs courage, but then I have already travelled a long way. I have cast off all nonsense... I have also experienced most things in myself and have lived through every degree of emotion. I have been much loved and much envied, much admired and much calumnied. I have been encouraged and discouraged. I have been faithfully served, but also foully betrayed. I have been praised and criticized, flattered and laughed at. I have been understood and misunderstood. I have been helped and hindered, hurt and consoled. Passion has been thrown at my feet and I am supposed to have had many adventures, which is not true; but I *have* been much loved — beautifully, faithfully. And no man who has loved me has ever turned against me, because also with

**Queen Marie
during World War I**

these was I upright and honest, never offended because they told me they loved me, but also explaining why a Princess, a Queen, a woman, a mother, must hold herself back, remain within certain bounds.

These are spirit talks — so I can say all this — besides, I am nearly sixty — and yet, well, it seems, so I have been told, that I have some radium in me, something beyond age, a force, a magnetism. But within myself I am aloof, not indifferent, but just a little far-off, if I may so express it, too wise — I know too much, have seen and felt too much...

What sort of pen do I write with? It is simply a Waterman, but all the mystery lies in the nib. It is a nib in a thousand! It is broad and as soft as a soft lead-pencil, and it runs so smoothly as though it *were* a pencil. It is more precious to me than the pearls round my neck...

One of the sore complications of my life was that men would never remain friends... Even the women I was friends with became over-sentimental. They wanted to separate me. There were scenes of jealousy. They tried to bite others away from around me. And I am a lover of freedom. I do not want to be stifled, compressed, urged, adored; I want a frank, natural, unsentimental, but deep, true, and honest friendship. Well, ever again I had to put people out of my life. There was something about me that made people desire to be the only one. They made me go through agonies because of their hungry need of emotion, whilst I wanted calm, intelligent inter-course, perfect companionship, unaccompanied by scenes of jealousy. And I hated to have to say, 'You may love me this way, but I do not, that way, and unless you understand this I must put you out of my life, because you stifle me. You throttle my liberty, and impose upon me a feverish sentimentality I cannot live up to. I want frank naturalness, no clasping of hands, and looking me tenderly in the eye. Such things are reserved for supreme hours in life and can only be mutual.'

June 17

My previous solitude was invaded by many guests, too many all at once... I have a very simple way of receiving. Of course I am not a conventional Queen, like dear Queen Mary; and my kind guests are not quite sure that they sanction my ways. When they are with me they cannot quite resist me, as there is a vitality and good humor about me which carries even the stiffest off their feet. But when they think about me, they disapprove.

The Prince of Wales had tremendous charm, but he has to go through his tricks too often and today his face is no more that adorable boy's face, and, he must be getting stale, even to himself! The times are difficult for Princes.

You say the glamour of Roumania suits me — that I am the right Queen for this charming peasant people so full of dignity and picturesqueness. I think you are in a way right. We suit each other... Politicians spoil Roumania, and my boy imagined he must cap my popularity because the love people had for me might put him in the shade. It was a mistake... When I appeared this year at the head of my regiment on the tenth of May, their old love and enthusiasm awoke anew and they gave me a tremendous reception... You ask if I can ever go to the theatre like anyone else? Yes, when abroad I always insist on sitting in the stalls. In my own country I must stick to my box, and neither can I run about the streets and the shops as I can when on a holiday...

Bran, July 18, 1934

In the summer of 1934, the Queen had "forsaken" the castle at Balcic for her "little old fortress on the other side of the Carpathians — an enchanting place..." She complained, "...but we are having too much rain, which prevents my flowers blooming as they should... I am distressed to see them so soused."

Her American friend had sent her some photographs and in thanking him, she wrote, "I missed Virginia when I was in America, as I had to hurry back home, because of the King's illness. There is much I would still like to see in America, but I doubt I shall ever come over again."

Queen Marie during her visit to the United States (1926)

Queen Marie's visit to the United States had suffered, partly because of her enthusiasm which so often warped her caution, and partly because of the self-seeking advisers she gathered about her. She recalled this in her letter:

The enormous publicity one is subjected to is difficult to live through. You cannot keep your own footing in America when people are eager to receive

Queen Marie in the United States

or see you. There is no privacy, nor can you ever do anything you want. You just have to allow yourself to be rushed along. It was a very interesting experience, but terribly breathless and you felt yourself on exhibition all the time. American hospitality is rather bewildering and one must have an iron constitution to be able to get through. I had caught cold and all the first days in New York it was only my royal training which kept me on my feet. It was a colossal effort not to break down and to appear everywhere according the overwhelming program, having to talk publicly on every occasion, and this with an aching throat! Besides, I had never talked publicly in my life!

Luckily, I have found a comprehending doctor who treated me, so to say, 'standing.' It was my one condition, as I explained to him: I *cannot* be sent to bed.

But it certainly took every inch of my energy not to collapse, as I was feeling physically wretched. A real training, however, had taught me to give the maximum of effort — never mind what my own feelings were. How I ever had to courage to face those huge assemblies, sometimes only men, today still I can hardly understand, but I did! And blessed nature as I am, I even overcame my sore throat, having submitted to cruelly severe treatment, and ignoring the pain. It is wonderful what a human body can stand when the will is dauntless.

Yes, Russia! It fills me with a feeling of horror... Alas, our country has accepted the Soviets at last, and I am miserable about it. We are so terribly near to them, and I think it is a huge and dangerous mistake; but I certainly do not mean to receive in my house those who murdered all my mother's family.[4]

---

[4]Queen Marie was the daughter of the Duke and Duchess of Edinburgh. Her father was Queen Victoria's second son; her mother was the Grand Duchess Marie, daughter of the Tzar Alexandre II. Her parents became Duke and Duchess of Saxe-Coburg-Gotha.

In August, Queen Marie was staying "at a little place in Transylvania" where there was "a warm salt lake particularly good for everything that is rheumatic." She wrote from Sovata, on August 7, 1934:

I was interested to hear about your visit to New York and the sort of discontent which followed, making you wish for wider scope, even if it means risk at a period when a safe place means daily bread. I suppose youth must spread its wings and venture — that is life. 'Life is afraid of the brave,' says a French dictum. One needs courage more than anything else, I think. I generally had courage except for saying disagreeable things and for scolding even those who most needed scolding. It is agony for me to scold. It is a weakness which has cost me much trouble in my life; that terrible horror of causing even a passing pain and the almost morbid aversion to seeing another ashamed of himself. I always preferred taking the blame. I never could have the very human satisfaction of the 'I told you so.' To me the hour of victory was always sad, because victory is always over someone and I cannot bear to contemplate the beaten man, even if he is my enemy. This weakness has all through life prevented my being a really strong woman... Curiously enough, I have had the really Christian spirit, but it is inborn, not an effort. With me it is never an eye for an eye... try as I may, I cannot be careful and calculating. I am spontaneous and rash...

Yes, friendships are no easy matter. They can be the finest thing on earth, but they can be stifling, and in my case there is the complication of my being a Queen. I once had a great attraction for an exceedingly spirited young lady... We met by chance and felt greatly in sympathy with each other... As long as she did not live under my roof it was all right... Soon I noticed there was a great difference. There was a bite beneath her good humor... She wanted to bite others away from around me — the others who had faithfully served me for many years. She thought she had come in as a winner who was to be a ruling favourite, making sport of the feelings of all those around me, turning them into ridicule and showing up their faults. She tried to sway my will and make me listen solely to her advice with an unjustifiable presumption as though she could teach me my own 'trade.' She wanted to draw a circle and within that circle we were to be alone, she and I, beings of a rare essence. And worst of all, even after I had said good night to her, she would steal down again to my room when I was already in bed and needed my solitude, to clasp hands and tell me how she loved me... her greatest mistake was that she became insanely jealous of Ileana who was the one creature on earth I was most closely and beautifully in sympathy with, rare between mother and daughter, and into the bargain she tried to declare that it was Ileana who was jealous and when she could sow no discord between us, she began trying to show me all Ileana's faults, and tell me I was a fool to believe in her so completely... I had to shake her off... I was very frank with her; we have kept in touch, but I cannot live with her under one roof... I almost hated myself for awakening these unruly passions in women, whilst I myself cannot bear anything even on the outside edge of unhealthy sentimentality. There is a sort of manly independence about me... I like to keep a certain distance, a certain mystery — 'familiarity breeds contempt.' Of course this may also be a royal particularity, a sort of unapproachableness I cannot overcome...

Do you know any foreign languages, or do you only read and talk English? There are so many fine books in German. In general I like German literature better than French... I have not been able to settle about going to England for the publishing of my book in September... My professor friend[5] who is my literary adviser in London, thinks I ought to be there... The literary people want to give me a festive lunch to celebrate the occasion. It will make me feel rather shy as on the whole I am diffident about my writing... We are taking a cure of baths in a warm salt lake, surrounded by woods. Ileana, her husband, and babies are with me. She must take the cure more seriously, but it also does me good and the swimming about in the dark green warm water is very delicious. It is very easy to swim in as, being exceedingly salt, there is no effort to remain at the top — one floats like a cork!

I think most of the youth of Europe hate the thought of war. What a curious figure Hitler is. What shall we see still in Germany? I withhold every judgment, but mostly everybody is virulent against him abroad, and what Germany's real feelings for him are, is difficult to clearly perceive...

Bran, August 31, 1934.

We are back from our salt lake... I have returned very vigorous and full of energy to enjoy the almost overwhelming beauty of my August garden, where everything is in riotous, almost insolent bloom... I have a deaf gardener who wanders about amongst the work of his hands like a priest in a church. Hearing no sounds from

---

[5] Sir Stephen Gazelee

the outer world, he is more intimately in touch with his flowers, as no talk reaches his ears — none of the many horrid things people say and discuss. But his wife, who is fat and lame and entirely of the earth, has a tongue for two!...

Yes, I have read young Botkin's book... No, there is no truth in the Great Duchess Anastasia theory. Botkin is horribly unjust towards the Emperor's sisters and tries to make greedy creatures out of them; wanting to deny their niece for the sake of a fortune which they, poor things, *know* does not exist. They are resigned to their cruel poverty which they bear with admirable dignity. It was the people who grouped themselves around the so called Grand Duchess Anastasia (who was a half-wit) who believed in the fable of the great Romanoff fortune, stored away somewhere, and of which they hoped to grab their share if they had been able to prove that the half-wit was really a daughter of the Tzar.

The real relations all went to see her, and especially Grand Duchess Olga, who was mentioned as one of the hard-hearted and grasping aunts, had ben the dearest intimate of the Tzar's daughters; and she went several times to see the invalid, hoping that she might be one of the young girls she had dearly loved, but she was finally absolutely convinced that she was a fraud.

Also the Grand Duke of Hesse,[6] the Tzarina's brother, went and he too, who knew them intimately, had to recognize that she was faked...

The ex-Mrs. Leeds who is a niece of mine, for a time was convinced that this girl was, or might be, her cousin, but finally, after having had her for months under her roof, was obliged to give her up as a fraud. Besides, it seems she was a most odious personality and quarrelled with everybody. Of course Botkin writes with great eloquence. I wonder if he really believes what he says or if he wants to be sensational. It certainly makes an interesting book...

My journey to England is quite settled. I shall be in London on the 21st of September and remain a month in England, going up for a few days to Balmoral to visit the King and Queen...

The abominable murder of Dolfus was a wicked thing. Ileana was much upset. She takes a much more vivid interest in Austrian politics than her husband does. She is a very keen spirit and she has

---

[6]The Grand Duke Ludwig of Hesse-Darmstadt, a grandson of Queen Victoria and therefore second cousin to Queen Marie. His sister, Princess Alexandra, was married to the Tzar Nicholas II.

much of my impetuous generosity which tempts her to impru-
dences.

What both she and I find difficult is to cope with the ideas of our
Court... We offend their feelings by often having at our table people they consider too lowly to sit at a King's board. They look upon
it as an offence to their own dignity, and more than one has told me
'You consider all those beneath your rank equals, but for us they are
not;' I see their point of view, but it is very difficult to explain
ours... It is difficult for that class which so respects itself to comprehend our larger generosity and that spirit of not judging people by
their position or even talent, but by their humanity... One little
example... is so quaint that I must tell it:

When I first came to Balcic the population, which is very poor and
heterogeneous, was very excited and delighted. Amongst those
who showed their awed pleasure was an old Turkish woman of no
degree, almost a beggar in fact, living as best she could... it tickled
my fancy to have her come to see me, with her humble bouquet of
flowers or sometimes the gift of a few nuts or even a couple of
eggs. She was always dressed in a black sort of caftan over wide
trousers, a white veil on her head and loose slippers on her naked
feet. As she generally came about breakfast time, I would invite her
to take a chair and to share my early repast, and I would give her
large cups of very sweetened coffee and huge hunks of cake. Neither of us could understand a word the other said and all our conversation was carried on through pantomime. Her face was as
wrinkled as a walnut, she had few teeth left, but there was a look of
remembrance in her eyes and if one studied her features one could
see that she must once have been pretty. Occasionally, I had to submit to being kissed!

Well, later on, my followers discovered that this old crone had in
her youth been a 'lady of light repute' and, of course, I was hence-
forth expected to repudiate her entirely. Well, I just did not... but
this inconceivable behavior is severely criticized by those who consider themselves responsible for my Queenly acts!

...The cloud of uncertainty hanging over Europe is indeed a heavy
weight making all future outlook precarious. Even when I contemplate the work of my hands in the places I love an anxiety steals into
my heart and I wonder what my ultimate fate will be? Will I also
love to be uprooted and to become an exile one day, just at an age
when one dreams of harvest and rest? Who knows?

Queen Marie arrived in London late in September, 1934, to find that her book of reminiscences was "a great success." She was "terribly rushed but also most affectionately received everywhere" and she wrote a note to her friend, from the Ritz Hotel. "Everybody is reading it and the critics are good. Even an old highbrow like Lady Oxford, who writes herself, is enthusiastic about it, and she has a tongue for ten! Old England is glad to have me back... It is well-managed that I and my book should appear together... I sent affectionate thoughts to my young American friend."

Then came tragedy, to break the pleasant visit. On October 9, King Alexander of Yugoslavia was assassinated and Queen Marie had to hurry back to her bereaved daughter. She told the story in a remarkable letter, written from Belgrade, on October 28:

It is not easy to take up my pen again. A life-time seems to separate me from the happy hour before tea on October 9th... I was in my beloved home-country, England... I was drinking a cup of tea in an old friend's house. The telephone rings — my Minister calling up the gentleman of the house — then the news, no softening of the blow possible... no merciful doubt — just the horrible, bare, unbearable, truth: Sandro killed... Mignon a widow... little Peter, King!"

I got up from my seat. I felt as though someone had given me a tremendous blow on my heart and I felt like crying out for mercy: No! No! Not that,

King Alexander of Yugoslavia

do not let it be that! Do not ask me to accept this horror, this new, too great, too annihilating sorrow. Let this cup pass from me...

But it could not pass, it had to be accepted and it had to be lived, the bitterness had to be drunk, every drop. And since then we have been trying to live it, my daughter and I.

There are small mercies even in moments of most complete distress. One was that I was in England; that poor little Peter could be brought to me from his school, that I could break the news to him and take him to Paris to meet his mother.

The tragedy of those first hours after the news are a nightmare, trying to get into contact with Mignon, to know where she was, who would announce to her the ghastly news.

It was by purest chance she was not with him in that fatal motor at Marseilles. She had been ill, so her husband did not wish her to go by sea... The first meeting with the one who had once been her life-companion was at 5 a.m. — in a bleak dawn, led by strangers to the town-hall where the dead King had been brought after the crime.

There he lay, her King, in that stiff official salon, on a velvet sofa, the Serbian flag over his body, and the smile of welcome for the French not yet wiped off his face; he was killed so suddenly that death took him unawares, but brimming over with life and kind feelings.

There she stood alone on foreign soil — facing the one who would never more open his mouth — silence — no good-bye, no last look — everything torn to pieces in a single moment. She took it standing, like a soldier's wife. And my heart was crying out all the time — Mignon, Mignon! My child, — Mignon.

And now I am with her in this house which was his, amongst his things — and we seem to wait for his step, his voice, his smile, his fun, his feverish impatience, his impulsive imagination — his always new ideas, new plans, his big and active intelligence... For the moment, the grief has been too absolute, too huge, too stunning for tears. Neither my child nor I, as yet, have wept. We have only carried — carried the burden of his disappearance. We are not turned to stone, but living flesh defending itself against tears till we are in a condition to be able to weep. We hold each other's hands, and we remember. We talk of him, we do not relegate him to his coffin. We let his spirit move amongst us, we almost speak to him — Sandro — we cannot believe he has really gone.

He had such quick impulsive moments. He was here, there, everywhere — used to disappear and reappear suddenly, and Mignon, her head a little on one side, a gentle loving smile on her face, used to let him be as he was, just a little erratic, always in a hurry, sometimes very silent, almost distant, unapproachable, but Mignon always smiled and waited; the wife of a hard-working, preoccupied man. His rest, his comfort, never impatient, no caprices, splendidly unassertive, absolutely unselfish, never desiring honors or success for herself, nor riches, power, possessions, but rejoicing over all he did and had.

Now she is quite lost. Her helplessness hurts me. I know life, I know a widow's life. It is true, her children are still young; they cannot be unkind to her yet, but others can set her aside, will probably try to separate and influence the children — every possibility is there, and I feel I must protect her, guard her... I do not wish to exaggerate anything, to dramatize, to mourn or wail, but there is tragedy in our two fates, but hers has come too soon — she had, according to the laws of nature, the right to a longer happiness, and being as she is, Mignon is not one who will build herself a new life, a new fate — Mignon is statical.

Mignon is too good, too unselfish, too unimaginative to build, to create, to break through. Mignon is a follower, not a leader. She is not what I compared myself to: a tree which grows through a stone wall. She was made to be the follower, the admirer of a great man; his rest, his comfort, his home, his arm-chair... Spiritually I have lived with excruciating intensity all these last weeks, and I feel strangely in touch with Sandro. I understood him so well, so much more than most of them did, because the bigness in me understood his bigness. We were builders, and there is an inner loneliness about builders it is almost impossible to define.

I am speaking of things not quite in earthly dimensions, so they are almost impossible to put down in words.

I have also been for a week down with flu — and this has given me much time to think and to try and realize all I am going through; it is very big, very quiet, very deep...

October 31, 1934.

I could not finish. Now my 59th birthday has come and gone. Congratulations were brought to me with understanding tact. I was half in bed, half up, being still very shaky. My widowed little Queen found comfort in looking after me... I am very touched to hear my book has been put into Braille...

Before Christmas, Queen Marie was back at Cotroceni. She wrote, on December 21, from her "large and empty" palace,

I am inclined to fold my hands in my lap, to sit quite still and to ponder over the strangeness of my fate... Sometimes I see my life passing before me in a long pageant, and feel as though I must tell it all, in biblical language... "There was once upon a time a maiden born upon an isle lapped by the sea... and I see the little girl with her confident eyes who believed in life and in human hearts... To me all can be told. I am a live dream figure. We can hold *Geistergesprache* and yet both of us in our own corner are pulsing with life. You are at the beginning of your road, I am more than three quarters along mine... I am almost your conscience, but not a troublesome conscience — to me you can talk as you can talk to the best of yourself, without fear of being misunderstood, laughed at!"

...Yesterday I faced a man who believes enormously in my talent. A professor, once a Socialist, but who changed his ideas because of his belief in me, which upset his conceptions of royalty. A queer, dark fellow who occasionally translated some of my writings. Why I say 'I faced him!' is because beneath his outward mask of almost Buddha-like calm and indifference, a flame was burning which I always had to prevent from bursting forth. I knew that a dreadful struggle was tearing him to pieces, but my feelings for him, except only for his clever brain, are almost repulsion. Up to the present, I was always able to keep him from breaking a friendship which on my side could never warm to anything else, but it has needed superhuman tact.

I sent him my books. The reading of them almost killed him with emotion. It was a rather dreadful interview. He had often been unfair to me because in his resentful breast he nursed a grudge against me, first because I was a Queen who had upset his dearest theories about royalty, and secondly because I would not exist as woman for him. But in reading the simple tale of my life, something crumbled within him — he suddenly saw me in another light — and he hated every bad thought he had, but is at the same time torn to pieces with despair that he had never known the real me before, the me of my earlier days who was struggling as a lonely little stranger in his country, whilst he, with his Socialist ideas, wondered if I really ought to exist, or be suppressed.

It was a painful scene. I needed all my strength and tact. His heart was bursting, and my nearly sixty years (he is at least 15 years younger) was no barrier to his passion for me. All this burnt before me in intolerable pain and I had to be a stone, so as not to set light to the man's overwhelming emotions. It was rather terrible, but I got through it, but afterwards my knees were shaking. My book had been a joy and a torture to him. He longed to discuss it with me as critic, as admirer of my literary ability, but emotion was strangling him and I dared not let him have all his say.

We women wield such power, that is why the bad ones can do so much harm, like (name omitted)... My whole life has really been, besides all the rest, one long resistance against those who wanted to love me too well — too much. They saw in me the fount of all joys, of all realization, and yet I had to keep my riches to myself.

Hedged in my palace, surrounded by a thousand eyes, there could be no woman's life for me, and yet for many I shone as the supreme desire of their lives.

Why do I write all this? What grief has shaken my depths? Is it the thought of Mignon's bereavement which thus stirs up the past?

You must look upon this as a letter written by one who lately has been living through *too* much — whose heart is sometimes so intolerably heavy that she would like, occasionally, to take it out of her breast and lay it on the table beside her for a rest...

But this is a *Geistergespräche,* with one whom I have never seen, whom I shall probably never know in the flesh, which allows a sincerity which could not be if you, very young being, were really standing before me — therefore I am not ashamed of this sudden outburst of the living me, which has always to be buried alive!

Queen Marie's next letter was written from Cotroceni, on January 8, 1935, thanking her friend for a book he had sent her. Then she described her Christmas which she had spent "rather sadly alone." But there had been a "lovely festivity in a huge, long domed white room, with lovely indirect light, and tables for all the presents." Towards the end part of the very long room there is an endless table for all the servants (which in a palace are a whole regiment) and every most humble *serviteur* appears in his or her festive best, from the chief cook down to the most inconspicuous garden aid, going through the departments of stables, garage, washing, electricity, telephone, and telegraph, and all the rest.

When I first cross the threshold of the room there is no light except the candle-decked Christmas tree. In former days of course, I was surrounded by children. This year I was quite alone. I had my own tree on the 23rd so as to be able to go up to Sinaia on Christmas Eve for Carol's tree. There I had at least young Michael. Otherwise it was a tremendously military affair. Carol has become very friendly with me, but he lives a life in which I can have no share which leaves me with a feeling of unbearable emptiness.

The Queen then recalled her visit to England, before the assassination of her son-in-law.

I loved it and felt incredibly at home and I was given everywhere a warm welcome... It really is a wonderful country and my first roots have remained there. I return each time to my native country with overwhelming joy!

My friends, whom I had not seen for 9 years, gave me a wonderful reception and I loved being at Balmoral again — the first time since the Summer I describe in my book. Of course there have been changes since Queen Victoria's time. There is less tartan about the place, but much has been left exactly as it was in her time, including the Landseer pictures! There are more flowers, the gardens have been added to and improved, but neither George nor May really know the names of flowers and they much enjoyed my knowledge.

George has always kept an especial affection for me. I stimulate him, my uncrushable vitality makes the blood course more quickly through his veins. May feels it also. She likes being with me, and then I am never heavy on their hands. I know so perfectly how to look after myself and be happy over everything, finding interests everywhere...

May looks dull in the eternal photos we see of her in the many papers — always the same hat, the same cloak, the same parasol, the same smile, the same shoes. But she has a nice sense of humor, only there is this, she told it to me herself: she does not like uncomfortable things. She likes prosperity, ease, politeness, everything running on well-greased wheels. She does not like have to have her depths stirred. She is fundamentally tidy, orderly, disciplined. She likes possessing, collecting, putting things in order. She likes wealth and position, jewels, dresses. She has little imagination, but she likes reading; history interests her, and family trees. She likes to be amused, but decorously, though occasionally a risque little story can make her blush with the pleasure of having understood it. She has watchful but kindly eyes. She is always very smartly dressed, even in the early morning. Her clothes fit as though built for her. Her collars go up right under her ears... She has wonderful jewels which she wears without fantasy. Her brooches, necklaces, pendants, bracelets are worn in classic fashion and the color of the stones are chosen to match the color of her gowns which she wears in bright, light colors. She has endless diadems and wears them often... She is always pleasantly and easily busy — no scurry, no effort, no exertion. She looks into things in detail and is an excellent and vigilant housewife. She has excellent appetite, excellent health, and sleeps beautifully. A placid, undisturbed woman who keeps all that is unpleasant at arm's length. But she is kind-hearted, full of attention, and although she hates illness she is very kind to the sick and pays them stiff little visits and always sends messages of enquiry. Both she and he are scrupulously polite, but their demonstrations of pleasure of affection are always restrained and decorous. You can think, as contrast, impulsive, uncalculating, unconventional *me*. I am always astonished that they really like me, but they do!

"Their thrones are seats of peace," as I expressed it in my book... My last letter was, I fear, a little weird — but unlike dear Queen Mary I have to go through many emotions — and my seat is not one of ease and comfort!

The theme of solitariness increased in Queen Marie's letters and in March, 1935, she wrote:

The Winter has passed very quickly... in the evening I am always quite alone. I do not sup, but merely drink a cup of soup (I like soup, a Russian heritage) eat some orange compot, and generally I am reading the while. I have got very fond of being alone. When Ileana married I thought it was better to die than to remain all alone in the big empty house. But there is a sort of peace in solitude. Ileana was here for a fortnight with husband and children... She loves painting and wanted to learn from me — showing her how to lay on color, how to compose a picture, how to get the right lines — my old love for painting awoke anew, and now I have complicated my already over-busy life with a renewed passion for the art I had laid away... what I do today is better and has more force than what I did formerly — quite a pleasant discovery... Lately I have been fascinated by a book about Nijinsky, written by his wife. She adores him and the part when he gradually becomes demented is heart-breaking. One loves him, although there were such queer and also reprehensible sides to his life. It is so intensely Russian in its acceptance of life, events, circumstances good and bad, but having read it I feel I would like to have known him. In spite of certain things which upset one he is a clean and simple spirit... I was amused to see that Sullivan's operas had such success in America. Sullivan was one of the most intimate friends of my father.

The volume of Queen Marie's reminiscences had been published in America in the early spring of 1935 and in her next letter to her friend she resented the "tone of joking impertinence" in some of the criticisms. Some of them made her "royal blood squirm" and she wrote:

though you are an American I am saying this to you — the Americans are by far the worst, especially when they speak of a Queen; because from the first she must be ruled out from generally mercy; if possible, she must be turned into ridicule like a wax doll in a puppet-show. If this puppet dares to show signs of being a human being, then she must be ridiculed. It is as though those who scoffed were afraid of being impressed, or even touched in spite of themselves, so they laugh before they have even understood...

...Spring is coming very slowly. It is deliciously 'early green,' just that incomparable haze which lasts about ten days each year, just before the leaf is really leaf, and when the green of the trees is a light instead of a shade... Of course, I feel *too much* and that is why I am often misunderstood and even ridiculed... I am looking well this year, rather out of the way well — sometimes I feel almost shy when I see how well people think I am looking. A sort of Italian summer... Just because I am an animator they say I have a way of coming into the room which fills it with electricity. Of course it is important how Queen comes into a room, because everybody is always waiting for you — you are always *the* guest.

For the first two weeks of May, 1935, Queen Marie was in England for the celebration of King George V's Jubilee; then she hurried to Sonnberg for the birth of Princess Ileana's baby. "Well, here I am for the seventh time grandmother," on May 25 she wrote:

England was a joy, a deep joy. I love it with the love the roots of a tree have for their *own* soil, something deeper than reason, something fundamental, so to say — basic. Something deep down within me responds to England as it does to nothing else. To the soil, the people... I have had to battle, to grow through 'stone walls,' so when I am amongst civilized super-perfect content and ease I am only like a wanderer who rests awhile, rejoices, approves, but who knows that it is not for him, that he is only taking breath before new effort, new 'moving on.'

And yet I am like a fish in water, like a lizard in the sun; I bask, I stretch my cramped muscles, I relax from all tiring effort. I enjoy, deeply, take breath, being at home. I like the politeness, the taste, the habits, the discretion, the freedom, the unnoisy and easy hospitality. I like the loyalty, the deep feeling of respect for the crown, the royal family — no servility about it, but a happy, serene, natural acceptance about a beautiful tradition which does not depend upon the man on the throne, but on the people's will to venerate what they have chosen, elevated. It gives a solid, aesthetic, secure centre around which everything circles with a feeling of law and order...

In America it is smart to scoff at royalty, but in old European countries it gives beauty, a 'worthwhileness' which nothing else can represent. In a procession there must always be a culminating point, something one is expecting, waiting for, towards which little children, sad woman, and old soldiers can stretch out their hands — a happy excitement, a fine display, dignity, prestige, tradition, which in itself is a sort of religion.

Can you, young Democrat, friend... grasp what I mean?

There is also beauty in the English country, in the noble parks, the fine old country seats with their valuable old pictures, old plate, china, and glass, which is to be found nowhere else and which is perfect in a way not describable, but has to be seen. Something in the line, the orderliness, in the quiet green isolation which nothing elsewhere can come up to.

Many of the old families have now to live very simply — the women wear old dresses, a maid serves at table instead of the powdered footmen of other days — but the ancestral portraits look down upon you, the silver on the table belongs to the times of the Stuarts, the Georges — and all this is not astonishing, ostentatious, but natural — always was...

There is an indescribable dignity about it, and the manners are so quiet, so staid, so natural, the voices low, cultivated. Sometimes the men are a bit dull, a bit heavy, the ladies a bit dry, superficial, stereotyped, but they know how to behave, they are secure in their traditions, their politeness, their rights, their habits. There is a home-feeling about big and small English houses which fills one with content, and as to the gardens... But I shall not begin about the gardens, or I shall never end.

And in these days of deplorable insecurity and anxiety there was something comforting, reassuring, touching about the reception the King received at his Jubilee, in the way the whole nation took part and rejoiced with him and over him. No matter that he has no special personality, that she is stiff and something conventional — they were emblems — flags — the kindly father, the benevolent mother.

And it was such a fine day and the flags fluttered so gaily and the crowds were astonishing, astounding — good-tempered, well-behaved crowds kept in order by tall, kindly, patient police. The English mounted police on their superbly-groomed horses are one of the goodly sights of this world... a sort of delicious, warm pride bubbles up from my depths when I think of England. Everything

in me agrees with it, feels at home, at peace... My love for Roumania in no way makes me less proud of being English, of feeling
English, with every drop of my blood...

You ask about the Prince of Wales. For the moment he is inclined to
be a revolutionary, that is to say, one in opposition, especially to his
father's steadiness. David (as we call him in the family) kicks
against traditions and restrictions, without realizing that tradition
made him, is his *raison d'être*; he will have to find the right balance
between today, yesterday, and tomorrow. Not easy...

Yes, it is sad to see people destroy themselves because of jealousy... I
have two friends, women-friends, who destroyed themselves thus...
A queer feeling, or rather complication has followed me all along
my life's journey. Women have loved me as passionately as men
have. I mean this of course purely from the sentimental point of
view. They have absolutely tortured me with their love... sentimentality with a woman always gave me a feeling of nausea, because I
could never reciprocate it, and my very toes curled up in exaspera-
tion and my hair bristled with distaste at being sentimentalized by a
woman. And yet it happened to me over and over again. They
wanted to dedicate themselves to me, to live for me, sacrifice themselves to me, and what not else!... I had to strike them out of my
life... I was as indifferent as stone. Then came storming scenes of
jealousy, till finally I would have to sit holding their hands and telling them in plain language what no kind tactfulness was able to
make them understand, that even if I was a stupendous event to
them, an all absorbing thirsty need, they were not this to me and it
must be understood, or one day I would be capable of murdering
them.

I learned an awful truth: it is cruel enough to love and not to be
loved, but it can be endured. Whilst to endure love when you don't
love is *unendurable*. I cannot explain what there is in me which
awakens this passion... It could be funny, but alas it is sometimes
infinitely tragic. And age has nothing to do with it. It is just as bad
today, even worse than it was in my youth, coming perhaps from
that feeling of strength, fullness, which they feel in me.

In almost every letter, Queen Marie wrote to her friend of the books
she was reading, and they were strangely mixed. She gave her opinions on
The Strange Death of President Harding, a "terrible book," *The First To Go
Back* by Irina Skariatina with which she was "out of sympathy," and Francis Stuart's *Try the Skies* which "fascinated" her. The Queen thought Sin-
clair Lewis's *Dodsworth*, "exceedingly good," and she read Zweig's *Mary*

Stuart with "enormous interest." Sometimes she strayed into reminiscence, when a biography touched the fringe of her own world. She had read Corti's life of the Empress Elizabeth of Austria and wrote:

> How beautiful Empress Elizabeth must have been, but how selfish. She filled the world with her own needs, her own desires, wishes, and tastes. Judging her from one of her own caste, I cannot but condemn her. She lived unfairly, spending streams of her husband's money, but not playing the game — looking upon herself as a sacrificed martyr. She has remained a legendary figure because she was beautiful, original, independent of thought, because she was an Empress and as her Emperor was both rich and generous she could squander endless millions upon her marvellous settings. Whenever she wished to travel, she travelled in a spectacular way — yachts, castles, palaces, gardens, horses — nothing was too lavish, though she had a morbid dislike, even a horror, of being looked at, and always kept a fan between herself and the crowds, even when in her greatest beauty.
>
> Judging her from a colleague's point of view, I would say "No, she did not play the game." She took without giving, and never thanked for what she took, only wailed at being misunderstood. She forsook her worthy, hard-worked husband and though she had spontaneous moments of charity and good will, it was only when it gave her a sort of thrill or excitement. She was a poetic, also a noble, searching soul — but the morbid interest she took in herself, in her feelings, her likes and dislikes, her health, her figure, was unhealthy. She was absolutely ruthless towards the feelings of others. Of course, there is no doubt she was not quite normal and towards the end melancholia had beset her in a way which made all things unbearable to her. The truth is, she accepted no duties and no one forced her to do her duty, so she was entirely without aim, never without means of giving way to her very ruinous fantasy, and because everything could be bad, it became worthless — it simply became a chase after satisfaction, and no satisfaction possible because there was no gratitude for what she was given and because she had no peace of mind — never, anywhere. She was a woman who wasted her life and was never conscious of how she tortured others around her. And yet she had that strange faculty of awakening admiration and calling forth deep devotion amongst the few towards whom she behaved normally. In fact, a wasted life, and wasted treasures of beauty — both mental and physical.

In the same letter, the Queen turned once more to recollections of her American visit, the "worthwhile moments" and the "many thrills." "In a way," she wrote:

I represented the King, and was given a King's honors and this put me on my mettle, made me feel I must give my very best. Denver was one of the places my children and I liked best. We also loved Seattle. The schools there were wonderful, and I had been in touch with the girls of the Seattle High School... several years before I came, and they gave me a tremendous reception. It was of course the odious, trivial press which often offended my feelings of 'niceness' — a sort of familiar vulgarity and running down of all that had been nicest, which, be one as little inclined to offence as I am, the same hurt and left a bad taste. With that, both I and my children treated the reporters who were with us so kindly, in such a really friendly, comradely spirit — but they, in many cases, gave back evil for good and this hurt us. I also have a nice remembrance because in those days my son Nicky was my closest friend, and we shared things together. Later, a woman got hold of him and made him imagine he had never been happy at home, but misunderstood and ignored — whilst he had always been living in the centre of everything, the spoil favorite of everyone, and my dearest ally. *Tout passe...*

Often you have asked me about the impression Wilson made on me... I thought him pleasant, amiable, but according to my diary: 'I cannot help feeling that he exaggerates his own type...' He certainly had the type of a clergyman, exceedingly sure of his own excellence and superiority. Personally, I was rather irritated at Europe's attitude towards him, treating him as supreme arbiter of European affairs. No wonder it turned the man's head. He was treated as a demi-god and finally imagined that he was one chosen to redeem humanity. In spite of my every desire to like him, right inside me, I had the feeling he was a fraud, and that if put in the same situation as the clergyman in 'Rain' he would probably have behaved in the same way... I did not genuinely like him because I had not the feeling he was genuine, but playing up to himself... I also have the feeling that Harding must in reality have been a sympathetic human being. Inclined as I am to believe in others, I can understand how he was taken in, and how he *could* not believe that his dearest friends should betray him thus, and profit of his credulity... Seeing what happens to my son, I understand it even more. Men have strong appetites and often let themselves in with people, not always reputable, counting upon the idea that pleasures (even if shady) shared together will create a sort of happy fraternity which excludes every thought of betrayal... power pays its penalty. Everybody tries to abuse the one who wields it...

Talking about royal tradition, there is an excellent book called *Monarchy* by Sir Charles Petrie. He is a convinced believer in monarchy and argues it all out most logically. Of course I cannot but be pleased that a serious man should espouse a cause in which I believe. Curiously enough, he is unfair about King Alexander of Serbia... I read with interest the articles about little King Peter, but I could not help being annoyed with Mme Gruitch's article, because it is all self-advertisement and three-quarters of it bluff! The old lady never had anything to do with Peter, and her anecdotes about him are purely invented so as to bring herself into it. She is one of the Europeanized Americans who have become arrant snobs.

In the early summer of 1935, the Queen stayed with her widowed daughter in Dalmatia, in "a simple house in grey tones according to the style of the country." She wrote:

The sea is unimaginable blue, diluted sapphires, and there is no tide... My youngest sister, 'sister baby,' now Infanta Beatrice of Spain, was also there, and we were the most blissfully happy trio... My sister is nine years younger than I am, but I am very young in spirit and Mignon is ripe for her age, incredibly reasonable and absolutely selfless. My sister, though she adores her husband, has had a hard life... My life has not exactly been a bed of roses, and my child... must stand on her own, for the sake of her sons. Her own life is so to say — over. So we three women know the iron law of royal duty, no matter in what circumstances, and our three separate existences meet and blend without clash... The bathing was miraculous and Mignon took us also for long drives through stunning scenery, wild and grand, sometimes almost fierce... Mignon drove us herself, with almost masculine efficiency, unabashed by the terribly precipitous turnings... I was pleased to see her take to driving again — it is a good sign.

Towards the end, unfortunately, the children went down with malaria...We all three turned into sick nurses, I being the least efficient of the three, as medicine was never my specialty...

My people want to make a fuss over my 60th birthday. It is good they should remember how long I have been with them, but I do not want them to spend money on me. I did accept, though, from a very dear friend, a beautiful thoroughbred chestnut horse, a stallion; a gorgeous creature which shall go with me for autumn riding at Balcic... He is tall, slim, with divinely arched neck and a silky coat of the colour of beech leaves in autumn, and has a soft swinging gallop. It is like being carried on the back of a wave.

In her last letter for the year, Queen Marie thanked her friend for being so "very clever" as to arrange for his "birthday" letter to arrive "exactly" on the day, and she described the "orgy of remembrance."

My 43 years with my people suddenly rose up before them almost like a golden legend and they lived to remember when I came from over the seas, with all the glamour of a great name — of great relations, bringing down into this far-off little-known corner of Europe some of the great powers to which, by birth, I belonged... I suddenly stood once more before their eyes and they understood what I had been for the country and how even today, when they have shelved me, forsaken me, I was the one they had *really* loved.

The Queen had not conquered the strange jealousy that has, for so long, marred the relationship between monarchs and their heirs. She could not end the story of her birthday without bitterness.

"And my son," she wrote, "well, he could not bear that they should remember. He thinks it diminishes him. He was of them all the one who *would* not understand... The story is tragic, could be told with burning words..."

God bless you. You are a dear boy, your feet solidly on the ground which does not, however, prevent you from seeing the stars!

In her letter written on January 8, 1936, the Queen returned again to the unhappy theme of her son. "My Christmas was peaceful," she wrote,

But under this reign, everything has become over-official, too regulated, too strictly conventional, so as to mask the inner want, the irreparable loss of home-life and home-heartiness which nothing can replace. So it all feels sham, a smart lacquered screen, behind which things take place in which I have no share.

But there was "one family joy," during the Christmas celebrations at Sinaia.

I have made great friends with Michael, wrote the Queen. For many years a feeling of jealousy did not allow the parents to let me enjoy him. For some reason this jealousy has died down. Probably I also have become less impetuous, and so awake less apprehension. Anyhow we are now allowed to see each other more often. He has grown beyond all recognition and is sending out feelers. He wants comprehensive sympathy, senses that I can give it, so has a longing for my company. He is a darling and I anxiously watch his progress, guessing the many questions he is putting to life — and no one to answer them gently, carefully — and yet there I am, quite near with all my yearning, never discouraged love...

I much enjoyed *Victoria Regina* — most clever and witty, and though strongly satirical, much truth in it — cleverly done and even if sometimes, as her granddaughter, I found I ought to be annoyed, the wittiness of the whole thing outweighed any slight done to the great little old lady!

By the way, de Lazlo is coming to paint a large picture of me for the National Bank. I wonder what he will be able to make of my 60 years!

Queen Marie's next letter was written on January 29, soon after the death of King George V. It was "a great sacrifice" for her not to go to the funeral but, she wrote,

I felt it was the *one* moment when my son, considered to a certain degree like a pariah, could go and take his place amongst other kings. They could not cold-shoulder him at such a moment. It was good for him and the country that he should go so I encouraged him to go — and stayed at home. It must not look as though I were leading him by the hand or protecting him with my personality. Besides, he is of the actual generation. I, strong as I am, belong to the past and must accept this quite naturally. Besides, widowed Queens, even if they are loved, are difficult personages to place at official occasions and it is good they should remember this themselves without having to be told... I am so sorry for Queen Mary. He and she worked in such harmony. They were like a splendidly paired couple of first-class carriage horses, stepping exactly alike. She was such a perfect companion, dignified, patient, stately, contented with her daily round, with no strong desire to let her imagination rove. She agreed with, and loved her royal existence, felt no irritation against conventionality and routine. She told me herself that, above all things she liked ease, comfort, order, regulation. She did not like to be disturbed deeply. She was ideal for a Queen of England for whom everything is arranged by magnificent old tradition... She loved her George in an unemotional way and was the most faithful comrade — punctual, patient, tidy, even-tempered, placid, quietly intelligent and tactful...

I belong to those who believe in young King Edward and I wrote him a word to tell him so. He is quick, intelligent, loveable; he is certainly inclined to burn his candle at both ends, has an urge to amuse himself over-much. He is perhaps a little too modern, but the tremendous weight and strength of England behind him — put him on his honor. It is such a tremendous beginning — to stand out chosen, before all the world who expect you to carry on, to be a worthy follower of a loved father. The torch has been passed into his hands. A cruelly beautiful moment when the deceased King's body is lowered into his grave and for the last time he is given all his titles — then a pause — and the same titles are pronounced once more for the new King: Edward VIII, King, Emperor of India, etc. A magnificent, simple, moving moment, I only heard it over the radio, but it went right through me... It is a very dangerous moment for a change of regime — such confusion in Europe, such dark clouds everywhere...

The early part of February was devoted to Philip de Lazlo's portrait. The painter had arrived at Cotroceni, eager to paint "a really royal picture." The Queen wrote:

He cannot paint a Queen every day and dear de Lazlo is an inveterate but naive snob. He has come together with all the most famous people in the world; sovereigns, popes, politicians, aristocrats, professional beauties, bankers, millionaires, great actresses, generals, priests, dictators, and Indian potentates. He loves 'grandeur,' but has remained a simple, artless, confidential, amusing, kind man. Although naturalized English, he speaks it abominably. Sitting for him is very entertaining, as he can talk about literally *everybody*, of every nationality and it is talk, talk, talk, all the time. But my yesterday's sitting was exhausting as he insists upon gorgeous and official attire, a thing I have quite given up — so that I had to dig up the old gorgeousness of my royal days and this attire is exceedingly heavy and exhausting to wear... He has enough lovely models to paint from, probably some amongst them that look like Queens, but are not! So he cannot use upon them his Velasquez, Titian, Rubens temptations and ideals. It needs a Queen to be able to carry off certain overwhelming attire — a painter is justified when he paints her thus, and she is not 'dressed up,' she is really wearing her own clothes!... It is only because he is such a unique craftsman that I submit to his tyranny. I believe in his ability to reproduce the beauty of all burnished, lustrous tissues, so I just give in... he arranges a looking-glass in such wise that one can see the picture he is painting. So yesterday I saw my own face, in an incredibly short space of time, grow out of nothing — out of empty canvas. The firm, sure rapidity of his stroke is stupendous, never a hesitation, never a mistake, and it is all done with the brush straight off the canvas... It is pure magic. He knows no difficulties...

I agree with you in your contempt for the *average* reporter. They have falsified the everyday values. They have vulgarized life and encouraged the ugly side of human nature... The Lindbergh case is disgraceful.

Discussing royalty — King George's funeral was again proof of how Kings can told things together beyond the capacity of political men. This was why it was so important for my excluded son to take his place in their ranks.

I have, unfortunately, always the tendency to let him get his 'undeserved' successes too easily. It would be better for his character if I had the courage to let him *see* what I do for him, but I have a morbid horror of humiliating anyone... So I never hold up before my son either my patience or my generosity, nor his lapses, which allows him to continue believing himself a fine fellow when he is not. I see him with such dreadful clearness — torturing to a mother's heart, a mother's pride, a mother's love...

Yes, I think King Constantine and Queen Sophie were unfairly treated. I think also that both had very great limitations... Sophie always complained — life seemed for her a weight, a losing battle, her conventionality, her preconceived ideas, tastes, and prejudices withered all *joie de vivre* in her. She always felt defeated, so she attracted defeat... I confess she bored me. I felt stifled in her company. She made me feel as though I had corners, as though I were too healthy, too big for her over-tidy rooms, her over-labelled ideas. We were quite good friends. As a widow, she spent months and months in Roumania...

On February 19, Queen Marie wrote a hurried short letter to her friend in America:

My favourite sister, Ducky[7] is dangerously ill. I am called suddenly to her bedside...

On March 21, the Queen wrote again:

Yes, Ducky has gone forever... A companionship, a friend, an assurance, and also all the dearest memories of an incomparable happy childhood. To us sisters Ducky was our conscience. She was the proudest, strongest, most upright, most capable, most law-abiding, but also the most unforgiving of us all, and this inability to forgive

---

[7]The Grand Duchess Victoria Feodorovna, wife of the Grand Duke Cyril of Russia.

was what finally broke her. She had no understanding for weakness, could not accept compromise of any kind. Her ideals were absolute, not to be discussed.

There was something of Lucifer's pride about her — magnificent but dangerous. This will give you an idea of her way. Once she said to me: 'If I say something is good taste, it is not that I *think* it is good taste, but that it *is*.'

...Unbending, authoritative, almost domineering, she could accept no half-measures. Untruthfulness she could not even understand... Her great fault was that she gave no one a second chance, being in this my direct opposite. She could not forgive, once a person had disappointed her, or not lived up to what she had expected, she would put him or her aside... Three of us sisters were born leaders, but each in a quite different way. I used gentleness and a deep understanding of the other man's side of the case. Ducky used strength and withering contempt when disappointed. Sister Baby used and uses diplomacy. We were a strong race — the mixture of Russian and English was a strange blend, setting us somewhat apart from others, as, having strong and dominating characters we could not follow, only lead... The meeting of the four sisters, for the last time at Amorbach, was tragic... She was literally dying of a broken heart... Ducky could not forgive, and her nearest and dearest had betrayed her. She discovered that her whole life had been based on a lie... He had *always* deceived her... Like a beggar he stood on the threshold of her room and dared not touch her hand... When told by my sisters that I was there she immediately connected the thought of me with flowers, and murmured something about lilies. We both loved our gardens. I also had the consolation to hear her say, when asked if she was pleased I had come — 'It makes all the difference in the world...'

She died at midnight... The next morning I went to her for a last time alone. We had wrapped her in a long soft white silk robe. We had few flowers at Amorbach, but I had some white lilacs which I laid around her head and shoulders, and Sandra put a bunch of freezia in her hands... We buried her at Coburg... It was a cold day, half-snow, half-rain. I hate funerals... I am not of those who like weeping on graves...

And now I am at Sonneberg and my face seems to have shrunk, to have become pale and gray, but I do not carry my grief outwardly with me...Thank you friend... for two letters, and also for your sweet and comforting understanding of my pain.

I quite understand that you want to keep me in the spirit. Some shyness might come over us if we met in the flesh. As it is there is no barrier of separation, of any kind — neither of age, caste, distance... We are just two human beings.

A month later, Queen Marie wrote of Philip de Lazlo's portrait which she had not seen "quite finished," but those who had, told her it was "superb, at the same time dignified and simple, extremely royal."

He realized by being with me, talking with me, learning to know me really, what I really was today, and understood that I had stripped off so much belonging to those days when I was shining before the world as a brilliantly successful and glorified Queen. He understood that, if I had lost in brilliance, I had gained in depth, purified by all the grief and the many renouncements... I had to be purified and to learn how much of my old life was vanity... It is not in vain that, on decline, so much is taken from us. It is so as to prepare us for the end. To sow the seed of longing for another life in our tired souls...

Portrait of Queen Marie by Philip de Laszlo (1936)

...de Lazlo also painted a rather wonderful smaller picture of me in my mourning veils... the expression is sad and thoughtful and I have hung it opposite the brilliant Queen of ten years ago. All in gold, with the crown on my head, and the contrast tells its own tale...

Queen Marie's friend had told her of his plans for a summer holiday. Her reply reveals the curious memory and affection she had for people who never came in the horizon of her royal interests.

If you should go or rather stay longer in Denver, I would be glad if you could find time to visit Miss... at Colorado Springs. She is an invalid, was a teacher, and I have corresponded with her for years... I have spoken to her about you. If you manage to see her, ask for her in my name and afterwards write to me about her. We have never met, but her letters are clever and interesting and she seems to have a brave spirit... I loved Denver and there I received one of the warmest receptions. I liked the place and the people... what terrible floods you have had in America! I read about them with distress... Have you noticed that my hand-writing has become much less tidy? There is fatigue in it...

In June 1936, Queen Marie was at Tenha-Yuvah, the place she "loved best." "It is the most enchanted season of all," she wrote, "first the irises, now the roses, and many flowers to come... I want to make out of one of my new grounds a memory-garden for Ducky. It is to be in a small meadow studded here and there with rough fruit trees, overlooking the sea... In the middle of the walled garden is to be an old stone peasant well, enormously heavy, rustic, and attractive and beside it an old stone cross... I was lucky enough to find this old well in a part of Bucharest, once quite countryside, now eaten up by spreading town..."

In the same letter Queen Marie wrote of Mr. Frank Buchman, "who started the Oxford movement" and who had stayed with her at Sinaia.

I was much in sympathy with his creed, but one or two little incidents with Buchman himself put me off. One was just about personal confession in public. He wanted me to make a confession in front of my children, at a moment when he was rather under the influence of one of them, who did not quite played fairly towards me... I seemed to discover something rather sly in his way, which somehow upset me. Also, when I went to America he was on the same boat. He was tremendous friends with my children and we were all very happy together, but when in America I had the miserable feeling that he wanted to use me as a "reclame" because I was a Queen, and it ended with a little soreness on both sides, although I tried to be as loyal as possible. In those days he was being much attacked and those playing host to me did not want to have me mixed up in controversy. *He* tried to secure me as a manifestation and the whole thing was rather uncomfortable. Somehow I did not feel rightly or wrongly, that I specially needed reforming... I felt the snob in him and this put me off. But I approve of any moment which can help people to become better and all the people Buchman brought me together with were first-rate people...

In his recent letter the American friend had asked the Queen some question about Mr. Herbert Hoover which prompted her to answer,

Yes, I think Hoover was prejudiced against Roumania. This had much disappointed me as for a time he had worked in Belgium with my uncut diamond friend, Joe Boyle the Canadian, and who had a great admiration for Hoover. He imagined Hoover would be my friend...

As to a gramophone plate of my voice, reading some of my own writing, I *have* been asked to do it; but as yet I have always hesitated. I have become strangely shy about publicity. I was often so spitefully treated... Today I am not easily to be had for anything! I consider my public day over and think it is a great rest... I greatly shrink from all publicity, as all those who had been hard hit and had to remain silent... In July I hope to go to England...

The Queen wrote her next letter from Lord Astor's house, Cliveden, on July 27, 1936. She returned to the theme of her love for England.

Here I need make no effort. All within me agrees with the habit, soil, landscape, and the English conception of life. Their sense of honour is mine. I come back to my kind... I drift down quiet waters, and exquisite sensation and harmony relaxes the strain which sometimes is over-great in the country of my adoption. Here all is beauty, accomplishment, everything is smoothed out for you, made easy...

Cliveden is one of the most beautiful places in England and is something of a home to me. The absolutely perfect house, grounds, setting, the unique view over stretches of emerald-green carpet-smooth lawns, down upon the Thames, over the beauty of century-old trees — is indescribable. I love it all with an intense love, not quite free of pain...

Lord Astor is a born angel. He was always my friend. Life has not marred our friendship and he adopts those belonging to me with a charming simplicity given only to those whose hearts are large, generous, and unselfish. Lady Astor is the most stimulating company and she too is deeply good beneath her somewhat domineering attitude. Her tongue is occasionally over-witty and outspoken, so that she is sometimes misjudged, but she has a noble spirit and I love her... they all accept me as though I were one of them which is inexpressibly comforting. Also Ileana is beautifully at home in their house. We are just as good friends with the young ones as with the parents...

As to the Oxford movement, here some are ardently for it. Others don't like it. I must say I like Mr. Buchman's methods less and less the more I know of him.

...Be happy... You are very real to me, although we have never met.

The next letter was from Bran, on August 31. "...here I am," wrote the Queen, "all by myself and have actually begun to work at volume IV."

Stirring her own story into life made the Queen despair over what had happened in Roumania since King Carol's ascension. "Today, what have they made out of my poor country?" she wrote:

> ...it makes me sad, because although the kernel of the country is still healthy, administration and governments have rotted over-much. And the King was too young, too much exteriors, for quick and easy successes, for outward show — paying too little attention for the means used, even in his own palace... He has great qualities and is very intelligent, but — well, the world had cried that 'but' to all the winds, and being myself set up as a contrast is no consola-tion; because his is the present and also the future if he does not, aided by disreputable councillors, blow us all up... Like the ostrich he puts his head in the sand, believing that thus he is safe... there is a sort of unreasoned jealousy against my past, against what I have been to the country... I am a sort of living reproach. I cannot admire all he does; I know his *métier*, I alone in the country know it, and he knows that I know it and this, for some reason, infuriates him... Personally I consider that an honourable family life is best for Kings, and safer. But I cannot force upon the young ones a standard of morals which no more fits in with their ideals and needs...

In October, the Queen was at Balcic again, "...the sun is shining brightly," she wrote,

> my precious, spacious room is full of roses, gladiolus, and early chrysanthemums. A lovely, peaceful room with which my soul is in harmony... From Bran I went to Milocer and spent over two weeks in that marvellous place with my dear Mignon... Mignon is incredi-bly restful company and I needed her soothing atmosphere... I had been having rather a bad time at home and arrived very depressed. For the first time I am obliged to make a mighty effort to preserve my optimism... I am continually hit in the back and subjected to ugly and unnecessary humiliations by those surrounding the mas-ter. They egg him on the maltreat me because I will not bow down to what I consider wrong and harmful. My very silence and retreat from everything is a reproach. No end of *misères* are inflicted upon my dignified little household... It has become the reign of evil, and I am an outcast... I never thought it would come to this!

> Besides the cruel grief, there is also much danger. Sometimes I can-not even pray! So I went to my excellent motherly child to recover

my balance. I simply asked her to have patience with me. Morally I was very sick... And hardly had I reached Milocer than I heard that my favourite gardener *et homme de confiance* here in Balcic had died quite suddenly in a few days... He loved working with me, loved and understood my flowers, knew how to plant them, keep them, improve them. He helped me to create beauty. He was honest, faithful, dependable, and immensely capable in every direction. He was the keeper of the whole place, house included when I could not be there myself.

Well, Mignon let me wallow also in this grief... blessed little Mignon, with her staunch attitude towards life — loving, but not sentimental — not passionate as her mother... gave me back my balance... And whilst I pace my terrace, adore my roses, saunter through my vineyards and go to the places we had still planned to embellish, it is as though Yavin were keeping pace with me. I actually hear his step beside mine...

King Edward VIII was still in Britain; he did not abdicate until two months later. In the same letter, written on October 12, Queen Marie recalled her visit to London and her impressions of the new regime.

Certainly the young King is much more modern in all his conceptions, also they say he is very stubborn. Personally I think he is perfectly fascinating. Of course, he must go forward, but I hope he will not destroy all old royal traditions. England is a land of tradition, and it is part of her strength. If the young King finds the right balance between the old and the new, he will do well, as he is both clever and charming. Our lunch at Buckingham Palace with him and the Queen was a very pleasant meal. Ileana and Anton were also with me and conversation flowed freely on many subjects. David, as we call him in the family, is many-sided and much less insular than my old friend, his father. He can understand also a foreign point of view which was almost impossible to his father. He has a charming face, though a little faded now, and a delightful laugh.

Queen Mary, though very sad, is exceedingly quiet and like Mignon she is unsentimental and staunchly bears her loneliness. Her position is assured. She has every possible worldly good and honour; everything is done for always with magnificent order and plenty. Her own son behaves beautifully towards her, although, of course, being of a different generation, they do not always see eye to eye. Certainly, there is always a certain sadness in being in the past, but she has had long years of prosperity and calm happiness and she told me that she looked upon it as a benediction that George was called away at the right moment — before he and others could be aware that his faculties were lessening, and his strength giving out. All in Queen Mary is quiet, unemotional harmony. She passes smoothly through life — honoured, guarded, appreciated, recognized. Her health is perfect and she still loves life in the form which it remains to her. I returned to her a second time for a long *tête-à-tête* tea and we had a long heart-to-heart talk.

Welbeck belongs to one of the most prodigious English establishments. The Duke of Portland, now already 60, is like a King in his own domain — a wonderful old gentleman who lives royally and is a type bound to disappear. His park and woods are simply magnificent and he loves very inch of his ground and is fond of entertaining on a very large footing. Duchess, who was very beautiful in her day, has become very deaf — but is exceedingly gracious. De Lazlo made beautiful pictures of her in her day of glory. She still a grand air...

Perhaps you are right not to go to London during the Coronation. You would of course see grand sights, but the prices will be double and the town too full. London can be terribly crowded...

What I mind most about myself just now is that I feel defeated... Even Ileana has been torn out of my life. Her brother behaved... so unkindly that this year I did not even try to get permission for her to come — and you know she was my purest joy... I have also at the head of my household, an absolutely devoted man, who does all in his power to guard me from persecution — thereby drawing the thunder down also upon his head. As he is an officer, there is always danger that they will try to take him from me. Today I am absolutely defenceless and it is sad to be treated thus in a country for which I worked with so much love... I shall probably spend Christmas with Ileana as she has not been allowed to come here...

Queen Marie's despair over her son was an increasing obsession. The letters she wrote during these last eighteen months of her life became less brave; her robust spirit began to fade. "He tries to subjugate me and those who serve me," she wrote, on November 27, "but he cannot banish me... there is a spirit of tyranny and despotism in him which others foster for their own interests, making a hell out of my life... My own son ought not to try to humiliate and darken the last years of my life. It is ugly... It is a sort of jealousy of all I was..."

Grief closed in on the Queen, bitterly, during these months. In November, her nephew, Alonzo was killed on the Spanish front.

"He died heroically during his first battle," she wrote, "His plane was shot down in flames." She liked "to think of him flying like Icarus with flaming wings up into the heavens..." In December her "favourite lady-in waiting" died, and her old maid had served her for 30 years, died in Berlin on Christmas Day. At the same time she had to lament the death of her "devoted and perfectly charming young A.D.C." by "a horrible abcess on the brain." He had served her "with utmost and unchanging devotion," staunchly standing up against "the flood of iniquity" surging around her. She wrote of him, "Incorruptible, intelligent, good-looking, devoted... an excellent officer, everything promised a brilliant career. I had chosen him four years ago. He did not disappoint me. I had even made a perfect gardener of him, and had taught him to love and understand flowers as I did. He was an apt pupil and I felt I was developing his mind and intelligence in a way he had never dreamed of. He loved to serve me and looked after me in every way, as though I was something very precious which must be lovingly guarded, protected. He hated to see me suffer." The Queen was at Sonneberg when she wrote this letter. She paused to complain, "all the deaths this year seemed to accumulate around me." Then the powers of courage came back again. "There is an enormous source of vitality in me," she wrote, "so I shall set out anew." The "ugly intrigues" and the "abominable prospering of unworthy upstarts" in King Carol's Court still depressed her. "I look on, and am horrified at the danger he is conjuring up... there is nothing but self-interest in their so-called devotion, and their spirits are the spirits of slaves who will betray their master if an evil day comes upon him... But for all my grief I am still alive." The Queen turned then to the subject of King Edward's abdication:

Personally, I am too royal not to look upon David as a deserter... There is too much poetry in my heart and soul to be touched by this love story. She is an uninteresting heroine... The whole world was open to him... it seemed so unnecessary to stand the whole British Empire on its head, to compromise the throne, and shake the foundations of monarchy... Perhaps I am full of royal prejudice... though I dearly love him I cannot help doubting if he was really *à la hauteur* of his royal mission. But what will be his life today?

In spite of his wonderful charm, David is perhaps really frivolous at heart and not of the stuff of which great rulers are made. I am disappointed in him. I thought he would have been a good king. But charm alone, if not linked with something more solid, does not suffice. Bertie (George VI) has perhaps more solid qualities.

I have just read a quite magnificent German book by a man called Otto Gamelin — *The Life of Frederick II of Hohenstaufen*. It is a mighty story, beautifully told. Frederick II is my real idea of a King — not all virtue, certainly not, but big, strong, grand, almost overwhelming. He had to fight the Popes, but did so heroically, magnificently — although he would rather have reconciled himself with the Church... Already my mother loved Frederick II and used to follow up his traces in Germany, Italy, and Sicily, and together, when I was a child, we visited his grave in Palermo... The Germans write wonderful historical books. Last year I read the life of Charlequin (Charles V) by a German called Elert — a splendid book full of strength as well as human understanding... There is a sturdy strength about certain German writers which is magnificent. The language, when well-used, is grand, sweeping, with tremendous depth of sound and thought.

The head of my household, General Zwiedneck, a great personal friend... reads these books to me aloud. A convinced monarchist, he sees in me a luminous star among royalties, and suffers acutely when Kings do not live up to the heights expected of them — so we read these books with special emotion... We also read a splendid book about Cromwell and, though monarchists, we gave that great revolutionary his due. We are not one-sided, but have become thinkers, and, by force of circumstances, also to a certain degree philosophers, when we watch the strange and dangerous actions of Kings of today. They do not seem, as yet, to mix democracy with Kingship in a good, harmonious way. Good King George V did so, although himself not a particularly interesting personality. Let us hope that George VI helped by his charming little Queen, will follow in his footsteps. David... wanted everything too much his own way. For all his charm and ways with the poor, he was not really guardian of Kingly dignity, and this was felt by the larger part of his subjects, especially the steady, responsible ones — and caused probably more anxiety than loyalty allowed them to express; because he was at the same time their darling from the time when he was the golden-headed, sunny boy, the irresistable Prince of Wales... I always remember how he was after the war, in 1919, when I visited his parents in London, and we all lived together in Buckingham Palace. He was the most irresistable young man imaginable. We were great friends in those days and he was allowed to go out with me to theatres and dinners. I also gave him big teas in my own rooms when I united gay and charming young people around my table in his parents' house. They all smiled upon me. I was a refreshing addition to staid Buckingham Palace, and although at first a little anxious about my free attitude, being less boxed up in conventionality than they were themselves, my harmless good humour and high spirits won their hearts and they let me go ahead...

...Is this a career, an end for the golden-headed Prince? I could weep over him...

...For Queen Mary it must have been a dreadful blow. I personally felt the deepest sympathy for her. I only envied her for having stately and steady England behind her in perfect dignified loyalty in her hour of distress, a luck which was never mine. The Roumanians are a much younger people and their morals more mixed. The way the whole country felt for her during the crisis must have been consoling. My people stoned and denied me in my days of darkness, but the story is too sad and tragic to tell...

Some of Queen Marie's letters to her friend were two and three thousand words in length. Her constancy as a correspondence did not pale and in February, 1937, she wrote another long letter, from Cotroceni. "It is Sunday," she began, "outside my park is packed in wooly masses of freshly fallen snow... It is lovely, but there are no children in my house today, which is sad." She wrote of the chaos of Europe and of feeling that there was also "a blind groping for something better..."

But if this instinct of destruction wins the upper hand, then Europe will go down and all the horror of Russia and Spain will sweep over everything that was beautiful and worthwhile living for... in England there is a curious blindness about the real meaning of Bolshevism, and to them Fascism seems a greater danger... Fascism, although also a tyranny, leaves scope for progress, beauty, art, literature, home, and social life, manners, cleanliness, whilst Bolshevism is the levelling of everything... Every drop of my free blood rises up in protest against such an abominable conception of life...

The Queen turned once more to the theme of "friendship" and gave the opinion that "in the case of royalty" the dropping of a friend is complicated by the efforts of the friend to cling... not to be put aside, so that the world should not look down upon them as one fallen from favour." She remarked that for royal persons, "friendships are more precarious" because the friends wish "to profit by royal favour."

"They begin to need, to ask, to wish for things for themselves and others. We see they are digging their own grave and yet it is so difficult to cry out a warning." The Queen recalled her friendship with "a young girl poet,"

...her gratitude was great and everything seemed ideal. Although of a poor class, I saw her often, and we worked together and her love for me seemed weather-proof... gradually the temptation came to her to profit of the situation. Ever more and more demands for help on her side gradually undermined the pleasure of our being together... although I still stuck to the illusion that there could be a friendship between a Queen and one who was needy, our times, or, rather our hours together began to fill with dread of what she would be asking next. All pure pleasure in her company was at an end, and I began to see her... a person whose main object was to exploit our friendship. She *was* fond of me, but greater than her fondness was her desire to climb by my favors...

Two days ago I sent off a small painting of a white lily to hang in your room. It is certainly not a work of art, but my love of flowers glows out it and in a corner of your room it will always be a fresh little splash of white, a flower which will not fade unless you let a too violent sun pour in upon it. I hope the glass will not smash on the way and scratch the paper. I had it as carefully packed as possible, but it had a long way to go.

I have just finished reading *Gone with the Wind* and must say, though so enormously long, it fascinated me beyond words. It became a real friend and all the personalities so real that I felt I was living with them, and I was really lonely when I had to close the book and hear no more about them. It was a sensation of personal loss. And then it is so clever to keep us continually interested in a heroine who is so detestable... my invalid friend in Colorado wants to tempt me over to America; but I hardly think I shall go to America any more in this life. I could not stand today all the noisy publicity which would pursue me... The Queen of Spain managed more or less to be left in peace. I wonder how she did it?

Thank you also for the articles upon the Tzar. What a simple fellow he was, so loveable in many ways, but with something child-like about him. *She* was his fate. He adored her and her influence was disastrous. *She* was one of the few people I was never able to really get on with. There was a governessy attitude about her which had a freezing effect...

More than two months passed before Queen Marie wrote again. Her friend in America had to depend upon newspapers for reports of her life; and they were alarming. On March 15, the Queen was reported to be "partially paralysed." Another cable on the same day, from Bucharest, stated that she had been poisoned. On April 9, Prince Nicholas, Queen

Marie's second son, renounced his "rank and title" because King Carol would not "recognise" his morganatic marriage.

Queen Marie's devotion to her American friend survived these sorrows, and she dictated a letter to him, on April 19. "I do not want you to remain too long without news," she said.

> I am so glad you like my painting... My recovery is slow. I consider it odiously slow... I have, however, been several times in the garden, half on foot, half rolled in a chair, and had the satisfaction of seeing my beloved flowering bushes in full bloom... I have had the great joy that both Mignon and my sister, the Infanta, came to be with me for a time, and Ileana has just been here for a week... This is not really a letter, but I did not want you to be long without a sign of life...

Again on June 22, the Queen had to dictate her letter, from her small castle at Sinaia. The doctors promised her "complete recovery" if only she showed "unrelenting patience." She said,

> Unfortunately, this means: bed, bed, bed for an indefinite period, till my red globules eventually predominate again... Your letters continue to be a great joy to me, so don't cease writing even if my answers are scarce and short...

On July 25, Queen Marie wrote once more with her own hand, a letter of more than 2,000 words.

> I know you will be pleased to see my writing again, as it is a sign that I am really better... Your letters were a great pleasure to me. I read out of them such a breath of affection and appreciation of our rather unusual friendship that after reading them I felt each time refreshed. I am putting all your letters together, that they should be returned to you when I am no more, so that you can put your letters together with mine, which will be so interesting for you in your later life. In riper years you will enjoy reading through those long talks you had with a far-off Queen...

In this letter Queen Marie recalled the Turkish beggar woman at Balcic.[8]

> She has a sort of dog-like adoration for me... one day when Ducky was with me, and Shefica had finished her huge cup of coffee, some sort of remembrance of her gay youth came back to her, and removing the modest veil-cloth from her head, she revealed small tight plaits of brightly dyed, almost orange hair, and to our great

---

[8]The palace of Queen Marie.

amusement began to dance and sang as an accompaniment. An Oriental dance, slow, rhythmic, monotonous — as was the song which was sung in a nasal voice. It was a ghost dance; some vague nostalgia of former times, of her giddy youth, had awakened within her... and we saw a fleeting vision of a young and once comely Shefica who had danced 'for man's delight' as the Bible would express it. Shefica, however, in spite of her recommendable past, never let me down, nor did she profit over-much of her royal association; but when, on my birthday, the whole of Balcic public comes to congratulate me, she never mixes with the crowd, but stands well apart nearer the royal presence than any of those she otherwise associates with. Shefica loves flowers and when she departs I always fill her hands with flowers which do not grow in peasant gardens...

Queen Marie wrote of her children; of "Elizabetha"[9] who had "arranged her existence exactly as it suits her."

She is exceedingly talented, is very shrewd, and although rather silent she can be very amusing. It is our mutual love of beauty which is the strongest link between us... Since she divorced King George she has become more or less a private person, so no one has any right or even desire to disturb her queer existence. With that she retained a most imperial attitude which is in great contrast with her way of living. She is both attractive and provoking, and never tries to be a companion... Now we are excellent friends...

As to my Nicky, I am afraid I have lost him forever, not *de coeur*, but he has been torn from me and about this I am inconsolable... We were such very close friends and companions, had so much in common... He has become a sad wanderer who does not know where to settle down...

In August the Queen was at Bran, trying to mount the "many little steep stairs" in the castle, "eagerly ascertaining if everything was exactly in its place." She wrote,

I love arranging everything and even the angle at which an object is placed is important to me... I hate any neglect in this way. Considering the hundreds of quaint objects I have collected through the years, it is rather astounding how my caretaker... manages to keep everything as I like it, without shifting things about in wrong places.

---

[9]Ex-Queen of Greece.

The Queen complained, "Decidedly my poor legs are still shaky... I still need a certain amount of help from my neighbors... I feel humiliated, as though I had lost a large part of my personality."

I have done a good deal of reading lately. Alfred Noyes's book on Voltaire interested me enormously and he certainly makes Voltaire a very sympathetic personality... my childhood conception of him was sketchy and certainly to his disadvantage. We only saw the revolutionary in him, ignoring the philosopher... General Zwiedineck reads to me aloud in German... We have read the lives of Hannibal, Caesar, Heinrich der Löwe, Empress Constantza, Queen of Sicily, Marie Antoinette, and all so the lives of more recent history — Napoleon, Fouchée, Robespierre, which freshen up one's memory, as many of these had only been remembered through badly digested history lessons one was too unripe to really understand.

And all through the centuries war, bloodshed, love, passion, hatred, physical torture, mental anguish, treason, betrayals, strange heroisms, and brave deeds — for humanity is never at peace, alas, and the church forever playing a selfish, cruel, and unchristian part, augmenting human strife and misery. What inconceivable horrors have been committed in the name of religion!

Will you give your sister the enclosed card. Music seems to be a real happiness in her life. I do wish you could one day hear Enescu play the Lekeu Sonata. He really moves one to the very depths of one's being...

I enjoy the description of your different friends... There are people with whom one likes being, but one's recaptured solitude after a large dose of their company is greeted with an instinctive sigh of relief. I have had "swamping" acquaintances of this sort and found them generally a danger, because they dragged me along with them... In my special position any "let-down" on my side, after even more or less enforced intimacy, becomes for the other a humiliation... There is one part of my life which has always been difficult to talk about: the effect I had upon others. There is a certain flame burning within me, quite outside my own control, and this something made people long to be with me, long to take more of me than I wanted or dared to give... few were able to understand that I personally, isolated by my royalty, hemmed in by jealousies and restrictions, gave much more impersonally than they did... when they stretched out their hands to grasp me, it was to find that I could not be held or possessed... But enough about this subject, which is too personal and too difficult to explain...

You enquire about our Michael. He has become a splendid boy, so tall and good-looking, taller than his father who is tall, and topped by an innocent, almost baby-face. He is shy and rather silent and has instinctive tact. He knows wonderfully how to hold his peace. They liked him very much when he went to London, for the Corona-tion. It had been my idea to send him although he was so young; but I so wanted that something quite unspoilt should come from Roumania whose name has been too often dragged through the mire.

I have great sympathy for the new young King and Queen of England. He improves every day it seems, and he is a brave man, as he was very shy and retreating. But he has all the qualities asked of an English king, so as to uphold

Prince Michael
Great Voievod of Alba Iulia

tradition. He has a look of great breeding, although his brother George[10] is much better looking. George and Marina are really an out of the way handsome couple.

As to Queen Elizabeth, she is wanting in stature and classical royal looks. If I can so express it; she looks rather 'private' and certainly the royal regalia crushed her, while he had the look of an old missal. But she has an inborn sweetness and is in reality much more attrac-tive than on the pictures taken of her. She has a most lovely com-plexion and her eyes are like blue lights... She is not imposing, but she is sweet and loveable. Yes, he has a look of his mother, espe-cially about the mouth, but as he is exceedingly, almost over-slim, it gives him quite another type. Queen Mary is a wonderful old lady

[10] The Duke of Kent.

— she adores her royal round of duties and loves to go everywhere and do everything. When asked what she would like for 70th birthday she said 'A Court Ball!'

...I admire her. She is what I call 'game' and her faculty of suppressing emotion gives her a long lease of life and health.

...Excuse the occasional messiness of my pages, but my brain moves more rapidly than my hand, and as I have often told you, there are days when I have no vision of correct writing, and my words have funny faces and shapes.

You speak of Mount Vernon. We had it almost completely to ourselves when we visited it, and no one marred the atmosphere — it was still and undisturbed by crowds. There was a homelike, dreamy feeling about it which I loved; the simple rooms, the lovely view, the old English gardens, the quiet tomb...

I am taking up my fourth volume again, which is a sign of returning vitality...

In October, Queen Marie had to dictate her letters once more. "I had a slight set-back," she said, "and I am obliged to be more careful again." The "intolerable red globules" had "diminished again," overwhelming her "with an odious feeling of weakness." On November 7, four specialists were flown from Paris, Vienna, and Zurich, to confer over the Queen's state; there were intestinal hemorrhages and her life was in danger. Even then, she did not forget her friend. Her secretary wrote to him:

Queen Marie in 1938
One of her last photographs

She has asked me to thank you for never forgetting the second of November... Her Majesty came at 11:15 to the Cotroceni Chapel for a few minutes prayer... then She was able to walk and see her beloved horses. As the Crown Prince of Sweden was to lunch at the Palace, She wore her lovely grey gown of a delicate pearl shade... She was in high spirits, so much so that the Swedish guests were dazzled and fascinated. Unfortunately She had a very bad night and feels so fatigued that she has asked me to send you a word in lieu of the personal letter she would like to write.

Sixteen days later Queen Marie wrote, with her own hand, at the time when the newspapers were describing her as being "critically ill."

The letter had to be written in "little bits." "I am decidedly weak," she said, "I had to leave Balcic earlier than I intended, but before I left I did, with heart-rending precautions, still manage to get to one or two of my favourite spots, carried like a Mandarin in a chair by a dozen willing soldiers... I was thus able to have a last look at the 'Ducky Garden' where the autumn roses are in full bloom." The wish to build and create had not diminished. The Queen had bought "a new piece of ground" at Balcic and there she was "constructing a queer sort of building — a freak, a cross between a Turkish bath and a tiny Byzantine church (sounds horrible and sacriligeous) but it is really a charming form of architecture, and it is to be christened the 'Marienruhe,' that is to say, 'Marie's Rest'... I hope it will come up to expectations and that God will allow me to see it standing next Spring..."

I have a good deal of time to read of course... I have got through many volumes, including *Anthony Adverse*. Parts of it are lovely, and one feels deep sympathy for Anthony. I confess I can not bear the odious type of society man or woman created by modern literature, those cynical, godless, shameless types Huxley is so fond of; that absolutely 'degenerate' society which is full of beastliness which is, alas, the word which rightly describes it. And when today any book is quite specially beastly, then it is declared that it is disagreeable reading but that the author has 'genius.' Thus did a book come my way these days called *The Apes of God*. I tried it and really thought it frightful and at the same time intricate and utterly disconcerting...

I see poor David has been told not to go to America. What humiliations he meets at every turn. He is really paying heavily for his desertion of the British throne... And that cruel rebuff he received on Armistice Day in Paris; I thought that quite unbearable. I suffered for him... He would like to devote himself to a cause, but no cause today is really his, and he is too handicapped to be able to devote himself to humanity, for that he is not big enough, not abstract enough. I am horribly sorry for him!

Yes, it is true about the ballet. It is going to be given or rather danced at Warsaw and as the Polish ballet has all the good traditions of the Russian, let us hope it will be good. I invented the subject which came to me because of the sadness we Princesses endure in having to marry into foreign countries. Also I wanted to give a young Roumanian composer the chance of making himself known... Anything I may make out of it goes to help the poorer dancing girls of our ballet, generally over-worked little creatures who have always to smile, even when hungry... Beautiful roses are still being sent to me from Balcic... here the days are dark and in bed they are long... I am, however, as staunchly good-tempered and uncomplaining as possible... I have just heard that our dear friend Laszlo died the day when his great exhibition in London was to open. I am awfully sad that such a pleasant friend and great artist has passed away...

During late December and early January 1937-1938, newspapers all over the world published reports of Queen Marie's weakening strength; the coming of death. It is curious to place these reports beside the letters the Queen wrote to her friend, and beside the diary of my own visit to Roumania, which provides the material for the early part of this chapter.

On January 10, 1938, some of the newspapers, in America and Europe, announced, "Queen Marie sinking," "Family abandons hope." On that day I sat with her for more than an hour, and we talked of her friend in America. That afternoon, her secretary wrote to him:

Your telegram came today. Our beloved Queen told me she was going to write to you personally, but she also asked me to write to you, giving news about her health. We laughed this morning. Mr. Bolitho came to see Her, and he expressed the wish of wanting to be rich so that he might send 'many, many telegrams.' Exactly like...,' I said to Her Majesty.

When I recall the January morning, the snow outside, the warm golden room with the endless bowls of extravagant flowers, and the Queen talking, talking, in high spirits, I cannot believe the report for the day; of the "terrific fight... the painful injections, the headaches and disquieting nights... the horrifying hemorrhages...

I had not realised that the hour of reminiscences and good humour was compelled with such courage.

On February 14, Queen Marie was well enough to write a long letter to her friend in America:

I am glad you are sticking to the idea of visiting my beloved old England... I am really better I believe.

Anyhow, I am considered well enough to risk the journey to Merano... I want to get off... I have had much time to think... There are so many things that make my heart over-full, but they cannot be written or said... There are times when I dearly wish I could be ruthless. But I could only be so with shut eyes, my face turned to the wall... Forgive this little cry of pain, but there has been over much lately and human beings, even the best, are not always easy to live with... I seem to be a personality whom no one can approach with indifference, so conflicts are suddenly there before I have even time to grasp them. I mean *too much* to people!

...A change of atmosphere and *milieu* will do me good... I hate leaving the country for a longer time as my very existence is for many a reassurance; simply to know that Cotroceni is not empty, that their faithful Queen Marie is breathing behind its walls helps them, gives courage...

On February 28, the Queen sent her friend a post card, with view of the Sanatorium San Martino at Merano, whither she had gone, for rest... "I am here since a few days," she wrote, "...the change has already done me good. The air is wonderful and the sunshine a joy..."

The next letter was dated March 13. "I love getting your letters," she wrote.

As to the progress I am making, it is despairingly slow and needs much patience... Flowers are continually brought and sent to me, so my room is gay with color, although it is not a very pretty room... some of my own things are here and they give it quite a homelike appearance... I am emancipating myself as much as possible from all doctors who like to cluster around me, cost a fortune, disagree with each other, hold my pulse, feel my heart, lungs, liver and what not, then depart, their pockets well lined with my money and having not done much more than prescribe some new sort of medicine or a dull diet... So I have put my foot down, refusing to continue to enrich them whilst I become poorer without having gained much by their advice.

Then Hitler's forces entered Austria. The Queen wrote:

Ileana has been over two weeks with me and has now just left me to fall upon the *anschluss* of Austria with Germany, an event she always dreaded as it meant the final annihilation of her adopted country of which she had become immensely fond.

Hitler is certainly masterful and a colossal organiser, advancing ruthlessly, but each time so well prepared that no other country is able to stand up to his ever more Napoleonic decrees. Now he shouts his Austrian origin which has finally obliged him to rescue the *oppressed* Germans of his first fatherland. Yesterday evening, when I called up Ileana to know if she had reached Sohnberg safely, I at first could not understand what she was saying, imagining that she was talking English, I could not grasp that she was saying in German that we must talk only in German. This was the first evident sign of Hitler's deadly efficiency... I, fervent lover of freedom, felt my blood boiling, but was obliged to keep my emotions to myself, knowing that at the other side of the wire she was doing the same...

Queen Marie wrote her last, long, letter at the end of April; a letter of more than two thousand words. "I am sure you will be sad to hear that I had another rather severe relapse," she wrote:

> We really had thought that I was getting on. I had even been able to go for a short while to a 'concours hippique' to see some officers jump their fine horses. The next day, alas, there was a fresh hemorrhage... I am not allowed the slightest movement... I have just had the tremendous emotion of meeting my ex-daughter-in-law, Michael's mother, for the first time again after 7 years. We had always been, although she too had not been without faults, great friends; and had suffered from the violent separation. Besides, since then, we have both had to stand cruel persecutions, and much of the good work we had done together was torn up and destroyed... Well, Helen at last received permission to come and see me and I must say I found her quite charming, still so pretty, elegant, gentle, refined. But the meeting was an immense emotion for both of us. All these dumbly stood sorrows surged up between us and though neither of us gave way to tears they were there, burning but unshed.

> This and the meeting with Nicky and the listening to his troubles, all my dear Ileana's grief at the sudden uprooting of her life, peace, freedom, all this came upon me at once with certain unsatisfactory results for my health...

> ...My niece Kira's wedding is to take place at Potsdam on the 2nd of May (Orthodox marriage) and the protestant marriage on the 4th at Doorn, presided over by the old Kaiser. I would rather have liked to meet him again...

Next day, April 26, the Queen added to her letter. "I am rather better. The moment I can be moved I want to go to a well-known, even a celebrated Sanatorium in Germany, called the Weisse-Hirsch..."

> I was amused at Carmen Sylva's fairy story book. To our more modern conceptions her tales are decidedly prosy and what as children we would have called 'goody-goody...' There is imagination in them, but somehow they bore me, whilst Andersen's, Oscar Wilde's, and also simpler stories often enchant me. Perhaps I am unfair, because I knew her too well and she was always fond of too

much trimming... Perhaps I like best the one in which she relates why she called herself 'Carmen *Sylva*.' She really loved the forest..."

The last letter — a card only — was sent from Weisse Hirsch, on June 20, 1938.

I am gradually crawling up hill again after a very bad two months of complete exhaustion... I have undergone strenuous treatments which left me no strength to hold a pen... I so enjoyed your last letters... I do want to be my own independent self again. People are awfully kind but I have to depend upon them and this is irksome as I love being free...

Princess Ileana wrote to her mother's friend next day,

...Mummy has read me so many of your letters I feel I know you quite well.

Princess Ileana

It is really in Mamma's name that I write... I am glad to say that she is feeling much better... Alas I cannot hide from you that the doctor considers the illness *very* serious indeed... she has reacted wonderfully to his treatment and so with care there is no reason why she should not return to normal... I think she has suffered overmuch sorrow. She is of a patience and endurance which in anyone so active as her is truly wonderful to behold. Her thoughts are always for others. For instance, when an injection into her veins (they are almost inaccessible) does not succeed, she is sorry for the doctor and not for her pain!

I must tell you that her correspondence with you... gives her the greatest pleasure you could imagine. She loves your letters... Your friendship really means a lot to her and she follows all your thoughts and activities with joy. I must personally thank you for this as during her illness your letters have been one of her chief sources of pleasure.

You one day will have to write a book about her, and my greatest joy would be to help you with sidelights when you should want them...

Early in July, Queen Marie became dangerously ill again. On the 18th, she died, in the late afternoon, at Sinaia. "No one should wear black for me," she ordered, "but my favourite colour — mauve. All flowers placed on the coffin should be red." Her heart was buried at Balcic; her body beside her king.

The story ends, in a room in Washington; the room of a middle-aged, shy, devoted scholar, with a painting on the wall, of a white lily.

> My love of flowers glows out of it and in a corner of your room it will always be a fresh little splash of white, a flower which will not fade unless you let too violent sun pour upon it... I had it as carefully packed as possible, but it had a long way to go.

Letters from Ray Baker Harris
to Queen Marie

I

December 19, 1933

Your Majesty,

Please forgive a typewritten letter, but I have used a machine for so long that my letters in longhand are practically illegible. And I do hope that you may read this letter.

By an odd coincidence your pictures arrived on the same day that the first installment of your memoirs appeared in the *Saturday Evening Post* magazine. I am delighted that the story of your life is now being published. To hundreds of us it will tell the many things we have always desired to know about Romania's great Queen, and will only confirm and increase the respect and deep admiration we have for your majesty.

I can see, however, that in your writing you do not hesitate to reveal your true self clearly. And many will not appreciate this, and some will misunderstand. I am sure you anticipate this, and that such criticism will not touch you. Because any one who is a force for good in this world, or who possesses sympathy, honesty, loyalty, and understanding is target for the criticism by the unthinking. It is the penalty imposed upon anyone who achieves real greatness.

It seems almost absurd for me to be telling you this. Because I am in my twenties, and most of life is still before me. Your majesty knows these truths so much better than I do.

Also, it is odd that I am writing a letter to you at all. I have never written to any other sovereign, except the contacts I have had with several of the Presidents of my own country. But you sent me an inscribed photograph when I was a very small boy, and ever since then I have felt, somehow, that the great distance between a Queen and an American boy could be, in a way, bridged by my respect and admiration. People without imagination or understanding cannot appreciate how this could be, and so I seldom speak of the several kindnesses which you have shown to me.

It was such a gracious thing for you to include that beautiful and recently taken picture, when you returned the one I had sent you (the one of your majesty as Crown Princess, taken in 1903) for your signature. I am delighted to have the both together — 1903 and 1933. They symbolize the thirty years which form the larger part of your majesty's memoirs. I am framing both pictures together, and they will hang in my small library, just above the several of your books which I have and of which I am very fond.

I have sent to your majesty, by registered post, a little trifle Christmas gift. Knowing of your great love of gardening, I have sent a copy of *Down the Garden Path*, a charming and very informative book by Beverley Nichols. I do hope that you have not already read the book previously, because I should like to feel that you might enjoy this book as a gift from me... in those moments in your very busy life when you can find the opportunity to read books.

Word has just been published today of the birth of your granddaughter, Maria Ileana. This must be a great joy to your majesty, and I desire to express sincere felicitations.

I realize that with Christmas messages, the birth of your granddaughter, and the beginning of your published memoirs, your majesty will be deluged with correspondence. But I hope perhaps this letter may find its way to you sooner or later and that you may find the time later to read the garden book, because it tells so much that I am sure will delight you, and because, also, it is about an English garden.

Meanwhile I am eagerly reading the chapters of your memoirs. I have always been deeply impressed by the combination of *Great Sorrow* and *Great Happiness* which has been in your majesty's life experience; and I cannot tell you adequately how stimulating it has been to have received the photographs and the book with your majesty's inscription to me. It is more inspiring than you really can know, because your majesty represents in reality so much of the ideals and vitality of life.

Wishing your majesty many good things during the holiday season, and the very best of health to enjoy the opportunities and happiness in the coming New Year,

Ray Baker Harris

Her Majesty, MARIE
Queen of Romania
Bucharest, Romania

II

April 4th, 1934

Your Majesty,

The wonderful letter, the beautifully inscribed photograph, and that intensely interesting article about "Stella Maris" all arrived the day before Easter Sunday. Of course this added a great measure of happiness to the joys of the season.

I immediately read the article on the "smallest Church in the Land" and it has impressed me deeply. How very much I wish I could step inside the little chapel, and see with my own eyes the beauties that you have created. Of course, rending your description of it is the next best thing to visiting "Stella Maris" myself. I enjoyed every word of it, and I took it with me when I went to see Eleanor Horton last night. She is just back in Washington after a short Easter vacation at home.

Did I tell you that Eleanor had previously loaned me copies of several of your articles... the one about Czar Nicholas, also "The Child With the Blue Eyes", and "Is Royal Blood a Blessing?". All of these interested me very much, and, in fact, I asked Eleanor's permission to make copies of the articles so that I could add them to my little collection of your majesty's writings.

And today comes your very nice letter in reply to the long one I wrote to you several weeks ago, together with the "Spring" photograph which naturally pleases me tremendously. I was especially fond of the little photograph you sent me some time ago — just the head profile. That informal little picture had a great deal of spirit about it.

I rather regretted having sent you that picture of myself. It was just a "scrap"— and it was taken back in 1928, and I imagine I appeared *quite* young. But it was the only print I could lay my hands on, and I had the feeling that you ought to know what my face is like! When I can find a recent print, I'll send a better copy.

I don't quite recall what I wrote to you about President Harding. He is an interesting study, very contradictory in many ways, and my experience in assembling and studying material has been a real education to me. I want to present a *true* portrait. My attitude toward President Harding is a sympathetic one, and I am anxious to do full justice to his admirable qualities and attainments. But, on the other hand, I should do him no service by ignoring unpleasant facts; although I shall gladly ignore inuendo, unsubstantiated gossip, and slander.

Under separate cover I am going to send you a little volume which Congress had published shortly after President Harding's death. When you may have some leisure, it may interest you to read the memorial address delivered by Chief Justice Hughes, who was at that time the Secretary of State. This outlines President Harding's life, and does it rather well. Also there is at the end a very appealing editorial, entitled "Back Home."

Every President has to put up with a certain number of unpleasant political associates — the political system being what it is! President Harding's trouble was that he was seldom less than friendly with anyone, was easy-going, tolerant, and overly trustful; and this tolerance for a group of low political associates put it in their power to damage his reputation and thwart his efforts.

How wonderful it would be if I could sit down for a talk with you, show you some of my material and tell you of my plans for presenting it; because you would give me so many inspiring ideas.

The second series of your majesty's memoirs starts next week. I have been very impatient for these to begin again. Volume II ought to be even more interesting than the first. I am genuinely enthusiastic about the book, because there are so few really great autobiographies. And your majesty has also been so generous in permitting me this great privilege of knowing you through your kind letters. You cannot know how greatly I appreciate this. It isn't possible for me to believe in you any more than I already do. Eleanor Horton and I agreed the other night that we believe you to be the greatest woman in the world. This is honest conviction, based upon what we have learned of your great generosity, understanding, intelligence, and friendliness.

It is an extraordinary trio — your majesty, Eleanor, and myself... and how pleasant and inspiring for us to have the privilege of knowing you in this manner.

Does it seem strange to you that a young man writes to you in this way? I cannot quite place the way I feel about it, because it is as though I were writing to a spirit rather than a person. I probably do not write half so freely and easily to my friends as I do to your majesty. Many of my friends could never understand this — would be astonished that I should write any letter at all to a monarch, a Queen. And yet, to me, a physical personality doesn't seem to enter into it at all — and that's what makes it so easy for me. The fact that Eleanor understood this also was surprise enough to me, but that your majesty understood the feeling behind the words I put on paper is no less than amazing. And so, that is why I think the trio is so extraordinary and amazing; and I thank Heaven that such a trio is possible in this overly practical world. It restores a great deal of faith!

I have wondered to myself sometimes, as I play golf with men who are my friends, or as I ride with them occasionally, what their astonishment would be if I should tell them of the quaint friendship Eleanor and I have with your majesty! Of course I do not speak of it, because I regard it as a privilege which is very personal to me.

It was most unusual the way Eleanor and I became better acquainted through our mutual enthusiasm and understanding for your majesty. I always thought Eleanor was charming, but not until "the ice was broken," so to speak, did I appreciate what a delightful companion she is. She has a quick way of observing everything, deep sensibility, and a wonderfully keen sense of humor. We have really become excellent friends, and it is a pleasure being in her company.

Friendship with a girl very often becomes something of a problem, but thus far Eleanor and I have been so frank and understanding in our relationship that I am sure neither of us can be hurt if we continue thus outspokenly.

As a friend, I think I can help Eleanor more by urging her *not* to *center* her affections on any *one* for as long a time as possible, but to *recognize* infatuations, or, one might say, personal enthusiasms, as they come — and to try to regard them objectively and thus form a real sense of human values.

I know I told her the other evening that in recent years I had been enthusiastically fond of certain people, and that while the infatuation lasted it supplied all the virtues which the person really lacked; and that now, as I look back, I wonder what I possibly could have seen in them. This sounds almost disloyal, and even quite fickle — and sometimes it has troubled me that I could change my attitude so completely regarding someone I had once been fond of. This honestly has troubled me, because I think I prize friendship and loyalty much more than love.

I have observed so many unhappy and miserable marriages — and I think it is almost a crime to bring children into wrecked homes — that I would want to feel very sure before I attempted to unite another life with mine. There has to be so much more than just the first infatuation to sustain a lifelong companionship.

I don't know why I have suddenly gotten off on this track! Do I sound very immature or silly?

* * * *

By this time you have received the copy of my article "Regina Maria," and I am naturally anxious to know if it pleased you. I have done nothing about arranging for its publication, as I would first want to be sure that it had your approval.

By the way, I was especially interested in the article which your majesty wrote about Czar Nicholas. I read a great deal about the Russian Imperial family at one time, and my imagination was of course very much stimulated by the drama and tragedy of their lives.

Was there ever any shadow of truth in the claims of some that Anastasia escaped? A Gleb Botkin, son of one of the Russian Court doctors, who escaped to this country, wrote a book some time ago (I do not at the moment recall its title) in which he gave full credence to the alleged Grand Duchess Anastasia. Did you read the book by any chance?

Of course, to me it seems unbelievable that the relatives of the Czar would unanimously refuse to recognize her if there was any possibility of her claim being true. But the story is fantastic enough to be appealing, and I know many people who firmly believe in it.

I imagine you are glad that Spring is putting in an appearance. Eleanor tells me that you usually go to Bran or Balcic, and she has shown me some of the beautiful pictures of your houses at Balcic, the gardens, and also of Bran which she has. She also showed me a very beautiful book of views of Romania which included some views of Balcic.

I hope very much that you do write a fourth volume of memoirs — *Pages détachées* if you cannot tell the entire story. I have followed very closely the unhappy events in recent times, and it was these happenings which really aroused and intensified my admiration for your majesty's bravery and dignity throughout such trying times. But even if these had to be touched upon only lightly, there is a great deal which only could write about really graphically.

What a long letter this has turned out to be — and I'm afraid not a very carefully written letter. I have just "talked on and on" and have not concentrated on the writing.

With a great many very good wishes always,

Ray Baker Harris

Her Majesty, MARIE
Queen of Roumania
Bucharest, Roumania

III

April 8th, 1934

Your Majesty,

Of course I do not know how true the descriptions are, but I think the enclosed article from today's New York *Times* magazine will interest your majesty.

It has just occurred to me that I should like very much to write an article about your majesty as you are today, the activities and interests which now absorb your time from day to day — making your hours just as full as in other days when State problems crowded for your attention. I could write it as though it were told to me by those who know your majesty personally, and that would give me the advantage of writing as only an interested observer.

I should like very much to do this, but there is no special haste; and so if you ever have the time to send me some material and information about your present activities, with perhaps a picture or two which would make good illustrations, I'll be delighted to go ahead and write such an article.

I'm enclosing herewith also a picture of one of the exhibits at the Flower Show recently held in New York.

There is a very picturesque old Canal — which dates back to George Washington's day — near my home here, with quaint old locks, and there is an old mill very much like the one in this picture. It is a very attractive place (and of course the canal has not been used in many years) and I shall take some pictures of it later this Spring and send them to you.

The first time I met Eleanor Horton was when some mutual friends invited me to join them in a long afternoon walk along the canal's bank paths. I formerly had many times ridden on horseback with friends along these paths when I was in college — back in 1926 and 1927. After this particular walk which I mentioned, one of my friends, who had been in college with me, stopped off with me for supper. He was looking over the books in my own small library, and noticed the copy of *The Magic Doll of Roumania* which you had inscribed to me so beautifully. He asked me about it, and then said — "Do you remember Eleanor Horton whom you met this afternoon? She knows the Queen, and is one of her great admirers." So the next opportunity I had to do so, I asked Eleanor about your majesty and, as you know, became very good friends through our mutual interest and enthusiasm for the Queen of Roumania.

My friend had known Eleanor for several years, having met her here when I was living in New York. His name is William Harrison, a very interesting fellow who is, by the way, a great grandson of former President of the United States of the same name. He is a very brilliant young man, and is at present Secretary of the Library of Congress and the Supreme Court. I don't think he quite understands how it is possible that Eleanor and I have this direct contact with your majesty, because he is of an essentially practical turn of mind himself, rather a self-sufficient person. But both Eleanor and I have found him a very loyal and satisfying friend.

I don't know if I previously sent your majesty a copy of an article I wrote about three years ago, and so I'm enclosing the pages in this letter. I'm including the index page, and call your attention to the line which reads: *"Walter Hines Page, Appreciations by Herbert Hoover, Lord Cecil, and Ray Harris."* This amused me very much at the time — I, an almost unknown young man, placed in such famous company as a co-author. It was just the idea of the three names together that way which amused me. Perhaps it will give your majesty a smile also.

But I did not intend to write your majesty a long letter today, and when I started I intended only to enclose these clippings.

With every possible good wish always,

Ray Baker Harris

Her Majesty, MARIE
Queen of Roumania
Palatul Regal Cotroceni
Bucharest, Roumania

IV

May 4, 1934

Your Majesty,

Your wonderful letter and the four delightful pictures of Balcic came yesterday. I have read the pages of your letter several times, and have the pictures out where I can see and enjoy them for a few days before placing them in a folio for sake-keeping.

I am sure you know that your letters give me deep pleasure, but you cannot realize how really great the pleasure is to me. And it is not only pleasure alone, but strength and inspiration as well. It is wonderful that our thoughts can reach out above age, the years, the spheres and worlds that separate our physical lives, and talk freely and frankly, without hindrance or embarrassment. I am more grateful than I can possibly say for all your kindly, helpful interest in one whose physical presence will in all probability never enter your life.

The fact that your generosity and understanding permits me to enter into the world of your thoughts and feelings, and that you share some of them with me, is a rare privilege I cannot ever possibly repay — except by continued loyalty to my belief in your majesty, and by trying my best to return, in a measure, the understanding you so wonderfully have offered to me. I feel a sense of utter frustration in trying to tell this to you in words. Great thoughts and feelings invariably seem rather small when reduced to being only as big as the words one has to use. But I hope you may understand, and that you may feel I am sincere.

It is all especially unusual... because even before I knew much about your majesty's life I had an almost instinctive sympathy and feeling of loyalty for you... quite unexplainable then. I remember quite a few years ago, when I was in school, I made a speech before all the students in which I assailed some unfair things which had been written about your majesty. It was, I think, probably the most dramatic speech I ever made. I outlined your life, your part in the war, that tragic departure from Bucharest, and other similar things which I had read. It created quite a little sensation and I remember I was asked how it was that I knew about these things, and why I felt so strongly on the subject. And in those days it was before I had any first-hand information — it was just a very strong feeling of admiration and sympathy for your majesty. The things I have learned since then have only confirmed those early feelings — but the *feeling* was there long before I knew the facts which justified those feelings.

I do think I understand your spirit, because so much that you have said in the story of your life, and in your kind letters to me, strikes very responsive chords in me. I find myself saying — How well that thought is expressed — or, How many times I felt exactly that way about people, about things... and then again my understanding is just instinctive rather than knowing, because my life and experience lies so much in the future.

The very recent chapters of your memoirs are especially interesting, and I have been delighted to hear others say the same thing on every side. A very astute editor whom I know asked me to have lunch with him when he was in the capital for a visit recently. He knows absolutely nothing of my acquaintance with your majesty, nor even of my interest and enthusiasm for your book; and he asked me if I had been reading the articles, and went on to say he thought them the best memoirs he had ever read. This was frank, honest praise, because he had no way of knowing how much his praise pleased me.

I think you have said very poignant and powerful things with real tact, grace, and effectiveness. If I did not like your book I would probably avoid saying anything unpleasant about it, but also I would never express praise unless I honestly meant it. I always feel extremely uncomfortable when I occasionally find myself saying things I do not mean. That is the thing which often makes me wish to dash unceremoniously out of drawing rooms where people are saying polite nothings to each other.

I was a house guest a number of years ago, during my vacation from school, and recall I was rather in awe of certain other guests who were well-known. I remember feeling beforehand that I could not possibly join in their conversations intelligently, they were such celebrities! Well, I found I could not join in their conversations, but not for the reasons I had thought! Instead, I found them saying exceedingly trite, polite, small-talk things. I remember my disappointment with amusement now. But although I see something beneath the surface (perhaps not very far yet) today, and have a little more mature perspective, still I much prefer the informal company of a few friends where there is friendliness and where I can be myself... and as this is not always possible, I even prefer being alone.

But this is an almost endless topic, and I had better stop this time before I get too deeply involved in these conclusions. It is a miracle that your majesty, whose life is so full, whose hours are so crowded with the actual presence as well as the thoughts of those many very near to you... it is a miracle that you should be interested at all in these rambling thoughts of one so comparatively insignificant and so far away.

You speak of the story which you could write of the recent years, a story that would be so powerful as well as tragic. Have you ever thought of writing it now, and making some arrangement with a trustworthy publisher that this last volume would not be published so long as any of the principal people involved are alive? This would give the story to history, so that its power and its lessons would not be lost, but it also would inflict no hurts in this generation. The true story should be told, and who else is there who could authoritatively tell it?

I am pleased you think I could be of help to Eleanor Horton, and it would be a very happy task. She is a delightful and satisfying friend. I want very much to see her make the most of all the possibilities her life has to offer — and for one of Eleanor's quick mind and deep sensibilities life holds very much indeed. Of course there is much I do not understand and which is confusing — even in my own younger sister whose growth I have watched from the very beginning. Women's minds and hearts are not easily made tangible — there seems always elusiveness and contradictions!

We hear a good deal here lately about political unrest in your part of the world, and I always read these reports with careful interest — making allowances, of course, for press exaggerations. Naturally I seize upon everything concerning Roumania — ever with the hope that the difficulties do not touch you directly... but I realize too that you are always affected when events involve those whom you love in spite of everything that recent years have unfolded. Roumania had her very best years, her greatest good fortune in the years while you were reigning Queen.

I have a very special liking for the picture you sent me which shows you seated in the Cloister at Balcic in the place you call "The Waters of Peace." Because that beautiful little cloister, as well as the chapel, will stand there by the Sea for hundreds of years — a place which you built, which has your spirit about it, and which, in a manner of speaking, represents for all time everything that has been in the *Story* of your life.

Queen Marie's Palace at Balcic

And it may sound sentimental: But, someday before I die I *shall* visit Balcic in memory of the happiness and inspiration you have given to me in these younger years. The years ahead may alter my outlook much, impulses may be more staidly bounded — but thoughts of your majesty will always bring back youthful feelings and a happy heart. And so, someday I shall go to Balcic and visit the little Cloister, and I'll look about at all the beauty you have loved, gaze through the arches at the Black Sea, and as I stand there I shall meet your majesty and talk with you... because it would be then just as it is today — only our spirits would meet. Oh, I've said it very clumsily, but do you understand my thought?

I'm amazed at myself for writing these thoughts. But they just "come" and I feel no embarrassment in setting them down in a message to you. I have never expressed my feelings in this way to anyone else, and I could never say them even to you if I were talking to you personally. But it is a joy to express them to you in this way.

...And to be less serious for a bit: Did anyone send you clippings from the newspapers about the reception held here in Washington at the Russian Embassy? Not, of course, that it was important, but it was an amazing revelation of the wide gulf between the "ideals" of the so-called proletariat Soviets and their practice. They employed the greatest display. They have taken the old Czarist embassy and spent a fortune redecorating it in the most luxurious style. It may seem uncharitable of me, but when I saw a photograph of "Madame" Troyanovsky (wife of the Soviet Ambassador) I said aloud — "What a face! What a figure!" That is the absurd tragedy of most Soviets I have seen: They may win possession of castles, but they cannot possibly win the appearance of belonging in them!

It is really quite ridiculous the way the Soviets have "splurged" in America since their government was recognized. The magnificent old embassy building was restored, but the Russian government also leased another beautiful, aristocratic mansion here in Washington. They will use this to house the various attachés! They are trying to outdo all the other embassies in lavishness.

Then in New York City the Russian Consulate leased the home of Mrs. John I. Pratt (whom your majesty may know of... she is better known as Ruth Pratt, and was for several years a Member of Congress — America's Lady Astor!). Mrs. Pratt's husband built this mansion with Standard Oil dividends! So that the house, every stone of it, represents capitalism, wealth, and social aristocracy! The Soviets might just as well have leased the house of Mr. Rockefeller himself! I don't know why Mrs. Pratt leased her town house to the Soviets. Of course, she is now more or less alone... her children all married, and she has a beautiful country home where she lives the greater part of the time.

I wonder if ever the Russian masses will wake up to their exploitation under the present regime. People who know the country well have told me that the Russian character *needs* royalty — in much the same way your people in Roumania do. The true Russian peasant has been submerged apparently by these colossal Jews like Stalin... but can it last? The Soviets have taken away so much that the peasants, with all their former poverty, once had and longs for and wants.

I read a great deal about Russia at one time, and everything I could find in print about the Imperial Family. I especially like the article you once sent Eleanor about the Czar, and I made a typed copy of it for myself.

And by the way, I think you have in reality included in your memoirs a little biography of Queen Elisabeth — Carmen Sylva. She was always just a name to me, and I never read any of her writings, but your descriptions make her a real person and curiously enough you allow us to see all sides of her personality — a whole book about her could not tell half as much as your graphic paragraphs.

Here again I have written such a long letter — and such a poor one in return for the marvelously interesting ones your majesty writes!

Many thoughts rush forward asking to be put into this letter, and questions come to mind — but I must not tire you, and I can only look forward to our further "talks" together. *Please* write *anything* which comes to your mind to say to me — my interest will always be very strong and I am forever in your debt for your kindness in admitting my spirit to this fine acquaintance with your majesty.

With every possible thought and wish always,

Ray Baker Harris

Her Majesty, MARIE
The Queen of Roumania
Palatul Regal Cotroceni
Bucharest, Roumania

V

July 7, 1934

Your Majesty,

Just as I was leaving for New York ten days ago, your beautiful, deeply touching letter from Balcic arrived. I took it with me and read it several times while I was on the train. Almost as if I were experiencing the same sensations myself, I could understand so well how you felt in reading Hoppe's chapter on *The Castle of Dreams* about those wonderful, active days filled with life and joy and purpose. It stirred me very deeply.

And because time passes with such unrelenting swiftness, I am now back in Washington, and my visit to New York is in the past. I returned here late at night — and on my desk was the package containing Hoppe's book. I opened it immediately, although I left the other mail until morning, and read at once the wonderful inscription you had written so graciously. It said so much with poignant feeling.

It all makes me so proud to have your majesty's friendship and trust. I feel that very fortunately I have found a new and lasting friend, who comes to me bodilessly, from the "high places" of the world, with friendly, kindly, helpful interest. And they have become a very important part of my life — your letters, and the privilege I have in writing to you.

But I do not agree with your feeling that perhaps now is your time for rest. Perhaps for the moment, but for the moment only. I have a feeling that your people will call to your majesty again — at a time when their need will be most great. And I feel that their King will come to you, because you will be the only one who can help. It seems to me inevitable that this should come to pass. So perhaps that is the purpose for which your majesty is permitted to have rest now.

When I was in New York, I went over to Paterson to visit Eleanor in her home. I went to lunch and remained all afternoon, and almost to supper time when I had to dash off to keep another engagement.

It was the most enjoyable part of my entire visit in New York. They are really a very unusual family — and they seem to just properly complement each other — a beautifully balanced sort of family.

Eleanor's sister, Jane, is really a genius. She is very young — about fourteen or fifteen, I think, but extremely brilliant. Often when very young children have extraordinary talents and mental gifts they have a sort of unpleasant, unnaturalness about them which suggests the abnormal. But it was most certainly not this way with Jane. Her entire manner is charming, very frank, easy, natural, and unaffected. Her conversation is delightfully original, and she is a priceless mimic... never unkind, but displaying real insight into character, and a beautiful sense of the ridiculous. She does really quite good painting — both in oils and water-color, and also nice pen and ink subjects. It is all life-like, with a fine sense for color and design, and has none of the crazy treatment given to so much modern work.

Aside from that, she plays the piano beautifully, and even composes some nice songs with quite good lyrics.

Eleanor's mother has a nice sense of appreciation, and is a perfect audience for her talented family!

Eleanor's father is a wonderful musician, and a most interesting man to talk with.

My visit in their home was unusually pleasant. I have never visited any other family for the first time, and departed from my first call so reluctantly, and with such a strong feeling of friendliness for each member of the family.

I can understand very well now why Eleanor often feels that her life at the school is unsatisfactory and superficial. Because in her home there is such genuine friendliness, such a fine tempo of quick, intelligent living... and they are the sort of family which attracts many interesting people as their guests.

At a school, of course, and especially a fashionable girls' school, there is bound to be a great deal of obvious pose, affectation, and a certain sacrifice of friendliness to the needs of discipline.

I think it is absurd that the *Saturday Evening Post* thinks the third volume would not appeal to the American public because it is a War book. After all, it is not, strictly speaking, a war book... it is rather the story of your life throughout the days of the War. You would be the dominating, central figure for the readers, and in your figure would be the central point of interest.

It is true that there have been so many war plays, and war motion pictures, and war books, that the American public is weary of the general tone of War. But, after all, they have never before had a viewpoint of the War from the pen of a Queen — the Queen who, without a doubt, had the most active, dramatic part in the drama of those days. Certainly no other Queen ever saw the conflict from such close range, played so determining a part in her country's policy, and who suffered more from the personal loss. It is all such a *great* story, so moving, so powerful, that I cannot imagine *any* reader being indifferent to it.

I think I shall write a letter to the Editor of the S.E.P., just from the viewpoint of the average reader, and say how much I have enjoyed the recent installments, and add, casually, a word as to how I am anticipating the reading of your story of the war days — just as though I were taking it for granted that they would surely publish it. I shall ask some friends to do the same thing. I do not know if it will accomplish anything, but it can do no harm... and I know that a good many people are anticipating the third volume. Of course, it may be too late now — as the books will be coming out soon. I am very impatient for the volumes — with the *complete* story.

I have already written many of my friends and acquaintances, urging them to read the books — telling them how great I think it is from what I have read in the *S.E.P.* articles... and I think those who do read the book with interest and fairness will be greatly benefited by what you have written.

In New York I had lunch with a young but already very well-know American writer — whose work is too good to be successful, although he has had two very popularly successful books. Those two books I liked least of everything he has done. Anyway, he has a very brilliant mind and deep sensibility. We were talking about how few really genuine autobiographies there have been — for the reason that most autobiographies are merely the reminiscences of an older person "looking back" — they show nothing of that person at the various stages of his or her life. We agreed that a real autobiography would have to come from a diary, or letters.

For instance, when Beverley Nichols was only about 20, in Oxford, he wrote a little novel (which was obviously autobiographical) called *Prelude*. That novel *was* Beverley Nichols at twenty. If he hadn't written it then, it never could have been written later... because five or ten years later he of course felt so much differently, and wouldn't admit to the earlier feelings, even if he were capable of recalling them accurately.

And I observed that this was the unusual and the wonderful quality about your majesty's memories — because, whether you were helped by your diaries or letters or other material — you *did* capture the feelings of the earlier years, and in reading your *Story* one *feels* the gradual change in your outlook and impulses. Of course, I think this is partly because you have retained so great a portion of your youthful spirit, so that you can recall earlier days with an accuracy of which most people become incapable in later life.

I was interested and pleased to hear of the tremendous and spontaneous ovation given to you when you appeared at the head of your regiment on the 10th of May, but I am not surprised. Hoppe mentioned in his book how deep and enthusiastic was the affection of Roumanians of all classes for their Queen.

I have just seen a new book of photographs of Roumania — by the German photographer, Kurt Hielscher, published by the Brockhaus press at Leipzig. This has some very marvellous views, and some especially attractive photographs of Castle Bran and also of Tanya Yuvah at Balcic. Also many photographs of interiors of peasant homes, and I am surprised by the beauty of bed coverings, tiled stoves, embroideried costumes, etc.

Doubtless you have seen this book. Some of the peasants themselves, as pictured, look like Anglo-Saxon types, although of course in most cases they are of dark complexion... but one cannot be sure from pictures.

The pictures of Churches in Bucharest are very beautiful.

There is really not much to tell you about myself in this letter. Although I had a very enjoyable visit in New York, it was more pleasant than eventful. I saw a number of old friends, and I lived in New York a long time as a boy, and then again in 1928 and 1929 I was with a publishing firm there, so that there are many recollections — and places I wanted to see. However, in recent years I have said good-bye to a great deal that was once quite important in my life — and one cannot always resume a relationship where it last ended, or feel the same about places which time has changed. It is a little distressing sometimes to see certain parts of one's past so completely made to disappear.

My first day in New York I left in the afternoon and went up into New England to stay overnight at the home of a friend who has a nice summer cottage on the Shore — and it was cool and restful and friendly. I had to return to the city the next morning and had two interviews with people who had material to give me for my book. Then I went and stayed with some friend on Long Island, and the next day went to visit Eleanor. And so a week passed very quickly in the same tempo. And all the time I was there I had a certain sense, or rather a wish to see again other people who were still in or near New York and whom I had once known well. It seemed strange I should be so near and not try to do it. But one cannot revive old friendships at a moment's notice, and actually I had little more than moments. And, after all, I am leading a different life now than I did then, and so too, probably, are they... there would be such a bridge to cross.

Which reminds me: I can so well appreciate your irritation with the people who have tried to close in around you, possess you, make their affection a smothering thing. Jealousy causes so much suffering. And everything dies when it's smothered, even the object of one's affections. I understand what causes them to act that way, because I have recognized those feelings in myself at times and have had to fight with them. When one intensely loves someone there does come a sort of instinctive possessive desire that is a little blinding. But when one has learned what the consequences are, there is no further excuse for giving in to such impulses. I can realize that your majesty has had to go through a great deal of this because people are naturally drawn to you and want to feel that they are especially favored.

And although one understands and sympathizes, it is impossible to permit others to smother us, even with affection, to take us into caverns away from the normal daylight... because life has to FLOW!

I read a very nice description by an English writer once... He likened his life to a river. The woman in his life was one bank of his flowing life, and the world was the other, and WITHOUT BOTH his river of life would be a marsh! The woman whom he loved, and the world he had to know, were the two banks... and unless there were the two banks together his life ceased to flow and be complete.

Your letters are a very wonderful help to me just at this time when a good many things of my boyhood have gone out of my life. Those things must be replaced in the new life I am entering into — the life that will carry me into middle and later age. When one has given up so much, it is a great strength to find a relationship that gives so much inspiration. I am not sentimental when I say that I admire and am really devoted to your majesty. It is a fact. There, far away in a world away from mine, is an ideal in actuality. By a combination of circumstances that ideal became a friend — a bodiless friend; still very far away — but a close friend in understanding, in appreciation.

Sometimes I have had strong feelings about things, and have written extraordinary letters to friends in my own world — BUT NEVER SENT THEM. I had to destroy them and write a more conventional letter, and put my feelings in words that were less free.

But I can write my feelings in a letter and sent it to you, because it is the same as if I had destroyed it. It ceases to be a material letter after it is started on its way — that is, it ceases to be a letter going to a material person. I might just as well be sending it to the moon. I have expressed my thoughts and feelings, and sent them out — even if I destroy the letter itself. But the perfect part about this relationship with your majesty is that, a little afterwards, my feelings and thoughts receive a reply, and understanding, friendly response. This is the wonderful part about our correspondence.

From your letters I know that you have understood why I write to you as I do. And, recognizing my impulses, you also respond and it becomes a mutual thing.

Well, there is no purpose in my stumbling for words and phrases to express how I feel about these letters we exchange. I do appreciate how wonderful you are about it. And I do want so very much to retain and deserve your friendship always.

Here, I feel, is one strong relationship in my life that will never become a disappointment. It is free from all material things that bruise and injure. I am so grateful for it.

I hope you will not have thought me greedy for sending those three pictures to be signed. I sent them about ten days ago. I have in my small library a very nice portfolio of photographs of your majesty, and of things Roumanian. These nicely complement your books that I have.

Balcic must be beautiful and restful at just this time of year.

With all possible good wishes and thoughts — ever,

Ray Baker Harris

Her Majesty, MARIE
Queen of Roumania
Palatul Regal Cotroceni
Bucharest, Roumania

P.S. I hope this letter does not seem *too* serious to you. But just these last days I have been conscious of the absence of several of my best friends, which makes the days less satisfactory. Eleanor, of course, is at her home in Paterson. A young fellow who has been one of my best friends since college days has just departed for his home in Montana to be done several months... Friends are a great moral assurance, and their absence is of course felt.

But I do not want to write you "heavy" letters, because I always feel a definite happiness and pleasure when I sit down to write to you.

VI

July 22, 1934

Your Majesty,

Several days ago I especially wished to have one of those talks with you, but my mood was too restless and disturbed to make it possible for me to concentrate on a letter.

Last Saturday I went to New York again — remaining there only for Saturday night and all of Sunday. I went up to visit with a former college friend who has just taken a new position there. We had a fine visit: an almost endless dinner Saturday night, talking over old times and getting acquainted again. The next morning we took a boat that goes down through New York bay and out into the ocean — about a two hour sail — and it landed us at a small town on the Atlantic coast. The day passed by aimlessly, but with such friendliness. We visited an old lighthouse station on the hilltop the "Twin Lights" — one of the first lights that ocean vessels see as they approach New York. Then we walked along the shore for quite a distance, went in swimming in the late afternoon, and returned to New York by boat again in the evening. Back in the city, we had another long and perfect dinner, and talked and visited until time for my train.

It was a visit of leisurely, contented, friendly hours — immensely satisfying and stimulating. And so, when I awoke on the train and found myself in Washington again on Monday morning, I certainly was far from happy about it! To make matters even less satisfactory, each of my best friends here in Washington has departed for the Summer, and so my work was the only thing to turn to. Of course I had more work than I could handle at my office, but all the same there were too many moments in which to recall the ocean shore friendly companionship.

And working in an Institution has its limitations... too much divided authority, too little individual responsibility — every individual personality being effectively submerged to the personality of the Institution as a whole, so that satisfaction in one's own work is very much reduced to a minimum!

Anyway, you see the state of mind I was in? There is nothing to compare with feelings of loneliness and longing to make one utterly dejected and miserable.

So, instead of writing to you with reckless words, I read again that wonderful, beautiful, and very wise letter that you sent to me from Balcic just after you had read Hoppe's book. And I found in that letter everything that I needed. I have read it very many times since it came, and always I am moved by the beautiful way in which you express your thoughts... and there is such calm wisdom in it! "Humans are small and often nasty, but they are also often very unhappy, they would rather be nice if they could..." And even in casual phrase you say things so beautifully — "...an overwhelming sadness came over me when I remembered *the immense energy and glad assurance* of those days..."

And so, as I read all that you had so graciously written to me, my longing and a certain sense of despair was lessened and feelings became easier. Consequently, I have been able in the last few days to give some quiet and serious thought to my present circumstance. It has given me a certain determination to try, during the next few months, to arrange some change of both work and environment. After all, I have been here in Washington, and at the Library of Congress, for more than four years... It has been, of course, security during four years of business depression in this country. I have had a continuing and fairly satisfactory income at a time when many people have been deprived of any income at all, through no fault of their own.

But I need a feeling of accomplishment, I need the presence of at least one or two good friends who like me and of whom I am fond. Without these I begin to feel like a marsh!

If I knew when I was well off I suppose I should "settle down" here indefinitely. Life here gives me most material things that I could desire; but this last visit in New York, and the contrast in returning here, has made me conscious of the things in life that I am permitting to pass by.

And so, instead of being just miserable — your letter has steadied my thoughts and given me a strength to look to my problems calmly.

In reading your letter again I was so very much impressed by what you said of the necessity, now and again in your life, to set aside those who wanted to be "the only one" — who wanted to bite others away from around you, who were jealous — wanting you to have only their stifling adoration.

Of course I am still too young to have experienced very much of this sort of thing... but I know very well what it is. I think it very unusual that your majesty should *recognize* these tendencies in those who have surrounded you in the past, and that you have insisted on maintaining your complete freedom. So often people permit themselves to be walled in by the hungry affection of just a few.

I know that a few times in my life I have met interesting people whom I have felt I would like to know better... and then, as soon as our relationship passed the stage of more acquaintance, jealousy would show its head and let me know, in subtle ways, that I had better not "poach"... and that if I persisted in ignoring the warnings, and continued to come closer to my new friend, they would find ways to misrepresent me, to put in a word here and there that would soil the new friendship before it was strong enough to withstand the darts. This sort of thing can be very distressing.

That is why I have ceased, somewhat, my more youthful tendency to seek new friends... that is, really close friends. It requires too much. And so I have come rather to prefer to keep the few old friends who already know me and who have already seen me at my worst as well as at my best advantage. In college days, of course, I went through that period of instability — which I suppose is a part in the life of any emotional or sensitive person. Naturally, at that time I did things now and then which were impulses and thoughtlessness. And so, looking back, I especially value the few friends who have remained with me from that time. There are two or three, and I have always been able to count upon them.

This is speaking of Friendship, of course — and I really value it more than love. One takes too many things for granted when in Love... too many things seem all right which are not all right... it is a little insane, and one cannot be sure where one stands until the tempest has passed. But with real friends one has sane, inspiring, contented assurance.

Eleanor Horton I met through one of my best friends. And then your majesty became a strong bond between us, so that now — when I am not seeking close friends — I suddenly found that I had another good friend. But this was an extraordinary combination of circumstances. And you have made possible for me a very friendly and also intimate relationship with Eleanor, although it is not disturbed by a deeper and more disturbing feeling. I hope that it can be maintained this way... at least for some time to come.

By now you will have received my letter in which I told you about my visit to her family, at Paterson. It was really a delightful, genuinely pleasant experience... so much friendliness.

My, what a serious tone I have been writing in! I hope you do not mind my writing to you in this way. Because the thoughts just come, as if I were writing my feelings without any intention of showing them to anyone. It is because you have been so very generous and understanding in the past that I have come to the point where I never hesitate to send these letters to you.

Washington is incredibly warm. It is no place to be in Summer. Each day the temperature climbs a bit higher, I have the benefit of a Westinghouse fan, and a small army of cold drinks, but still I feel as though I were very gradually drying up! To go out of doors in mid-day, it is just like stepping in front of an oven that has just been opened.

Had you heard that Grand Duchess Marie has written another book — to be called, I think, *Family Portraits*. I should not think, from her former work, that she would be especially good at character portrayals... because she seems to be always on the surface... an attractive lacquered, hard surface. And I think occasionally she forgets why the public is interested in what she writes.

I'm enclosing herewith a recent editorial on the War Debts that appeared in one of our magazines. It seems to me the most sane statement of the facts that I have read. Politicians, trying to curry favor with their constituents, have deliberately beclouded the debt issues. If the debts could be settled by the various heads of the Governments involved, a settlement could be reached in short order. But the politicians tie the hands of public officials, merely for their personal political advantage. I thought you might like to read this.

Sometime, when you can do so, I should especially like to have you tell me how youth reacts in Europe to the constant menace of War. It has always seemed to me that their ambitions and desire for personal achievement would be clouded by the possibility of another War which would ruin all they had attained... thus making achievement seem less worth striving for. Is this so? In America, of course, we are free from the *immediate* dangers of War. There is no enemy at our gates, so to speak... we have wide oceans and a friendly neighbor in Canada, and an indolent neighbor in Mexico.

With every possible good wish, and greatest appreciation for all your kindly, helpful, friendliness....

Ray Baker Harris

Her Majesty, MARIE
Queen of Roumania
Palatul Regal Cotroceni
Bucharest, Roumania

VII

July 29, 1934

Your Majesty,

My thoughts have been very often with you during the past week. All these troubled, stormy reports from Austria must be causing you the greatest anxiety, since they involve so many things dear and important to you, aside from the tremendous political significance of what is happening. I hope with all my heart that the Princess Ileana has not been directly touched by the apparently widespread disturbances. I have watched the newspaper dispatches closely, but have observed no reports from Sonnberg.

I have been rather surprised also not to find any dispatches in our New York papers from Bucharest. Roumania, and all the Little Entente, is so directly involved, but I have seen no reports at all concerning the attitude of the Roumanian government in this crisis.

It must be a fearful complication, which we cannot entirely appreciate here, except in a general way. These must be especially anxious days in Belgrad, because of the close proximity to the actual conflicts.

I do think this whole situation is the greatest possible reason for denying Germany the arms equality she has been demanding. If Germany were well armed at this time, there would certainly be war. Germany, well armed, is peaceful only so long as other nations do not interfere with her ambitions. Whenever her ambitions are opposed, Germany cares nothing for peaceful settlements. It has always been this way, and the record is conclusively set down in history.

France often seems unreasonable, but I think she knows this very essential truth about her neighbor. Only a short time ago, there was a feeling of sympathy for Germany in this country, a feeling that she should be allowed arms equality. But the events of the past ten days have proved very conclusively that an arms equality for Germany means an arrogant, ruthless Germany. Lack of full arms equality is the only thing which makes her respect the policy of the other powers. It is the only thing that is keeping Europe from a general, devastating war.

Of course, this is only my personal opinion, formed from a great distance and entirely on second-hand information, but I am strongly of the belief that Germany must never be granted arms equality.

In some ways, however, the next war in Europe may not be as horrible as is anticipated — although it will certainly be brutal enough. But the agencies for destruction are so powerful that I can foresee only almost immediate surrenders, humiliating peace for the protection of whole national lives.

The element which always disturbs me deeply about Europe is the ever-present threat of War. It seems to me it must be a germ as deadly as cancer, and as malignant. Because inevitably it must cast a great blanket of futility over the natural ambitions of Youth — the Europe of the future. What good is there in striving toward ideals, toward real accomplishments; what good is there in marrying and establishing homes and families; what good is there in creative art... if, by political machinations, all those things may be swept away in an avalanche of black war, almost overnight.

I think all the courage and glamour has gone out of war! What bravery is there in marching into a cloud of poison gas? It is suicide. There is no chance to fight, no possibility to win... nothing saved, nothing at all accomplished by the effort. Poison gas deprives War of its heroes of the personal combat. It is only foolhardiness, not bravery, that sends men into a cloud of certain death — fighting an enemy that cannot be conquered, that cannot even be seen!

Honestly, I sometimes think that Europe is completely and forever doomed... unless this pall of *futility* can be lifted... the futility which comes by the ever-present spectre of War... and the completely devastating character that all future wars will have because of the new agencies of destruction.

Here, in America, we are only just at this moment escaping from the influences of that same quality of futility. Our post-war generation, mostly young people who had been in the war, had that cynical, futile philosophy and put it into books and music and the drama, etc. And consequently, the generation coming just after, my generation, received an awful dose of this sort of pessimism and cynicism. It naturally influenced us. But today, the work of young men of my generation, of young women's work too, is taking on a new tone. Belief... Confidence... a definite change in outlook, because the future seems worth striving for. War doesn't threaten America directly in the future, and our feet are free from the last War. My generation is a FREE generation, looking forward hopefully, confidently... sometimes a little uncertainly, with goals that are not clear... but with Belief and Confidence again, not doubt and cynicism.

I wish with all my heart that this were possible for Europe too. But is it? Only twenty years... your young men of the World War are now in their forties. The infants of the World War are now young men just facing life, and in their youth they are privileged to experience no security — faced with the already *immediate* presence of War — which, if it comes not today, will surely come tomorrow... the figurative tomorrow of the immediate future.

Oh, I *am* sorry to write such a letter, so gloomy in its prospect for your part of the world. But I feel so strongly about it that I could not stop until I had written down what was in my thoughts. I know you will understand.

Aside from the disagreeable implications of the present trouble, the political implications are, of course, very interesting. There is much rumor here of an impending restoration of the Hapsburgs in Austria, and political writers seem to think the position of the former Empress Zits and her son is strengthened by present conditions; and knowing the attitude of the present Roumanian government toward the Hapsburg dynasty... such endless complications! It is a wonder to me that European diplomats keep any semblance of sanity whatever, considering the endless maze in which they live!

But I shall not write any further of disturbing things, or of the political matters.

I'm enclosing a picture of Prince Michael that appears in today's New York *Herald Tribune*.

Photograph of Queen Marie Dedicated to Ray Harris

Also I am enclosing a postal card photograph of your majesty, taken evidently on the occasion of Princess Ileana's wedding. And your majesty is much the loveliest of the four! You seem to have all their separate qualities. I am adding this attractive little picture to my collection, and would appreciate so much having it signed.

You will think me very greedy, but I am sending another large picture under separate cover — a portrait taken shortly after the death of His Majesty. Would you sign this for me too? I am always on the watch for interesting photographs of your majesty, and of Roumanian places with which you are associated, and I have begun this portfolio in which I keep all these photographs. The photographs tell a story in themselves, and it is the only collection of this sort that I am keeping. I haven't the time for others, but this collection concerning your majesty gives me a great deal of pleasure and satisfaction, and I am very proud of the several pictures which you have sent to me from time to time.

With many kind thoughts and affectionate wishes — always,

Ray Baker Harris

Her Majesty, MARIE
Queen of Roumania
Palatul Regal Cotroceni
Bucharest, Roumania

VIII

August 13, 1934

Your Majesty,

Several days ago I telephoned my house in the morning to say that I was having lunch downtown, that I was going into the country for the afternoon, and would not be home until late in the evening. But before I could give this message, I was told that a letter had come "from Sinaia." So I forgot about my plans, and went home for luncheon! And there waiting for me was not only your very interesting letter written at Bran, but also the three large photos.

I cannot tell you how delighted and pleased I am by the wonderful substitution which you so generously made. I had not especially liked the flashlight picture myself, but then I have never seen a photograph of your majesty which was less than attractive, so I had sent it anyway. But no photograph I have ever seen even begins to compare with that beautiful picture with the Stella Maris chapel in the background. I want so much to tell you how much it pleases me, but I cannot find the words. It is very beautiful, and, as you say, it looks more like a painting or a very fine print than like a photograph. There is nothing you could have sent me that would have pleased me more.

I shall not frame the nurse costume picture, since I like this other one so much better. I have ordered a frame with a very light brown, highly polished wood, with an inside border of gold, separated from the brown wood by a thin black line. It matches very beautifully the tones in the picture, and I shall be so proud to hang this picture just above my bookshelf — with your books just beneath it.

It was so nice to have the picture of your majesty riding at the head of your regiment; and with your letter were those charming small pictures of Bran. It is really not quite fair to be so generous to me, because it leaves me completely without ability to thank you adequately.

What you say about your visit to America is very interesting. During all your visit here I experienced a sort of dissatisfied feeling, because it seemed to me that you were unable to do the things that would have most pleased you, and that you were not seeing the sort of things which are most genuinely American, nor experiencing any of the best that American hospitality can offer. It seemed a shame that your precious time should be taken up by banquet after banquet, reception after reception; that when there were so many whom it would have been a real joy for you to meet and talk with, that it was necessary to take the time to be greeted by countless dull officials.

The Carveth Wells book, *Kapoot*, was mailed several days ago. Many passages of the book are acutely distasteful, but I think it is necessary for the author to have adopted this tone. Because only in this way can he really convey the true sensation of disgust that the scenes in Russia aroused. I hope that none of the book will offend you, but I think it probably will be a satisfaction to you to know that one writer has had the courage to tell of Russia just exactly as it is.

I quite sympathize with your determination that you will never receive the Soviets in your house. King George of England, I believe, has never received the Soviet ambassadors, but it has always been done by the Prince of Wales instead.

American recognition of Russia was supposedly done to counter the aggressiveness of Japan in the Pacific, but I think we have already had reason to regret our action, as has every other nation that entered into official dealings with the Soviets.

I particularly call your attention to that chapter in *Kapoot* which describes what Lord Bryce wrote of the Russians under the rule of the Czar. He said in part that although many peasants were terribly poor, they all had a certain freedom, and that they always had at least huge pots of nourishing soup. Today thousands have nothing at all either to eat or wear.

It will be amusing to see if I am a good Prophet! But I have a very strong feeling that quite soon I shall have some new opportunities opened to me, and that I shall probably be leaving Washington. This is, at the moment, pure speculation, because I have nothing definite upon which to base such conclusions. But always in the past I have made my changes very quickly, suddenly without much advance notice. And I feel that such a time is just ahead.

For four years, and beginning the fifth, I have been here in Washington... and so it is really about time for me to move ahead. I cannot ever "settle down," I'm afraid. It will be a little difficult to tear up the roots that have started here, and my mother and sister are living here probably permanently; and I have several very valued friends here. But my enthusiasm is so stirred by the possibility of new opportunities, new scenes, new work to do, that not until later will I suffer the longing for the satisfactions I have known here. But it has always been this way with me, I *have* to move ahead.

I shall continue to work on the President Harding biography in my spare time, but I am not in haste. I want to do a really worthwhile piece of work, and every passing month gives me new ideas and new material. My writing will always be a sideline, as I can never earn my income that way. Everything I have written that has been published in the past, I have done only because of my special interest in the subject — written mostly for my own satisfaction. And one cannot hope for a steady income when one writes that way! But I prefer it so, because I should hate to have to write things that didn't interest me — just for the income. And many writers do just that.

But I have found that my writing has often led me to paths that I like — to work that I like to do. For instance, in writing this biography of President Harding, I have met and talked with many interesting people and they have come, in a measure, to know me. The same thing has happened in the past, and has developed many interesting associations. My job with the publishing firm, where I remained more than two years, came about in much the same way. So any writing and my work are definitely related.

But wherever I am, and whatever I am doing, I do hope that always I may retain the generous and inspiring friendship that your majesty has given to me, and that I may always continue to receive your letters. I shall never cease to be thrilled and grateful when they come. This fine association with your majesty makes me less dependent upon my immediate material world, and that is a very great help. It gives an independence of spirit in meeting one's problems. I am sure that you can understand this.

And always it will be such a pleasure to be able to turn to you and write of my feelings, my successes, and my plans — knowing that you will always understand. And occasionally I may turn to you with a problem which your words could help — viewing it, as you do, with understanding and from the clearer perspective of distance.

In return for all your kindness and your inspiration, I can only pledge my loyalty and my deepest appreciation. It is very little to give in return.

It will be very nice if you can arrange to be in London when your book appears. I am so impatient for it to appear over here. Scribner's have promised me a reviewer's copy about two weeks in advance of its actual publication date — which I think is to coincide with the appearance of the second volume in England, about October 13th. The American edition is to be in one volume, I understand, which is a slight disappointment, because I think the two-volume idea is the best.

I am also very anxious to see the volume for the war years, and I hope that the *Saturday Evening Post* will reconsider and publish it. But I am sure Scribner's *must* publish it in book form in any event, and it cannot be too soon for me, because the ending of the first part leaves great expectation for the dramatic days to follow.

If you go England will it be only to London? Rural England has always fascinated me the most, as much for its associations with the past as its picturesque qualities.

I am going to New York again next week, and shall probably have an opportunity to call on Eleanor again. It is a very pleasant anticipation, because I certainly enjoyed my last visit tremendously. She will be coming back here to school late next month, I think, and I hear that there are a number of changes there — several of the teachers who have been there a long time will not be returning. I don't know how this will impress Eleanor, but I shall have a chance to talk to her about it when I see her.

Enclosed is a little picture which I have clipped from yesterday's New York *Times*. I think I can understand and deeply sympathize with many of the thoughts which must have been in your mind on that occasion.

It is worrying to see Roumania surrounded by so many dangers. Austria and Hungary are always, it seems, powder boxes... and then there is Bulgaria and the Dobrudja, and Russia and Bessarabia... and Yugoslavia and Italy... and back of it all the German tares being frantically waved by Chancellor Hitler, liable to do damage at any moment. It must be frightful to live in the shadow of such things, but I suppose it is an old, familiar situation in Europe and people there are probably too well acquainted with it.

The American newspapers have been reporting, as you may have read, that Princess Ileana and Arch Duke Anton have been very active in behalf of the return of the Hapsburg family to the throne of Austria. From a distance, it does seem like the only way to prevent German aggressions in Austria.

By the way, I have several times intended to inquire if you had ever read a book called *The Real Romanovs* written by a Gleb Botkin, the son of one of the physicians at the Czar's Court. I met him very casually and formally at a luncheon which his publishers gave, about three years ago, when the book first appeared. At that time he made a little speech, and talked about the supposed Grand Duchess Anastasia, claiming that she had been saved after the awful tragedy at Ekaterinburg. He seemed very sincere in his belief that she really was the Grand Duchess, but I think it is utterly impossible for Americans to judge such a claim — we are too much disassociated. But of course the claim is dramatic and appealing, but it has seemed to me that the relatives of the Czar would have exhausted every means to determine the truth; and it seems to me significant that none of the relatives who were so devoted to the Czar have in any way acknowledged this claimant. But I have wondered if you read Mr. Botkin's book, and what you thought of the arguments he made in her behalf.

I was very much interested in the descriptions of the visit which you made to the Russian Court as Crown Princess, and in what you had to say about the various members of the Royal Family. I always was interested in the Russia of the old days, and at one time read everything I could about Russia under the Czars.

That reminds me — you will notice in the *Kapoot* book that the Soviets have been careful to destroy all true knowledge of the Russia that formerly existed — Russian children today are deprived the knowledge of the freedom and advantages which peasants once had in Russia, and are taught the most perverted nonsense. The Soviets concentrate on the young, because they can make no headway with the older people who remember the Russia of former days. Therefore future Russia is being reared on a diet of lies and deceit.

Please forgive me for dwelling on these unpleasant subjects. But although they are distressing, they *are* interesting; and I cannot resist writing to you about them, because I know that you are so familiar with the truth about Russia, and know so much more about it than I do.

I hope that you and Princess Ileana and her little family will have a pleasant and restful time at the warm salt lake in Transylvania where you said you planned to spend some time. It sounded like a delightful, restful place.

Again I want to say what very *great* pleasure that lovely picture which you sent has given me. I always wanted a nice picture of Stella Maris, because of the things you had written to me about the beloved chapel, and it is perfect to have this beautiful picture of it, with the beautifully posed picture of yourself on the steps. It is perfect! I am really *very* happy to possess it. It was *so* kind of you to send it to me, and I hope you can understand just a measure of the happiness it has brought me.

With all affectionate thoughts and wishes — always,

Ray Baker Harris

Her Majesty, MARIE
Queen of Roumania
Palatul Regal Cotroceni
Bucharest, Roumania

IX

August 27, 1934

Your Majesty,

The wonderful long letter from Sovata came two days ago, and I have just finished reading it again. Also, as I write this letter I can look across the room and, just above a table lamp near my bookshelves, there is the framed picture showing your majesty on the path leading up to the Stella Maris chapel. Every time I look at this beautiful picture I send you a thought of grateful appreciation for your thoughtfulness in sending me such a perfect gift. I have a very special feeling for Stella Maris, and to have a picture of you in that setting is *most* satisfying.

It is exciting to learn that you have definitely decided to be in England next month. There is something unusually dramatic in your visits to England — perhaps because you were an English princess, and it seems a sort of "return home" despite all the firm ties in Roumania. I shall eagerly read the London papers for the accounts of your visit, and, when it is possible for you to conveniently do so, I shall of course be most anxious to hear about your London in a letter from you. How grateful I am that such a letter is even a possibility!

I am sending to London in the same post with this letter an order for the two volumes; because, although Scribner's have promised me an advance copy of their one-volume edition, I think the English edition is the one I want to keep in my library. I like the two-volume plan better. After you have returned to Roumania, I shall be sending the first volume to you, asking you to inscribe it to me. I am looking forward so much to having the complete *Story*, and volume III cannot be published too soon to please me!

You asked if I know any foreign languages, or if I only read and talk English. I can read French fairly well, but I cannot speak it. I wanted to study German in college, but permitted myself to be persuaded to concentrate on the French instead. I am sorry I did this, because there have been so many times that I wished I knew German. I also wasted a good deal of time on Latin in school, most of which I have since forgotten and it is so earthly use to me now — except that perhaps it is a sort of basis for other languages.

I never was an especially good student in school, and I had countless rows with most of my teachers. A very few I liked extremely well and did good work with them, but for the most part I heartily disliked school even though I managed to complete all my courses.

It was very interesting to read all which you wrote with regard to the two difficult friendships. Deep sentiment makes friendships all the stronger, but sentimentality spoils everything.

I had two very close friendships during my college days. We even shared rooms at various times, and living with a friend is a severe test! But the three of us were always very strong friends, and have so remained during the past ten years — through many disagreements too. I think this is because we always respected the independence of the other, and our expressions of sentiment never became in any way sentimental — only loyal comradeship and friendliness. Many other acquaintances, who were important for a time, have come and gone during those same years. And although we are no longer together (one is married and has his own particular world now) we do keep in touch and occasionally have very satisfactory reunions. I am very grateful for these two friendships.

In 1928 I went to New York and was an assistant editor for two years on a monthly magazine, and I met and came to know a good many people in the literary and artistic world there. You can imagine that I had to face many a difficult problem in the matter of personal relationships. In many ways those were two bitter years, because I was quite unprepared for much that I came to learn.

My father is a civil engineer who designed and constructed railroad bridges. I was born in the Philippine Islands, because he was the American engineer in charge of the construction of the first Philippine railways — in 1907. To my mother, her family was her whole world almost. Every influence was conservative, almost severe... and that was the only world I knew, aside from school and college.

But I have always felt strong sympathy for many sorts of people, and I instinctively understand a great deal. It is strange, but my father and mother have gone thus far through life totally unaware of certain phases — and if I were to try to talk to them about such things they would think me completely insane!

When I was a boy I was taken to church with poisonous regularity, but there is only one sermon of many I had to hear that I have remembered. It was an Easter Service, and the rector talked of Mary at the tomb of the risen Lord. He went on to describe how Mary, so very admirable in most respects, would not recognize Christ when he spoke to her, and asked to see the wounds, to see tangible, material proofs. And just so today many otherwise admirable people simply cannot recognize or understand anything which cannot actually be *proved* to them on their *own* short rule of material experience.

It is just as the young officer of your household said — many find difficulty in following your lead because they are not so really and truly kind as you are. They cannot fully understand you, because they have never been able to feel things in the same way that you do. They try to understand, because they are devoted to you, but it still must remain a mystery. I think the young officer made a very penetrating and understanding observation. It was perfectly pointed.

I have never permitted my friendships with men to get into any sentimental stage. Occasionally I have had the inclination to accede to some such importunity, because sympathy and understanding sometimes put up a stiff fight with one's better judgment. But I have seen too many examples, and there is no inspiration or good in any such associations — at least there would not be for me. Generosity and sympathy and understanding make me overly tolerant of others, but for myself I can never escape from the daily teachings of my youth... it is a sort of emotional tie which holds me in check, even when my mind is willing.

The two strongest emotional friendships I have had were both with girls. Those are strong currents and it isn't easy to keep one's balance. I can handle my relations with men more or less deliberately, no matter how much strong sentiment may be involved; but falling in love with a girl is entirely something else again, and can be rather overwhelming.

I am extremely fond of a most attractive girl, who was also born in the Philippines about two years after I was — and her family were friends of my parents when they lived in Manila. Her father was an Englishman, her mother the daughter of an American army officer. She was educated in England and in France, and I never really knew her until after her father died and she returned to the United States with her mother. She is not a beautiful girl, but extremely attractive and good-looking, poised, athletic and a really marvellous companion. There was wonderful understanding between us, and from the very first we hit it off wonderfully.

It became very serious, so much so that I had to face the facts squarely. We were neither of us honestly disposed to marry then, and I don't think I shall ever marry without the most definite assurance of financial security. And then I was more or less "experimenting" with finding a profession. As I look back, it would have been a huge mistake had we decided to "settle down" then. I left New York rather abruptly and came to Washington. It was far from an easy thing to do, and there were many long distance telephone talks and many temptations to resume the former tempo.

We both have been in and out of love again since then! As a matter of fact, she is visiting friends in Washington now, and we have had pleasant times again. She was here for a short time last Spring. Eleanor Horton met her, and they liked each other very much. Of course, there is nothing serious now, except some rather poignant memories — an occasional longing for those old days which went by like moments, with such complete contentment.

Please forgive me writing so much in this vein. I just started and couldn't seem to stop.

By the way, do others see my letters before you read them? I have somehow taken it for granted lately that my letters may reach you unopened. You can understand, of course, how it has come about that I have no hesitancy in writing to you so freely; but I do not think others would understand, and would think me a fool or insane to write such things to you.

I was interested in what you wrote about your friend believing in numerology, and wanting you to guide your life by her theory of numbers. You also mentioned in one previous letter that you had much sympathy of the Ba'hai teachings. When I was going to school here in Washington my mother had a friend, a very wonderful old lady more than eighty years old but with such an active mind and spirit. She was a strong Ba'hai, and had personally known Abdul Ba'hai (is that right?) and been his disciple. At any rate, she tried rather persistently to interest me in the Ba'hai. She knew of my admiration for you, and so she would always show me articles in the Ba'hai magazine which quoted interviews with you, and I think Princess Ileana also. My first acquaintance with the Ba'hai faith came about in that way! I was interested and sympathetic with their teachings, but I don't particularly like to have any form of religion "taught" to me. I think it comes instinctively, and from within.

You ask about Bermuda. Yes, I want to go there — possibly when I write the President Harding biography, which now seems an almost endless task! But I cannot go before Winter — which will be rather nice, because Bermuda is a perpetually agreeable climate.

I wonder what the Saar plebiscite will reveal. The people of the Saar are Germans, but they are free from all the heavy restrictions imposed by Hitler in Germany. They will be in a position to vote freely, without fear of reprisals... and it will be interesting to see if these Germans will wish to endorse Hitler when they are under no compulsion to do so. The press in America is solidly hostile to him. I think for a time public sentiment was turning toward him here, but after the Dollfus tragedy, reprisals against the foreign press in Germany, etc., he has lost most of his friends here . It is difficult to form worthwhile opinions from such a distance.

I received a delightful long letter from Eleanor today. They are moving from their house in Paterson, and going to a much larger house in the country with a good deal of grounds surrounding it.

This letter is becoming endless! I shall mail this directly to Balcic in the hope that it may reach you before your departure for England.

I do wish you a comfortable and happy trip, and I know that your book will be most enthusiastically received.

With every good wish and affectionate thought — always,

Ray Baker Harris

Her Majesty, MARIE
Queen of Roumania
Palatul Regal Cotroceni
Bucharest, Roumania

X

September 11, 1934

Your Majesty,

What you wrote about Grand Duchess Marie, in your wonderful letter from Sovata, interested me very much. Because, in spite of the real interest of her books, I had felt the tone of coldness and I remembered having been surprised at the very slight mention of her small son, of whose lonely tragedy you spoke, but she did seem extremely fond of her brother, Dmitri.

I have just been rereading parts of *Princess in Exile* and I like the way she writes of your generosity, your kindness, your love of beautiful things, and your youthful spirit; but as soon as she tries to analyze your qualities, she fails. She seems unusually observing of the surface evidences, but she reveals no real sensibility or understanding... her eye sees everything objectively. But it does, as you say, make extremely interesting reading.

The same publisher who brought out other books is presenting her *Family Portraits*, and it was supposed to come out this month but there has apparently been some change or delay.

I have been having a good many of my friends write to Mr. Lorimer of the *Saturday Evening Post*, asking when the third volume is to appear. Eleanor has also been urging her friends and acquaintances to write, and perhaps it may eventually do some good. At the moment, however, he says he does not think the third volume will be published serially by the *Post*, because it is all "war experiences;" but he does say that the *Post* is very much interested in a fourth volume of post-war recollections. Possibly, if a sufficient number of readers write in, he may change his mind and use the third volume also.

I have also been writing to numerous people I know who are in a position to help the sale of the book when it appears. A friend of mine is editor of an official publication of the American Library Association, and I have written to urge her to give a special notice to your book. This would go to every library in the country, and I think that every library in America should purchase a copy of your book; because many people who may perhaps feel they cannot afford to buy a copy will surely want to read the book at their nearest public library. The Library of Congress, for instance, will probably purchase many extra copies to meet the calls for it.

I am certain that your book will be very successful, and it gives me real happiness to have a small part in helping to increase its sale. Because in the pages of your *Story* is the real Queen of Roumania, and both Eleanor and I are extremely anxious to have as many as possible come to know the real Queen and not merely the legend. The *Saturday Review* of the Washington newspaper has asked me to do a feature review of the American edition — or rather, I offered to do the review (saying that the portions published in the *Post* had especially interested me), and the editor replied, saying that I might do the review and that he would feature it. Of course I shall write it as an average reader, without any hint of my special admiration for the author!

Since I wrote you last I have again been to New York! I went up with some friends and had a really enjoyable time, as the visit was mostly for pleasure, although I did remain over an extra day to attend to a business matter. I know New York so well that it is always pleasant to visit there, but I sometimes doubt I would be willing to live there again. If one works in New York, however, there is always the advantage of being able to live at some pleasant place near the city but entirely divorced from it... on Long Island, or in Connecticut, or even on the New Jersey ocean shore... and from which one can reach the city very quickly. I suppose it is inevitable that I shall go back there sooner or later, because New York is America's richest center of opportunities.

There is much news of the Balkans in our newspapers now — conferences in Belgrade, the restoration of the Hapsburg family, the marriage of Prince George of England to the Princess of Greece... all of which sounds like a great deal of activity in your part of the world. There are also very hopeful reports concerning King Carol, and my strong wish is that all the things your majesty hopes for may really come to pass.

I am so interested in your visit to England, and I know your book will be well received there. Of course some of the literary critics will have to indulge their vanity by being critical, especially of one so much higher in life than they are, but readers generally will find many satisfactions and inspirations in all that you have written.

Another quality which impresses me about your book is that your descriptions of people are all penetrating and graphic, but have neither malice *nor* flattery. Throughout it all is the sincere tone of Truth.

Eleanor will be returning to Washington within another week or so. It will be very pleasant to have her here again, because she is a delightful companion. During these early Fall months, when it is so enjoyable to be out of doors, we should have some memorable hours, and I am greatly looking forward to it. I suppose she has written to you about her new house at Little Falls.

I like the Fall of the year — even more than the Spring. Because in the Autumn there is renewed life, new activity, and the best things which have ever happened to me have come during these months. In the Spring there is usually a sort of disagreeable *thawing out* process, and I invariably manage to catch all the Spring ailments — including poison ivy! But in the Fall, there is freshness and activity. People end their vacations and turn their thoughts and efforts to work again, with new vigor. Children go back to school. The farmer gathers in his crops and prepares for the Winter. Everything is change and excitement and one feels stronger and more purposeful.

By the way, I always meant to inquire if you would tell me what your meeting with President Wilson was like? Perhaps I am being impatient in my interest, because of course you will doubtlessly describe this in your fourth volume. But it was such a dramatic circumstance. I remember Mrs. Daggett mentioning this in her book. It will be most interesting to read, in that promising fourth volume, all about those exciting and eventful days in Paris when your majesty did so much for the Roumanian cause. It would have been lost if it had not been for you.

Hoping to hear from your majesty soon again, and with every affectionate wish and good thought — always,

Ray Baker Harris

Her Majesty, MARIE
Queen of Romania

XI

September 16, 1934

Your Majesty,

Your absorbing, interesting letter from Bran came yesterday. Nothing comes to me through the mail which is more anticipated, more welcome, or more appreciated than these letters your majesty so generously writes to me. I am so grateful to you for them.

A few hours later the two photographs arrived by a special post, and I am delighted with the extra photograph which you enclosed. It is very much nicer than the one I sent. Of course, the several photographs which I have sent to you have all been copies, and so lack something of the originals. But they *all* mean a great deal to me, and are a great joy. The Stella Maris photograph remains my favorite. It is as perfect as a photograph can be.

Lately I have especially been able to understand your impatience with to much rain at this colorful time of the year. Because Washington has been having rain and more rain! We experienced a real cloudburst two days ago, and today is just a steady downpour. It spoils some of the Autumn blooms, but the flower kingdom seems to have marvellous recuperative powers, and a day or two of good weather sets everything to rights.

Your gardener sounds like a quaint character, and it was amusing to hear about his wife who "is fat and lame and entirely of the earthly, and has a tongue for two!". Has he always been deaf, and has he never heard the names of the flowers he loves and cares for so well? Do tell me something more about these two interesting humans, and also how he works with your gardens. Has he been with your majesty's service a long time?

I cannot understand *The First to Go Back*, as I started to read it and lost interest because it sounded like insincere propaganda. I cannot believe she can really mean the things to which she subscribes, but rather it seems perhaps she may have received some advantage from the Soviets for writing such things. I may be very prejudiced and pessimistic in my view, but it seems to me that the Soviets are breading an inhuman, unfeeling race, which, perhaps several generations from now, will eventually overrun modern civilization — as the hordes who destroyed the civilizations of Greece and Rome. Because Russia is a mighty nation with millions of humans who, if they are raised devoid of religion, family love, sentiment and sensibility, must eventually do great damage. But this is speculating very far to the future, and much can happen meanwhile. Perhaps the trend will turn, and great Russia will again be led and ruled by civilized, intelligent, educated people. Russia is the great human question-mark on the world's surface.

I read with deep interest all which you wrote about Gleb Botkin and the Grand Duchess Anastasia theory. A friend of mine summed it up very accurately several years ago. When the book first came out I had given my friend a copy to read, as she was most intelligent but yet disinterested in the subject matter of the book. When she had finished it she said — "I liked the book immensely, especially the first half, and I was interested in what he said about Grand Duchess Anastasia... but I wasn't convinced." And she had no reason to be prejudiced one way or the other. I myself fell somewhat under the spell of Botkin's eloquence, but cool analysis made me realize that there was too much unexplained. His theory has a dramatic appeal, and one could realize that the terrible suffering and the horrible experiences endured by any possible survivor from the hell of Ekaterinburg would be quite enough to leave a mind unbalanced, and particularly the mind of a young girl whose whole prior life had been in the sheltered, cultured environment of the late Czar's family.

But this line of reasoning is merely sentimental. As you say, the conclusions of the Grand Duchess Olga, the most devoted intimate of the Czar's daughters, who spared no effort to learn the truth, is entirely convincing.

What a terrible and horrible tragedy Ekaterinburg was. I read some reminiscences a year or so ago written by a daughter, I think, of the former British Ambassador to Russia. As I recall, she claimed that Premier Lloyd George had interfered and prevented plans which had been arranged with the provisional revolutionary government in Russia to bring the Russian Imperial Family, by British ship, to England. She claimed that Lloyd George did this because of fear of labor reprisal while the War was still going on. It sounds very heartless, and I wonder if it can possibly be true.

But to more agreeable subjects:

I am enthused and delighted beyond words to read your quotations from Mr. Keedick's and Mr. Scribner's letters. I knew Scribner's *must* pub-

lish your third volume, but I am especially pleased that they are so enthusiastic and want to do it very soon; *and* that they wish your majesty to
complete the fourth volume. I think it is inevitable that you must write
this fourth volume, because your majesty is the only one who can write
the true story in the way that it should be told.

I am sure that your first two parts (one volume) will sell very well in
America. Of course, Eleanor and myself will do everything in our small
power to help the good work along. Your *Story* tells of the real Queen of
Roumania, and it will make you countless new friends and admirers
among understanding people... and this is what Eleanor and I desire above
everything else.

There is also another side. I think that your *Story* is not alone for this
generation — for your own contemporaries. Yours is an autobiography
that will live, and probably will be even more understood and appreciated
by future generations than by your majesty's contemporaries. Because it is
a genuinely great book — the story of a Queen, the story of momentous
days and unforgetable events, the story of a great woman's life — and
written from *within!* Very few write from within themselves these days.
Instead they write only of their dissatisfactions with what they see around
them. It is perhaps the fallow spirit of the day. But you write for no particular time or period, because you write from within yourself — with a
spirit that is ageless. For that reason, I think, your book will also be ageless!

What I have just written may, to some people, sound like outrageous
flattery. But I know that your majesty feels that I am sincere, and for that
reason I have no self-conscious fear of writing exactly what I honestly
think.

It is the same, I think, with your novels. They also are written from
within, and not for any particular generation. And for that reason they are
not more widely understood. I cannot truthfully say that I entirely understand them, but I *feel* the things you write, and this completes a very sympathetic feeling. It is a little difficult to completely express this attitude
about your writings, but I think you may understand me.

I have not yet received the first English volume of your *Story*,
although I ordered a set last month and sent the cheque in advance so
that there would be no delay. I am impatient for it! I want especially to
read the parts which did not appear in the magazine series.

If the relations you speak about do not approve of your *Story*, it will
doubtless be because they are piqued to realize that their lives would not
make such interesting reading — even if they had the talent and the courage to write of their feelings and experiences.

I can also appreciate fully the difficulties which your majesty and Princess Ileana have had with those who are impatient with your democratic kindnesses. I can see their point of view also, because it is true that if your majesty were not so generous and kindly, and considerate of others, unworthy people would not find it within their power to take advantage of a Queen, to misrepresent you through their own lack of appreciation of your qualities, and to foster their own selfish designs.

But it makes your majesty all the greater, because in your character there are no barriers of selfish cautiousness, your spirit is big and naturally transcends all the petty boundaries and restrictions that humans set up. Because, as you say, Humanity — from the highest to the lowest — has many things in common, and Humanity itself is of never-tiring interest.

Doubtless you have rent the little book by Booth Tarkington, *Monsieur Beaucaire*? And you remember when the cousin of the King of France (who calls himself Monsieur Beaucaire, and who hides his real identity) falls in love with Lady Mary Carlisle, the famous beauty of Bath, England, he finds that she returns his love only so long as she thinks him of noble birth. When he is "exposed" as having been the French Ambassador's barber (which role he had taken to escape from the wrath of his cousin, the King of France) she treats him contemptuously.

It is then that he remarks, bitterly, — "Then, live men are just Names!" Of course, Lady Mary Carlisle learns too late that the French Ambassador's "barber" was actually not only a noble, but the first cousin of the French King. But the point is — to her his nobility was a name only, she could not discern nobility in the man himself.

Monsieur Beaucaire is a delightfully idealized, but beautifully pointed and penetrating little story. If, by some chance, you have never read it, please do permit me to send you a copy. It is a very small book and could be read entirely within an hour. And I think, in its way, it expresses your attitude so well.

To your majesty, nobility and character and humanity are not just names. You can find them, as you did, in the poorest and humble — in the old Turkish woman, scorned because of her early weaknesses. There is humanity in everyone, and humanity is many sided and interesting. And Humanity is God.

I admire so much the true greatness of your spirit, and comprehensiveness of your understanding.

Your story of the old Turkish woman was very human and delightful. I can picture her very clearly. And since God has given to you so richly of qualities and charms, you have not hesitated to touch the life of one of his most lowly creations with a refreshment that will make that quaint bundle of human poverty glad to be alive!

Yes, Eleanor's family gave up their house in Paterson, but they are thrilled with a new, quite large old house more in the country, with quite a bit of grounds, wonderful old trees. She has written me two or three very delightful letters about their happiness in fixing up this new home according to their ideas. This is, as you say, a courageous way of facing new problems and tackling them with enthusiasm. It's a power to make her own world. In this, I think you have greatly helped her with your spirit during the years you have given her so much friendship.

There have been many changes at the Holton Arms school during the Summer. Several of the old teachers have been replaced, and I don't know how Eleanor will react to the different spirit of the place.

I have not made any change as yet, but I am practically certain that one will arise quite soon. Where it will take me, I cannot now tell, because I do not know. But I shall be here when Eleanor returns to Washington, and wherever I go afterwards, I shall of course keep in touch with Eleanor. Through our mutual devotion to your majesty, we have become the very firmest friends — and I am sure it is one of those friendships, always rare, that will last throughout a lifetime. And the knowledge that we have your majesty's friendship is a great inspiration and help to us both.

I am enclosing rotogravure pictures from today's *Washington Star.* This shows three views quite near to where I live. I live in a part of Washington which is called "Georgetown". It was once a little city by itself, and then as Washington grew larger it naturally absorbed historic old Georgetown. The top picture shows the spires of old Georgetown University. I can see these spires from my window, and also the clock tower. It is very picturesque, and I rather like living near the college atmosphere — where life is always young and very hopeful. It is a Catholic school.

The lower pictures show two views in the countryside. The picture at the lower right is along the old Canal — no longer used, but very picturesque. In the Fall we take long walks or ride along the path beside the Canal — which goes for many miles into the countryside. I thought you might like to see these views.

You speak of the difficulties about planning for your fourth volume. This interests me intensely. You mention the one awful event which saddens all your recollections of those years. I do not know if it is a tragedy about which you feel that you can write. If it can be told, I should imagine that it would add great power to this fourth volume of your *Story* and make it the most poignant climax of your entire work.

But if it is a tragedy which you feel you cannot possibly write about at this time, then the "Pages From My Later Life" would be the logical solution — and it would doubtless be possible for you to make these "Pages" very stirring and a fitting climax, though not so strong as the full story would make.

I like the title "Pages From My Later Life," but perhaps while you are working on the actual writing of the fourth volume your material will suggest some other title. Doubtless you will keep an open mind about the title of the fourth volume, so that you can secure the one you like the best. But the "Pages" idea gives you an admirable working-title, even if you should decide on something else later.

"Stranger Than Fiction" might be an intriguing title — and suggests the old saying about "Truth is stranger than fiction" — and might suggest to the reader the anticipation of the revelation of heretofore untold facts.

But I do not think you should write your fourth volume with too much a tone of finality — hold the interest for the future. Because the years are long even if days do pass quickly, and the possibilities of the future are endless. I think this is a truth your majesty should not overlook. I am exceedingly interested in your plans for this fourth volume, and I hope you will tell me more about it as your work progresses.

I think I shall send this letter to you at London, in care of the Roumanian Legation, as they will doubtless know where to deliver it. I have sent to Bucharest two of your novels, *Ilderim* and *The Voice on the Mountain*, which will doubtless be held there until your return, when I hope you may inscribe the volumes for me.

Did I tell you that I have your volumes rebound in uniform style — a very heavy weave cloth, light gray, which appeals to me as being very attractive — and this makes a nice distinctive unit of your writings. I did not have the novels rebound before sending them to you for fear they might be damage in the mail, but they will be rebound as soon as they come back to me.

This letter has grown endlessly, and I shall not write more this time — in spite of many more thoughts that come to mind, asking to be put in this letter. As it is, I feel guilty in sending so long a letter to you while you are vacationing.

With the most affectionate thoughts and kindest wishes — always,

Ray Baker Harris

Her Majesty, MARIE
Queen of Roumania

XII

September 22, 1934

Your Majesty,

It must seem *very* inconsiderate of me to intrude with time-consuming letters while you are visiting in England — and especially to write so soon again after the young monster of a letter which I mailed to London only a few days ago! Please forgive me, but yesterday I received from Cassell's the first volume of the *Story* — so long awaited. I sat up reading it until 2 a.m. last evening, and tonight, just after dinner, I began reading the final pages. Just a few moments ago I read the last sentence.

Also, I received a telephone call from Eleanor this evening. She is still at Little Falls, but is returning to Washington on Monday.

There are so many thoughts about your majesty that I *must* write to you tonight. I am also giving away to the lusty temptation to send my copy of Volume one to you immediately — asking if you would write a special inscription in it for me? I had already sent to Bucharest my copies of your novels *Ilderim* and *The Voice on the Mountain*, and these will doubtless be held there until you return to Roumania.

But I simply *cannot* wait another six weeks before having my inscribed copy of Volume One, and so I hope very much that you will not mind my having sent it to London. As you know, this book means a very great deal to me, and, with the other volumes that are to follow, your *Story* will have the very first place in my small personal library.

I like the two-volume plan, and wish Scribner's were not going to try to combine the two separate parts. But they feel they can reach a larger public in this way, and I have no doubt they will produce a very handsome volume. How satisfied and pleased I shall be when I have *all four* volumes safely on my shelves!

By the way, I have made the suggestion at the Congressional Library that, as soon as possible, your book should be reproduced in Braille so that blind readers may enjoy your *Story*. Congress appropriates $100,000 every year which the Library uses to reproduce books into Braille. I think it would please you to have your *Story* reach that special public which would experience such unusual inspiration in reading all the things you have related.

The only Christmas gifts I shall make this year in this country will be copies of *The Story of My Life* by Marie, Queen of Roumania; and I don't think any of my friends will receive nicer gifts!

Oh, I have something amusing to tell you — although I hope you may not think me disrespectful. But it did tickle my sense of humor. One of the newspapers had a story about the visit to Scotland of Princess Marina, who of course is to be married to Prince George. Well, this newspaper dispatch went on to say that when Princess Marina arrived at Balmoral in Scotland, Queen Mary, in preparation for some social event Princess Marina was to attend, taught Princess Marina the Scottish dance — The Highland Fling! I am sure the instruction must have been entirely verbal, because even my fertile imagination simply *cannot* visualize Queen Mary herself dancing the Highland Fling! I hope you do not mind my telling you this, but the idea did seem so ridiculous!

There are so many thoughts about this Volume One, and I am delighted by the additional passages which did not appear in the *Saturday Evening Post*.

I wonder if the Kaiser will read what you say of him. It is very likely that he will, because I remember reading something written by the Princess of Pless, Daisy, in which she commented that the Kaiser had an insatiable curiosity concerning anything written about him. Your sentences about him are very frank, but they have the tone of truth without malice. He must have been an extraordinary character in his younger and more powerful days. I think it was the Princess of Pless who also said that he had a tremendous inferiority complex, greatly admired everything British but would never admit it except when he was *not* in England.

Reading through this first half of your *Story* again I have been further impressed by the way in which you describe everyone — so clearly, objectively and with real insight to their characters revealed in just a few words.

I was interested also in what you said, in speaking about Queen Elisabeth, "All through life I have had a curious faculty of sensing the undercurrent of other people's emotions, even when they were playing a quite different part to the gallery." I can understand this so well, and the slight feeling of isolation which that sense can create. Also I am afraid people have occasionally been able to tell from the expression on my face, or in my eyes, that I have sensed their affectation, and that of course can create a strain! But I am able to hide my conclusions a little more tactfully these days.

But there would be endless comments to make on all which is in this first volume, and I do not want to bother you with a long letter just now when you are traveling about. However, it all strengthens the one conclusion which I decided upon long ago — and that is the extraordinary "bigness" of your character, the great, understanding comprehensiveness of your understanding.

I have had, of course, in your wonderful letters so many evidences of your great spirit. It is so free, so compassionate that it is inspiring just to come in touch with it. I do so admire your philosophy, because it is the most thoroughly Christian spirit that I have thus far met in this world! And there is a real quality of admirable strength too — with the sentiment and the kindliness.

But it is rather futile to stumble about for the words to describe what I am trying to say... and also, I think, unnecessary. You have already generously shown me that you understand my appreciation of your spirit — and you give me a very happy share in the letters which you send to me. And it gives me strength and independence of feeling — it really and honestly does. It makes the temporary discouragements, irritations, and depressions of the day seem very unimportant. Do you understand this? I ask, because I am expressing a very deep feeling so inadequately.

I meant to ask you if you enjoy James Stephens' writings — *The Crock of Gold* and his poems? He comes to America nearly every year to visit a friend of mine who has a delightful country place in Kentucky — called "Freelands" after the Galsworthy novel. I met Stephens there two years ago. He was so insignificant appearing, so strange — until he spoke. He would curl up in a chair (and I say "curl" literally) near the huge fireplace, and then when he began to talk he became a really very big person.

The only thing of his that I had read before I met him was *Etched in Moonlight* — which, at the time, I had thought very dismal and morbid. But afterwards I recognized that they were not really stories at all, but such collections of phrases to capture certain physical emotions — hunger, fright, disgust, and the like... which was interesting, if not too pleasant literary diet. But later, I greatly enjoyed *The Crock of Gold* and I like some of his poems tremendously. I shall have copied, and send to you later, a poem which he wrote for me — a slight verse but very delightful. It was a very interesting experience meeting and talking with him. I may see him again this year, but it is improbable as he usually returns to England by October.

He spoke very beautifully about your majesty although, as there were other guests always about, I did not have a proper opportunity to talk to him about his visits to your majesty, as my impression is he said he had visited Bran. And of course, at that time I had not even met Eleanor, although of course I had a real interest in everything concerning the Queen of Roumania!

I have meant too to ask you what you think of Shaw? I was never a great admirer of Shaw — too much sparkle. But other people's views of his work always interest me.

But I will not prolong this letter — except to say once again that I do hope you will not mind my having written to you in England and sending the Volume One for an inscription... I simply could not put aside the urgent temptation!

With every affectionate wish — ever and always,

Ray Baker Harris

Her Majesty, MARIE
Queen of Roumania

XIII

October 5, 1934

Your Majesty,

What a quandary! My review copy of the American edition of your book came last night, and I am more delighted with it than I was with the English edition. Scribner's have certainly produced a very beautiful volume, and the sepia photographs are most satisfactory — very much more attractive than the black and white reproductions.

So I am afraid I shall have to keep *both* editions in my library! Sometime when you could conveniently do it, would you be willing to write a little inscription to me on a card which I could insert in my American copy? I shall of course have the inscribed English edition, but I am so greedy that I want to have a personal touch from your majesty in my American edition too. A card would be the simplest way.

Have you seen the enclosed circular. Scribner's have sent me a large supply of these, and I am mailing them out to a great many people whom

I think will wish to have the book — and in a great many instances I have also written personal letters urging my friends to buy the book.

I am very excited about the book, and I know you will be delighted when you see the American edition. I feel sure it will have great success here. It is to be formally released on the 15th of this month, and I have written a review which will be published in a Washington newspaper on the 20th, and I hope this will be helpful.

I have read the London *Times Literary Supplement* review, and although the review itself impressed me as being rather dull, I was very pleased by its favorable tone. It was not in the least critical.

Eleanor is back in Washington and frightfully busy with the "getting started" days at the school.

There would be much to write to you, but I shall save all my own news for a letter to Bucharest later, because I know your majesty has little enough time for letters while you are visiting in England.

With many good thoughts and affectionate wishes — always,

Ray Baker Harris

Her Majesty, MARIE
Queen of Roumania

XIV

October 15, 1934

Your Majesty,

What can I say? — from all the thoughts and deep sympathy I have felt for you during these past six distressing days. I know that your great heart will suffer all that Princess Mignon suffers, in addition to your own deep grief — and my sympathy and every understanding thought is with you each day.

On Tuesday morning I had just learned that your book would be put into Braille immediately, and would be available for blind readers in America before the end of year. The government is doing this. Each year, $100,000 is appropriated by Congress to be used for the manufacture of books into Braille for the adult blind, and these Braille copies are distributed to libraries in all parts of the country. I had gone to the Director of this Project, suggesting that your book should be made available for blind readers as soon as possible. He was not sure it could be included under this year's appropriation, but he said he would try to arrange it; and Tuesday morning he told me that your book would be put into Braille at once. I was very happy about this, and knew it would please you, so I sent a cablegram to you at London. And then, a few hours later the terrible news about King Alexander reached America. I cannot adequately describe my feeling of acute distress, because I quickly thought of all the suffering this tragedy must cause.

It is so difficult for us to understand here how such an awful thing could happen. Some reports say that the police protection for the royal car was inexcusably inadequate.

Eleanor long ago told me of what you had written her about the happy family life at Belgrade, and it tears my feelings to shreds to even think of the sorrow this insane deed has brought to your daughter's home.

I am enclosing a little article written for Americans by Princess Marthe Bibesco who is now visiting in Washington. There were many European visitors in Washington, attending the international aeronautical conference here, and as there were many among them who knew the King, and his work, Washington was unspeakably shocked. All social life stopped abruptly, and the grief and sympathy had a personal, quite sincere quality.

I am very much affected too by your wonderfully kind note from London, which has just arrived today. It had such happy news about your wonderful reception in London, the success of your book, and of the pleasant crowded hours. It is so cruelly unjust that all your deserved satisfactions should be interrupted by such personal sadness.

There would be much to write and to tell you — but this is not the time, and I shall wait until another day. Your book was released today and I think it is going to be immensely successful. I have this morning mailed out several hundred circulars to everyone I could think of who would be likely to buy a copy, especially here in the capital, and I have added personal letters to my friends. I have also loaned one of my handsome pictures of you for a window display in the principal Washington bookstore, and my review of the book will appear this Saturday.

But I shall write you more about all this a little later. However, I am enclosing a copy of a little verse which James Stephens wrote for me when I visited with him in the home of a mutual friend a year ago. This little poem is about a cat, and I think it may give you a smile, even in these dark hours, because it so perfectly describes the feline complacency!

Meanwhile, please know that if affectionate sympathy and understanding thoughts can help — all that my heart can give are sent to you
each day,

                                                        Ray Baker Harris

P.S. I commenced to write this letter entirely in my handwriting, but
I had to give it up, because you never would have been able to decipher it!

Her Majesty, MARIE
The Queen of Roumania

XV

                                                        December 23, 1934

Your Majesty,

There is so much to write to you! One thing after another has been
happening to me since my last letter, and this is the first opportunity I
have had in several weeks to sit at my desk for a time without the constant
threat of interruptions and distractions.

A few days ago I mailed to you a book which I greatly enjoyed, and I
thought you would probably find it absorbing too. It is called *Things to
Live For*, written by Francis Stuart — a young Irishman. It is an autobiography of feelings rather than of events — written by a young man of very
deep sensibility with a very rare gift for relating his emotions in words. I
read the book coming down from New York on the train, when I was not
very much in the mood for reading. But the first two paragraphs caught
my attention and I continued to read and finished the last chapter as the
train came into Washington. It appeals to me as a very beautiful piece of
work, and I hope you may enjoy reading it. I shall be so interested to
know how you feel about it. These are the two first paragraphs in the
book which held my attention when I opened the book without any intention of really reading it:

"There is an emptiness within the human breast, a hunger for we
hardly know what, that is the deepest and wildest of all desires. It is the
falling in love with life, the dark deep flow below the surface. Subtle,
crude, beautiful, terrible. A few have dared to open their arms to it, to
plunge into it, and always they are wounded and humiliated, but they have
been touched, have been caressed by those fiery fingers that curved the

universe and there remains about them a breadth, a spaciousness, a warmth of genius.

I, too, have felt that hunger. I, too, have been wounded and humiliated. Above all, I, too, *have given that yen to life,* and now I look back over a dozen years or so as one might look across a stormy sea at night and see white crest after moonlit crest and hardly notice the long black depths between."

And now to my news…

Have you ever heard of Will H. Hays? He is now president of the Motion Picture Producers and Distributors of America — which is an organization of the motion picture industry as a whole. He is a sort of mediator in the industry itself, and represents the motion picture business in its dealings with others. Before that, he was the Postmaster General in President Harding's cabinet. From 1914 until the time President Harding was elected to office, Mr. Hays was chairman of the Republican National Committee — and in many ways, of course, was responsible for the return of the Republican Party to power.

Well, I had some correspondence with him about my President Harding biography. He had been courteous and helpful, but not especially enthusiastic as I suppose I was only one of many who sought similar information from him. But he had assured me that he was interested in my project, and so not long ago I sent him a rather long report I had written — outlining all the material I had thus far assembled for my book, with the explanatory notes concerning my viewpoint on certain episodes and events. This report also contained all my endorsements from people who know me, as well as letters from one hundred of the principal libraries in America stating that there is a definite need for the sort of book about President Harding and his era that I propose to write.

Last month I went up to New York to see Beverley Nichols (who later came down here for several days as the guest of the Attorney General) and I had only been back in Washington a day when Mr. Hays called me by long distance telephone. He said he had just read my report on the train on the way back to New York from California, that he wanted to help me, that he was "prepared to do much more than merely give information," that he wanted me to come up to see him at once and he would pay all my expenses. I had no idea at all what he could have in mind. I could not return to New York at once, but I agreed to go up last week — and did.

His proposition is this: He wants me to undertake to arrange ALL his political papers (correspondence, memoranda, documents, etc.) from 1914 through 1921 in chronological order, with the same sort of sum-mary report as I wrote for my own material. At the same time I can use from his papers anything which is pertinent to my biography of President Harding! He is to pay all my expenses while I am doing this work, and has offered me a flattering "honorarium".

It is a wonderful opportunity for me, and if I make good with it I think it will develop into further opportunities for me — aside from the wonderful material I shall have for my book.

I was with Mr. Hays in his private office for two hours, and afterwards I went down to talk with a friend of mine — Mr. W.T. Howe, president of the American Book Company (which publishes most of the College and University text books in America). Mr. Howe is a very scholarly but also a very practical business man, and I wanted to get his reaction. He thought very well of the proposal Mr. Hays had made to me, and so I think I shall undertake the work shortly after the first of the year. I shall start off, I think, by asking for a "leave of absence" from the Library of Congress — so as to protect myself in the event the project doesn't live up to its possibilities.

But I am tremendously enthusiastic about it. The work will give me a wonderful knowledge of American political events during the time President Harding was in public life... with many facts never before published. As soon as I have finished the arrangement of these papers, I shall start in on the actual writing of my book — and hope to have it done before the end of the next year.

Please forgive me for writing so much about this, but I know you will understand my excitement in this new activity! Mr. Hays has sent a man to his home in Indiana to assemble all the political files and ship them on to New York. This will take several weeks, after which I shall go up to New York to look over the material with Mr. Hays, see how large a task it is, and make definite arrangements for undertaking it.

I found Beverley Nichols happy, healthy, and prosperous. He came over here only for a few weeks, to see the new plays, visit with a few friends, and to arrange some new contracts. He is to have new publishers in America after March of next year, which I think is a very good thing because his present publishers in this country have done very little with his books by comparison to their sales in England and on the Continent. *Cry Havoc!*, for example, sold more copies in the little country of Poland than in the entire United Stated — simply because the publishers here failed to advertise or secure proper publicity.

His new book, *A Village in a Valley*, is the third and last of the "garden" books. It is light, very amusing, and in parts very beautifully written. Occasionally, I think his books suffer a bit from lack of editing. He writes every book entirely in long hand, just as he feels about the subject at the moment. A secretary types the longhand, and Beverley is impatient about reading the typed manuscript — so that occasionally he lets "too much" creep in.

But of course I never read his books as disassociated from him personally and I naturally enjoy everything he has written, so that I cannot be a really good impersonal critic of his work. In the second place, I never criticize him at all to people who do not know him. And I never say anything which I have not already said to him. He has great talent, and as he is still very young, there are countless achievements waiting in his future.

Much to my astonishment and pleasure, his new book is dedicated to me. I mailed a copy to you as a slight Christmas remembrance, which I hope reached you safely.

I assume that Princess Ileana and family will be in Belgrade with you for the holidays, so that in spite of some shadows Christmas should be a very happy day in the Dedinje Palace! I shall be thinking of you, and wishing you much joy — and many satisfactions and happy days in this coming New Year.

Just a while ago I was looking through my engagement book. It is the only record I have of the past year, as I do not keep a diary. It is a little book, and has only initials and hours written in it — with now and then a word or two that has meaning for me. And so I have been seeing the whole year in this little book, and, everything considered, it has been a very good twelve months! The very greatest and most satisfactory experience of the past year has been this extraordinary opportunity to visit and "talk" with your majesty through these letters — to know your philosophy, to be inspired by your understanding and interest... no friendship with anyone has given me so much real and deep pleasure. I do say this with deep sincerity and entirely without affectation. It is one of the great privileges of my life to know your spirit in this unusual way.

I received a letter from Scribner's the other day, telling me that the second volume (the third in England) will be published here very early next year, probably simultaneously with the English edition. I am delighted by this, and look forward to its appearance impatiently. The first volume is still a best-seller in many cities here... and it is the sort of book, I think, which will keep on selling long after the first "best-seller" period. It makes a perfect gift, and most of my Christmas remembrances this year have been copies of your book. A number of friends, of course, already had copies.

Have you really started on the fourth volume? You will have one very fine advantage in the writing of the fourth volume. That is: you will be speaking, so to say, to an audience which already knows you. From the first three volumes they will have learned your nature, your spirit, your philosophy, and the events and people which have had a part in making your character. I should imagine that this would make it very much easier for you to write the fourth volume, in spite of the difficulties the task presents. You will not be obliged to explain yourself, because those who have read the earlier volumes will already, in measure, feel well acquainted with you. You will be speaking to friends.

When you may have the time to write me again, I hope you may tell me more about your English visit. Those first weeks must have been pleasant and exciting, and it is always a rare experience to see such things through your eyes — as I do from your letters.

I was interested in what you said in one of your letters about Lady Oxford. From what I have heard before, she is not the sort who would say she liked your book if she didn't — and I was pleased to hear of her enthusiasm for it. She has always impressed me as a highly individual, impulsive, and probably much misunderstood personality. Occasionally, she seems extremely self-centered, but one can understand that if one knows about her life. But she has had courage too, it seems.

Will you remain indefinitely in Belgrade? I hope the future for King Peter is in safe hands. We hear many political reports from Yugoslavia, but it is difficult to understand from this distance just what is going on. I can imagine that events have changed relations between countries in that part of Europe, but no one at this distance can really know very much about it.

The great controversies, in which there seemed to be so much *immediate* danger, seem to have quieted down; and the political writers here, who are supposed to keep in touch with European conditions, seem very optimistic about influences in the coming new year.

You would love Washington just now. We have had snow — for the first time at Christmas in the several years I have been here — and everything is very beautiful... the public buildings and the parks fit in perfectly to the Winter scene. I am sure you will remember the lovely, classic Lincoln memorial with the long reflecting pool... This pool is now ice covered, and many go there to skate — making it almost a carnival scene — and unusual in setting because of the long row of tall trees on either side.

Eleanor has gone home to Paterson for the holidays, and I wish I could call in to see them on Christmas Day in their new home. They are really a most delightful and usual family, and one feels happy and stimulated every minute of the time with them. When I was in New York the last times I talked to them on the telephone, but each time was so rushed that I could not get away from New York — as it is a rather long trip to that part of New Jersey and one would have to give over an entire day to it.

Eleanor has been teaching this year at school, as she doubtless has told you herself. And I think having a definite part in the faculty has given her a greater sense of responsibility, so that she takes a keener interest in it all. Of course, she always sees through sham very quickly, and there is always a certain portion of pose and affectation in the pedagogic life — a certain fear of being quite themselves before younger students. I think Eleanor finds it a little difficult to meet this, as she is always very frankly herself at all times, but she has tact and I think manages quite well. Anyway, it is excellent experience for her.

Oh, I intended to ask you before if you have seen the American edition of your book, and if you liked it? I think the illustrations are especially attractive in the sepia reproduction — and liked the book very much. I still like the two-volume idea best, and shall keep a complete set of the English edition.

I am enclosing an interesting article by Princess Marthe Bibesco which appeared last week in the *Saturday Evening Post*. Perhaps it has already been sent to you, but I shall enclose this copy anyway to make doubly sure. Of course all the facts she states are no new thing to your majesty, but I think you will like to see the way she has written her article. I found it very interesting, and it dispelled some of the confusion as to the royal "relations" which are seemingly so involved that I wonder even you can keep them straight. Do you never become confused by such a large number of cousins and nieces and nephews and in-laws?

I imagine you know very well the new Duchess of Kent? Her marriage to Prince George certainly gave the British public an opportunity to express their love for the royal family — a remarkable and stirring testimony. As I read the descriptions of the ceremony at Westminster, I recalled the last chapter in your second volume — when you faced your people, not on your marriage day, but when you were crowned Queen. Of course Prince George and Princess Marina faced no responsibility such as your majesty confronted... their life has more chance for continual happiness, as responsibilities and dangers will not press in from all sides.

One wonders how the Prince of Wales will be as King; if he will marry or be a bachelor king. Some have said he has no intention of being King at all, and that he remarked to the Duchess of York on her wedding day that she would one day be England's Queen.

It seems a little odd for me to be talking of Kings and Queens, Dukes and Duchesses — and to you! It is all so rather far from my own world. But then, as I have written to you before, writing to your majesty is very much as though I were sending messages to another planet — in these spirit talks; the only difference being that, instead of silence, an answer comes!

I am looking forward with intense anticipation to this coming New Year. Each New Year seems attractive, but this one more than ordinarily so. I have this new work promising so much of interest, the opportunity to write my book and do a real and worthwhile portrait of a man who has been much maligned and misunderstood (although my biography will not be a eulogy, it will be entirely fair, and nothing will be set down as a fact which cannot be proved as a fact); and the inviting possibilities of new acquaintances, associations, and new friendships. But now, and always, I think the most important friendship in my life is this one which is weighted by nothing material, which is sincere and a friendly meeting of spirits in exchange of ideas and thoughts — a friendship that will endure.

With many affectionate thoughts to you, and every wish that there will be many many satisfactions for you in this coming new year,

Ray Baker Harris

Her Majesty, MARIE
Queen of Roumania

XVI

March 16, 1935

Your Majesty,

Please do not consider it thoughtless of me to send you a photograph which was taken at a sad hour in your life; but there is about this picture so much of your spirit as I have come to know it. Although I had it copied from only a news photo, I feel very strongly about this glimpse of your majesty with little King Peter. There is courage and beauty in it. If you would not object to signing it, or perhaps adding a few words, I should be deeply proud to add it to my Roumanian portfolio.

I wonder if you are experiencing Spring days in Roumania such as the ones we have had here lately? It has been very warm, but Washington climate is incredibly treacherous, and more than likely we shall have a snow blizzard before March is ended.

Tomorrow evening my recently married friend and his wife are coming here for dinner. I have been very happy about their marriage, because in my friend's wife, Margaret, I have a new friend. And it might so easily have been otherwise. I don't mean any unfriendliness, but just a lack of mutual sympathies which would mean a gradual drifting apart from them. Instead of which, in these past few weeks, we have had several deeply satisfying times together.

A week ago we all went riding for the afternoon. The horses were frisky — not having been out a great deal in recent bad weather, and so we had our hands full but a fine time of it. The day was just right, the ground dry, but the March wind was about too!

There was one amusing incident which I must tell you. There were six of us all together, and in order to get from the stables to Rock Creek Parkway we had to cross one of the main motor drives, Connecticut Avenue. The horse of one of our party was being especially frisky and was somewhat ahead of the rest of us. Just as he came to the Avenue, a small roadster drove up near him and the driver thought he would be smart and make the horse more unmanageable by blowing his motor horn. It was very thoughtless, of course, and might have resulted in an accident to our friend. But instead the horse almost climbed in the car and just about scared the driver to death. He put both front feet up on the running board and snorted vigorously, and then turned and dashed across the Avenue and into the Park. It was all a very funny sight to the rest of us who were watching!

But there have not been so many such pleasant hours, because I have been swamped with work to do — both my own, and the work at the Library of Congress. Mr. Hays wanted me to come to New York this month, but it was out of the question and I had to beg a few weeks more time before undertaking the work he has in mind and which I am very anxious to do.

The Houghton Mifflin publishing house has asked me to send them a complete report on the present status of my biography of President Harding. A friend of mine told them about my undertaking, and they seem interested. I suspect they are principally interested in the fact that Mr. Hays' papers have been made available to me for my work. But I have been working very hard to get a report in shape to send them.

So these have been very busy days if not especially eventful ones. Everything has turned out so exciting and promising for me this year, and I am very optimistic about the immediate future, this year and the one beyond. There is so much to do, and it all seems clearly before me if I keep at it.

I was speaking a moment ago about my friend and his wife. You spoke in one of your recent letters about the power which women have, and what you said was so very true. This is an instance. Because, in spite of our long years of friendship in college and since then, the relationship could very easily have faded if his wife had not liked me, or I her. In just a few words, or even without saying anything directly at all, she could have put an end to an unusually strong friendly relationship.

And although I use this little personal example, it is a universal power I am speaking about.

The pity is that there are too few women whose spirits are as great and generous as is that of the Queen of Roumania. You are a force for good, a strong, direct, inspiring force. With many women I have met it has been quite the contrary — smallness, petty things, sharpness, unfriendly impulses, no matter how smooth and pleasing the surface personality. Especially it has often seemed to me that women are, generally I think, most uncharitable about other women. In commenting upon some action of another woman, I have heard women make the *least* charitable interpretation rather than the natural or generous one. Am I being silly to make these observations? Of course men do such things too, but speaking generally I think most men are inclined to overlook many small things which women generally pounce upon maliciously.

I am not making an all inclusive statement, because there are too many really fine and generous girls and women I have either known myself or known about. But I am speaking in a general away about the most one meets in the homes of one's friends, acquaintances, and business.

Will you think it presumptious for me to say that I have learned more from your book as to a women's heart and mentality than I have ever learned from any other source. But in your majesty it is the heart and mentality of a very extraordinary, a very kind and a very wonderful woman. And although I can understand and respond perfectly to your voice, it is not such a voice as I shall know more than a few times in my life.

It is incredible that I am writing to you like this. But to you, since have known your spirit, my thoughts find their way into words without halt embarrassment.

It has been experiences like this which have proved to me the presence of the forces, God they are called, which guide the universe and even small individual lives like mine. For time and again I have reached out to some attainment, and definitely and firmly my efforts have been frustrated by some combination of circumstances. And then when a little time has passed, my original objective is brought to me in a different but entirely recognizable form. Do you understand this? It isn't sentimentality, but *real* experience.

As I saw you when you came into the doorway of the Roumanian Embassy in Washington I longed for some opportunity to just meet you, to have a few words talk with you. But then your majesty never returned to the capital and such a meeting became entirely impossible. Years went by; I left Washington and was in New York more than two years. After returning here, I shared bachelor quarters with two college friends, one of whom knew Eleanor Horton. I met her several times, and then, by a sort of inevitable combination of circumstances, our "spirit talks" commenced — so much greater and fuller and more inspiring a meeting than would have been possible had I, as a very insignificant human being, joined in that endless parade of humans whom you met in America during your visit here.

This is, of course, the most wonderful experience I have ever had; but there have been lesser experiences that have been brought about and turned out to be so much better and more satisfactory than some original ambition or plan I may have had.

But it *is* amazing and extraordinary. Whoever could have thought (most certainly not I) that the one person in all the world to whom I could bring my thoughts and to whom I could walk most freely, would be the one I most admired but who also seemed the most distant — a *great* person and a Queen.

However, I seem to be getting too much into the First Person Singular!

Have you by now read the biography of the Empress Frederick just written by Princess Catherine Radziwill? I read it through at one sitting about a week ago. It is not a long book. To me, the book would do the Empress Frederick a greater service if it were not so obviously and vigorously partisan. But there seems much justice in her viewpoint.

The book begins with the romance of the old Kaiser, William I, who loved the Princess Elisa Radziwill. For the first time, I think, letters of William I to his sister, telling of his love for Princess Elisa, have been published. It seems that both families looked with much favor on the romance, but that the father of William I was obliged to forbid the marriage in the end because the Crown Council had ruled that Princess Elisa's family could not marry into the Royal Family without causing a misalliance which would alter the dynasty.

With this beginning, the author goes on to say that after William I married Augusta he never loved her, and she never understood him. So that when their son, Prince Frederick, married the Princess Royal he brought her from the comforts of Queen Victoria's court, and the liberal teachings of the father she adored, to the discomforts of temporary quarters in Berlin and into a household beset by feuds and jealousies, and bitter intolerance. Princess Catherine Radziwill portrays the Empress Frederick as having been independent, ill-advised, and probably often tactless — so that she had a very bad time of it in Germany.

The Empress Augusta is portrayed as an ambitious and politically active woman who, failing utterly to influence her husband, had found her son no more pliable but very much in love with his wife; and that in later years the Empress Augusta had flattered and spoiled her grandson, William II, and helped to estrange him from his parents.

I am telling you all this merely as Princess Radziwill sets it forth in her book. And as I say, the book is from beginning to the end a very strongly worded defense of the Empress Frederick.

The Empress Frederick seems a very tragic figure, and the victim of much denigration.

I think the book has also been published in England and you may have already read it. If not, I would be delighted to send my copy, because I am sure it would interest you. Naturally, I am interested in your majesty's impression of the book, since you know the true facts already. I noticed that in your book, however, you did not mention the Empress Frederick at much length, and that your childhood impression of her was a conflicting one.

Have you ever, by the way, read any of the novels by Claude Houghton? Hugh Malpole and Clemence Danc, and a few others are unusually enthusiastic about his work and feel he is one of the truly important writers today. I have just read *Neighbors,* which I think was his first book, and I am uncertain in my feeling about his work. The novel was brilliant really, but also quite eerie. It goes almost too far beneath the surface, if you know what I mean. I just wondered if you had read a book by him, and what you thought.

I am seeing Eleanor tomorrow. She goes home for the Spring holiday sometime next week, and needs the rest I imagine. This year she has had quite a burden of responsibility at the school, but seems to thrive on it too!

Will you soon be going to Bran, or Balcic?

By the way, Gertrude Stein is in this country, and has become somewhat of a fad. She is lecturing and being popularly received everywhere, and very much acclaimed. I'm afraid I cannot join the chorus. I think she is an unusual personality, and her friends are devoted to her; but do you receive any sensation but annoyance in reading her peculiar writing? I'm enclosing an article she wrote which appears in today's New York *Herald-*

Tribune. Don't you think it's awful? What she has to say, if you manage to struggle through what she has written, could be very clearly stated in one short paragraph — and the observation wouldn't be very unusual or penetrating either. It's clever, I suppose, but freakish.

On the other hand, I heard her make a little talk over the radio. She has a really marvellous speaking voice, low and full and rich, and I could gladly ignore the words for the pleasure of hearing the voice... but reading it is another matter!

Do things seem more optimistic in your part of the world? Reports here say that restoration of the monarchy in Greece seems almost certain within the next few months.

Tonight word comes of Hitler's armament announcement, which sounds a little ominous... but surely it is not a surprise to the rest of Europe.

But you hear enough of these things.

I have written to Scribner's to ask the definite date when your book will be ready. They had previously promised me an advance copy this month, but apparently the publication date has been delayed. I am most impatient for it, because of course it will all be entirely new — none having appeared in a magazine. It covers such tempestuous and dramatic and intense years that I am eager for the experience of reading about it all.

I have a very attractive and understanding aunt who lives in California. Her home is on a very steep hillside, overlooking a large and incredibly blue lake, backed by green hills, and then the higher ranges in the background mounting into the blue heights of the Sierra Madre mountains — in sight of snow-capped Baldy Peak (what a name!) a magnificent summit. I have had some very happy times there. Not on the peak! But at my aunt's house.

But what I start out to say was that at Christmas time last year I sent her a copy of your book. She had already read the parts which appeared in the magazine; and she knows nothing whatever of my "talks" with you. But a few days ago she wrote me again in appreciation of the book, saying in part — "...there is something very, very lovely about Queen Marie — a very brave and courageous woman; richly gifted, don't you think? I retain the vivid impression of sensitiveness, color, romance and so much that is truly fine in her rather rare and sympathetic character..." And this came very spontaneously, because I sent the book to her without any comment of my own; and as I said, she knows nothing of my "talks" with your majesty, or of my strong enthusiasm and admiration.

But this is the same response I have had from most people; and your majesty has of course received many such expressions from all parts of the world.

This has turned out to be a long, rambling letter of many different thoughts. I hope it has not burdened.

Every affectionate devoted thought — always,

Ray Baker Harris

Her Majesty, MARIE
Queen of Roumania

XVII

August 8, 1935

Your Majesty,

Yesterday I returned here from New York, and waiting for me on my desk was the perfectly inscribed three-volume of your *Story*. They were just the right lines from the Prayer, and pleased me so much more deeply than I can possibly tell you. The two photographs also came back safely and I am very grateful for your majesty's kindness in signing them for my Roumanian portfolio.

It has been nearly eight weeks since the last letter I wrote, and all the hours since then have been crowded ones. I went to New York to do the special work for Mr. Hays, and it proved to be a more burdensome task than I imagined. Of course it was interesting, and also it gave me much useful information for my book. I had only Saturdays and Sundays for weekend escapes to Long Island or to Connecticut. Mr. Hays seemed very pleased with what I had done, and before he left for California he proposed that I undertake some further work for him when he returns within a few weeks.

But at the moment I cannot seem to bring myself to decisions, and I have not much time in which to consider my impulses... If this letter reaches your majesty at a time when you may perhaps be free to write to me, I would greatly appreciate hearing of your reaction to a course of action which I have lately been considering with some seriousness.

Several possibilities are open before me at the moment. Mr. Hays' proposition is enticing, but, unaccountably, I have an uneasy feeling about him. He has been very gracious to me, but he is an elusive individual and I would be reluctant to place myself too far in his hands. I think, and this is of course expressed confidentially, that Mr. Hays is concerned first and last by the interests of Mr. Hays. His long political activity, and his present chairmanship involving him with the shrewd and selfish motion picture producers, make him an elusive business-diplomat. It is difficult to quite explain my feeling about him. I like to have association with people who are direct and frank and dependable, so that I know where I stand.

Ordinarily, I think I would enthusiastically take advantage of even a brief association with Mr. Hays, if only for the experience and associations with others in the business world that it would afford me. But lately another idea has been claiming my enthusiasm.

I have been thinking of returning to college! It has been fully ten years since I was last in school. I did not go ahead and finish college because of temporary financial difficulties. I probably could have managed it financially, but just when things were difficult I was offered a very flattering editorial job with a magazine in New York. Having been in school so long, I was anxious to be "on my own" and so left college and went to New York. That was in early 1928, and I have been doing editorial and writing work continuously since that time.

If I were married, or I suppose even if I were in love, my professional career would be too important for me to sacrifice my present opportunities and associations.

But I do not have anyone wholly dependent upon me, and as I look back at the past few years they have traveled with unbelievable swiftness. Why not, I have recently been asking myself, go back to college for a few years. The University training, the associations of the campus, would seemingly have a greater influence on my later life than the same time occupied otherwise. And life stretches so many years ahead of me. I am 27! Why not gamble a few years. Of course it is not possible in a letter to tell you the countless thoughts on the subject that have occurred to me during the past few weeks and months.

I am enclosing a letter which I received a short time ago from the Dean of Men, at the University of Stanford — in California. It explains itself. I wrote to him, gave him my past school record and an outline of my activities since leaving college and asked him if he thought I should attempt to return to school, after ten years. As Dean at Stanford for many years, I was sure he has many times met others in a similar quandary. His reply is friendly and encouraging, but this is not entirely a disinterested viewpoint.

Of course, going back to college will not be an easy adjustment. As he says, it will take a good deal of courage — particularly during the first year. I will have to take my place with many classmates much younger than myself — some studies will seem tedious and useless — many of my present enthusiasms, and much of my freedom now would necessary have to be sacrificed.

And yet, I have an inner longing to make the attempt. To finish the University, secure my degree, make new friendships...

It means giving up my present income — and, with very little coming in and a good deal being paid out for two or three years ahead. But I could manage it now.

These are more or less random thoughts, and I probably am not presenting the picture to you very clearly. But, merely on the face of it, I wonder if you believe I would be wise or foolish to "go back" to University?

If I do decide to do it, I think I shall undoubtedly go to Stanford. I would like to be on the Pacific coast. I have an uncle who is a Supreme Court (State court) Judge in California, and another uncle very well known in Southern California. But there are incidental considerations — as I should he closely confined to the University campus except for holidays.

But I have been so long in the Eastern United States that I would like to be in the different environment of the West coast — and it is a different tempo and viewpoint out there. Stanford is one of our finest American Universities. President Hoover graduated there, and is now a Trustee and lives near the campus — his home being nearby at Palo Alto.

It would be terribly difficult getting back to classrooms and lesson assignments again! However, I think it would do me good.

Really, I am imposing upon your majesty's kindness and patience with this long recital in the first person singular. Please forgive the imposition, and I shall mail this letter only because I know that the enthusiasms and problems of the young are of interest to your majesty.

This is, however, a decision which may very well change the entire course of my life.

Another consideration is that Mr. Hays is a good deal in California and my being at Stanford would make it possible to keep in some touch with him, though I could not undertake anything which would interfere with my studies. So I would not be losing that association entirely.

My first year, of course, I would have to drop nearly every one of my present outside activities and devote all my energy to making a successful "return".

But I could talk on and on about this, and become less and less coherent! So I shall close this topic. It is needless for me to say that whatever opinion your majesty may send me will help me to crystallize the feelings which I now have, and when next I write I shall doubtless have made some decision. Whatever is decided, this Fall and Winter will be intensely active for me.

To change the topic (which seems difficult now that I am "unwinding"!), did your majesty receive the book *The Belvidere Hounds* which I posted some weeks ago? I hope you found the book amusing. The dogs had been given such absurdly human expressions that the volume gave me much amusement, and I hope you may have found it amusing too.

I shall be in Washington for some time to come, going away only weekends to the Virginia ocean shore.

I wonder if your majesty is at work on the fourth volume. It is eagerly awaited, and I have already placed an order for it with Cassell. I imagine many others have done the same thing, so that I imagine the publishers in turn are importuning your majesty for the manuscript!

I have also sent an order to England for a copy of *Masks*, but the bookseller has not reported to me as yet so I imagine the publication date is not announced. I am deeply interested to read this "present-day" story.

No letter has come in many weeks, but I only assume this means crowded hours for your majesty. I mention this only because I hope that no letter has been sent that may have gone astray. It is ever a new and exciting experience when one arrives — as though it were the first one I had received!

One thing would make the difficult adjustment of going back to college somewhat easier — the privilege of writing my impressions and problems to you.

I saw Eleanor Horton some days ago — looking very well despite her summer studies in terrifically HOT Washington. She returns home to New Jersey Saturday.

I feel this is not a very good or successful letter — written as it is in some excitement and uncertainty. But I shall write a letter of more general interest another day.

With every devoted wish and thought always.

Ray Baker Harris

Her Majesty, MARIE
Queen of Roumania

XVIII

August 17, 1935

Your Majesty,

In the letter which arrived yesterday you say that it was written at Castle Bran, with a pouring rain outside. It seems almost as if that rain might have followed the letter all the way to America, because both yesterday and today have been very rainy and stormy.

But the storm outdoors, and every petty problem of the moment, seems very far away as I read again your wonderful letter and commence to "talk" with you. Just because our material lives do not come together, and because our friendship is entirely in these spirit talks, there is, as your majesty has said, there is a splendid freedom in our exchange of thoughts which would not be possible otherwise. I do appreciate and very deeply respect the trust which this privilege implies.

There are several subjects which your letter brings to my mind, and I shall refer to one or two of them during this talk. But first let me say how sorry I am to hear about the political ruling which prevents Princess Ileana and her little family from visiting in Roumania this Summer. It is understandable that important members of the Hapsburg might reasonably be excluded from the country under present circumstances, but when the Hapsburg royalty is a sister of the Roumanian King it does seem absurd and small to take such action. Politicians seem to be alike the world over!

A few days ago I wrote to you concerning my thoughts of returning for two years or so to University life, to complete my degree. I don't recall exactly what I wrote, but it was probably rather incoherent! It wasn't exactly an enthusiastic outburst, because I have long had the idea in the back of my mind. But only recently did I take any tangible action on the idea — writing to the Dean about my possible entrance at Stanford. I am very seriously considering this course, but I'm afraid it must wait for another year. It is only one month until registration closes for the school year which begins in the Fall, and there are so many matters of "unfinished business" to be attended to before I could cut off my present activities and enter into University life once again. And I would not want to begin on a new course with a score of things left undone... much as I should like to act without delay.

I hope very soon to have my book finished, and I could not very well take so time-consuming a task into days where every hour would be exhaustively consumed by the demands of the University courses. By this time next year my book will be in print — if it ever is to be published at all, which now seems so very promising. I have just had a letter from Houghton Mifflin again, offering to help me in every possible way in the preparation of the final manuscript.

I think I mentioned that Mr. Hays wishes me to do some further editorial work for him. This I could do "on the side" and it would be useful experience. I would not be willing to place myself very completely in Mr. Hays' hands, because he is much too much a politician by temperament. He has been astonishingly generous to me thus far, but I think I know the man. It is not a matter of much importance but, I think this illustration will convey what I mean. He may propose a project, enthusiastically, in a very specific way... and with every apparent intention of living up to his proposals. Then, a little later he may think of another course which would benefit him personally, and without further word he will promptly pursue the second course no matter how others may be affected by his altered action. Thus far, this characteristic has not touched me in any way, but I have observed instances of it that others have experienced. And I have observed that it is difficult to arrive at any definite understanding, such as an informal written agreement even. One has to be entirely at the mercy of his whim — as all his proposals are made by telephone or in personal conversation. So one must play his game, and keep independent. It is instructive, and also somewhat amusing.

But enough of this, except to say that I am not abandoning my plan of returning to University (to Stanford, in California), but I'll have to put my house in order beforehand.

I was deeply interested in all you mentioned about the Empress Elizabeth. It does seem as if she lived a selfish existence. What a great life she could have lived — her beauty and inexhaustible material wealth — if she had possessed perspective, if she had had strong interests beyond herself. I have not read the Corti book, but I want to do so and shall get a copy.

Thank you so much for giving me your impression of President Wilson. This interested me intensely. First, because I had never been sure of my estimate of him since I was so much prejudiced against him by all that I heard at home when I was a small boy during the War. I remember that my father would regularly "hold forth" at the dinner table with devastating contempt of the Wilson domestic policies. If it had not been for the War, he would never have assumed such stature — because he was widely unpopular in America for his domestic policies. But the War submerged all those considerations, and of course it became almost high treason to say a word against him during the War, because of his high position.

I agree entirely that Wilson at the Peace Conference was very much inflated! In the first place, he had no business at council tables. His representatives and ministers should have been there — with those of other nations. He could have been in Paris, so as to be available for immediate conferences, but for him to enter councils personally seemed very unwise to Americans, even then, and was the beginning of his quick decline in public support here. As president of the United States he had an anomalous relation to other delegates at the Peace Conference. They were obliged to show him all the deference due to a sovereign, and at the same time carry on the discussions of Ministers and Ambassadors. Wilson played the dual role of King and Prime Minister *in person*, and it gave him a unique and undeserved prestige at the Conference.

I was very interested to learn your estimate of him, because I am a great admirer of your majesty's ability to see people as they really are. Your portraits of people are never spiteful or bitter, however critical, but what you say has a mirror-like impersonal clarity. I have never read anywhere else such obviously *true* human portraits. So, I particularly wanted to know how President Wilson impressed you at your meetings in the Peace Conference days. The comparison with the minister in "Rain" was most apt, and I had never thought of it.

Also it was most interesting to hear about Princess Mary of England. The British Royal Family today is of course entirely worthy of all the great respect and admiration which their Empire, and many people of other nations, feel for them. But it is very interesting to hear a first-hand description of their characteristics as individuals. Prince George seems to be the most imaginative and interesting, although I do not know if this is true. But in recent years even the Prince of Wales seems to have taken on a rather "plain" attitude, even though he may be in opposition to the King's "steadiness". But, of course, it is impossible for one outside of that world to judge, and as I do admire the British royal family it is very interesting to me to hear about them from one who is in their world and, what is more important in such a judgment, also one of their own Caste.

By the way, I suppose you have heard that Lawrence's *Seven Pillars of Wisdom* is just being published — in an unabridged, full text. Till now we have only had the very abbreviated text of that work (*Revolt in the Desert*). It is not being published in America until September 27th, and I am looking forward to reading it — although it is a huge work and will have to be read leisurely if it is to be enjoyed or absorbed.

I was also interested to hear that James Stephens spoke at your majesty's literary banquet in London. He is really a genius, and a *great* poet. But when a genius happens also to be an Irishman, the result is usually entirely baffling. One cannot help liking the Irish nature, usually; but I have observed that on closer acquaintance one begins to discern a certain quality of insincerity toward the outer world. Do you believe this is a national characteristic? Of course I do not know about Stephens, I have known him only at his best — we both being guests in the home of a mutual friend. And I greatly like his writing. It has even helped me at difficult hours, and given me pleasure at other times. The sly wisdom in *The Crock of Gold* and the deep sensitiveness in his verse, not only sensitive but also often delightfully humorous. But as I said, the personality of the individual — the combination of Irish and genius is a baffling result! To mention only one other — Shaw!

I should think that a serious biographer of Bernard Shaw would lose all sanity! A good deal of Shaw is, I'm afraid, very much beyond me. Some of his earlier work I like very much, better than things he has written in more recent years. But who could genuinely understand so contradictory an individual?

I have never read Charles Petrie's book *Monarchy*, but it sounds very interesting. There is doubtless a copy at the Congressional Library, and I'll have a copy sent to my desk on Monday. It will be good to read a book on the subject which deals with it carefully and logically.

That is wonderful news about *Masks*. It would be good if some of the earlier stories were now reprinted, because the public now knows a good deal of the personality of their author from the *Story*, and could therefore read the novels with more understanding and enjoyment.

About friendships — It is helpful to me to read the thoughts which occur to you on this theme. Wherever a relation goes beyond casual acquaintance, the adjustment is not easy — and always there are different considerations with different individuals. And whenever the sentimental phase enters in — *what* disturbances life can provide!

Even between two men the quality of sentimental feelings can be a bad problem. I had not been out of school very long before I ran into some of these problems. These are thoughts which one seldom discusses, and this is *the very first time* I have expressed them on paper. But as your majesty has said, there is a freedom in our talks which allows for all subjects to be discussed.

My only friendships which have endured have been those free of the encroaching, possessive quality of sentimentality. Affection can be deep, but affection and sentimentality are distinct and separate, don't you agree?

When I first went to New York as an assistant editor on a magazine, I met a very personable young man of about my own age — intelligent, clever, and a pleasant companion. We had mutual acquaintances, saw each other frequently, and got on very well together. His manner and his interests appeared to be as masculine as my own, and so it was with some incredulity that I later began to observe a sentimental strain becoming more and more obvious. Finally he discarded pretense altogether and became openly so sentimental that he would take me to task for not responding as he felt.

It was extremely difficult for me. I knew how to recognize the usual individual of that temperament — the very obvious for whom one only feels a deep pity because Life has created them, through some quirk, as aliens in this world. But the friend I am speaking about had none of those characteristics on the surface, and he was liked and admitted in groups where that temperament would not be tolerated. It was difficult to grasp. But I liked him as a friend, and when he discussed his hidden feelings very frankly with me I thought it was possible to sympathize and understand. I recognized similar tendencies in my own nature — that is, I am inclined to strong feelings for friends, loyalty and affectionate impulse. But I very soon discovered that what was an entirely controllable impulse in *my* nature, was on the other hand an uncontrolled obsession with this friend. What made the relation all the more difficult was the fact that he was an entirely *decent*, well-bred, intelligent, and thoughtful person.

I cannot assume a superior, inflexible attitude toward others. For myself, it is impossible for me to escape — even if I should wish — from the influences of my home while I was a boy. It is almost a physical barrier to occasional impulses, difficult to describe. My conscience and a sense of good taste, and a desire to never hurt others, is all the moral rule I live by. Even so, I'm far from being as good as I could wish to be!

But the reins I keep on myself, I cannot hold in my mind when considering the actions of others. I have an instinctive sense of other people's points of view, I want to understand, sympathetically, different kinds of people — not to judge or preach. I would hate to go through life, as some others do, so infatuated with my own views and opinions that I would be figuratively wearing "blinders" which would prevent me from seeing and knowing any sights except those directly in front of me along some narrow road. This is rather poorly expressed, but I am sure you understand my thought.

Well, to get back to this friend. I could meet his feelings only so far and no further. I have retained his friendship, because he is a worthwhile person, and we keep in touch. But naturally the full, personal friendliness of our relation in the beginning had to be adjusted to an impersonal, although a friendly but independent relation. I have affectionate regard for him, but open sentimentality (as an every-day circumstance) made me acutely uncomfortable and it couldn't be endured.

That was nearly eight years ago, and in retrospect it doesn't appear as difficult as it actually was. Because in the beginning I tried to believe his temperament was merely impulse which I could understand and endure. After all, every one longs for affection and I could not but feel a pride in the regard which he had for me. But it was finally necessary to come to an understanding with him.

Since then I have had some similar experiences, but in very minor relationships which were much easier to handle. Of course one has all sorts of acquaintances, but when it comes to friends, there is one thing which I will not tolerate in anyone if they are to be more to me than casual acquaintances — that is: Cheapness. I am not thinking at all in material terms, but in terms of spirit. People who *think* cheaply, or who live by cheap personal standards. It is perhaps not exactly the right word, but once again I must depend upon it that you will understand my meaning

But as your majesty says has been your experience too, the most satisfactory friendships with my own sex have been those based upon complete mutual freedom, without sentimental qualities intruding. When I first went to college I shared rooms with three other young men. During two years we developed a friendship that has endured until now, and which I expect to enjoy all my life. Two of the three have lately married. All the many experiences we shared together, our affectionate regard for each other was never manifested in any sentimental way. Perhaps, in certain circumstances, a handclasp would have added pressure if we were parting for a time; or an encouraging word in some difficulty; or the happiness in each other's eyes at reunions later... those were the only surface evidences of our feelings. And always we lived independently, had other friendships and enthusiasms. But we understood each other, and our friendships outlived many of our friendships with others. That is, my friendship with these three has outlasted many other relationships which were important for a time but slipped away, as so many relationships do.

My relations with girls have been both satisfactory and difficult. I suppose I shall never really know and understand a woman's heart and mentality until I am married and have had the experience of living day-by-day in a woman's company... even then, I fear the woman I marry will probably prove as elusive of complete understanding as seems inevitable! A woman's heart and mind seems to have many unfathomable depths. But I shall want to be very sure before I do marry that it is much much more than infatuation.

It is almost ludicrous the rapidity with which people marry and divorce these days. I do believe that if two people discover themselves entirely, unsuited, they should free themselves. But a little longer courtship would probably bring such discoveries *before* marriage.

To be frank about it: quick divorces only mean, at least usually, that the marriage took place only to satisfy the infatuation. And when the infatuation wears thin, they say they are "no longer in love" and divorce. When actually, it seems to me in the great knowledge of my 27 years (!), that they *never were in love!* When I marry, I hope I shall have the sanity to look beyond the immediate fatuation for other qualities upon which to base an enduring companionship. When the first infatuation passes, I hope there may be continuing joy in new phases — in the experience of knowing, *truly knowing,* the heart and mind and soul of my companion... an experience which should be as diverse and satisfying as the first infatuation. That is, I hope that infatuation will be only the *first chapter* of love, and not all of love. Perhaps this may be impossible idealizing, but I hope not.

And just because I look at marriage in this way, I must carefully avoid going too far into the sentimental stage with women friends. I have been fortunate in having several friendships which are without anything sentimental. One relation was in the beginning, but later turned into one of the nicest friendships I have ever had — a fine understanding and good companionship, but complete independence. She lately married, as I think I wrote to you at the time, and is now in Europe with her husband — not returning here until next year. She had a marvellous sense of humor and we had many good times together...

However, all this is endless... the complications and the satisfactions of friendship! I doubtless have much yet to experience and to learn.

To return to the every-day topics:

It would seem as though Italy and Ethiopia are inevitably going to War. I am glad that Roumania does not seem to be involved in this in any way — and I hope that the American government will manage to keep itself free of the mess. In international diplomacy America seems to have a genius for getting into impossible situation! If we had as many large colonial possessions as England has, I think we would be perpetually in hot water. As it is, our holdings in the Orient are danger enough.

This reminds me to send you a clipping from the July issue of *Scribner's* magazine — an article by Beverley Nichols, "Stopping Wars and Starting Gardens," which has a lot of truth in it. I was especially amused by the line: "I don't believe that most of the livers of Europe's statesmen are working at all...!" I think the article will appeal to you, as well as amuse you, for it has SENSE.

You asked about Eleanor. Unfortunately, I have seen very little of Eleanor Horton this year. About three weeks ago we had a very pleasant evening at a friend's home. But both of us have had very little leisure time this year, and have never been able to tell in advance when we could be free. So it has been difficult to make appointments. Also I have been away from Washington, especially at holiday times. As I understand it, Mrs. Holton, the head of the school, wants very much for Eleanor to stay with the school and teach for a time. In fact, I think she wants Eleanor to take over most of the history classes. This meant that, in addition to regular duties at Holton Arms, she also had to take some special history courses on the side — at George Washington University here; and then stay on part of the summer to take a summer course. It was a pretty heavy schedule, but Eleanor set in to do it and her determination has won out as she told me she had gotten through all the courses satisfactorily. She has gone home for a few weeks to New Jersey, before returning here next month for the Fall term at Holton Arms; so I imagine your majesty has probably heard from directly by now.

Eleanor is a very clever girl, certainly much more intelligent and poised than most girls her age. She is still impressionable, of course, but I think she has a good sense of values, and that she has a wonderful future ahead.

My young sister, "little Eleanor," is active and busy too these days. She has been studying music very conscientiously and seriously, taking advanced lessons from a fine Russian pianist here. Four hours a day, at least! I am glad not to be in the house during *all* the practice hours, as "exercises" can be maddening! However, I am really very proud of what she has accomplished along this line.

Did I tell you that I had finally managed to secure a back number of the *Illustrated London News* — for January 21, 1893 — which was a special issue in honor of your marriage to Prince Ferdinand. It has, of course, many pictures taken at that time.

Except for the autobiography I have had all of your books bound in a special uniform way — an attractive gray cloth, rough finish. I am having the *Illustrated London News* issue bound in the same way, and will send it to you in a few weeks — hoping you will inscribe it for me; and you can see the binding style, which I hope you will like. But it takes a little time to get this special binding done, so it will be awhile before I send it.

But this letter *must* be brought to an end! It has been long and rambling, and I only hope not a burden...

All devoted thoughts and wishes always,

Ray Baker Harris

Her Majesty, MARIE
Queen of Roumania

XIX

October 14, 1935

Your Majesty,

There is so much to write this time that I am uncertain how to begin! This is my first day back in Washington, and the morning mail brings me your majesty's good letter written from Bran... which I am just now reading again for about the sixth time.

Much to my dismay, I found when I returned here that the copy of Housman's *Victoria Regina* had not been mailed. I had packed and addressed it, but somehow in the confusion of getting away it was overlooked. I am forwarding it at once and hope it may reach you without delay. It is an interesting, unique "biography" and I was impressed by it, but your majesty can judge the book more knowingly and I shall be curious to know how you feel about it.

This reminds me to thank you a thousand times for suggesting Ann Bridge's *Illyrian Spring*. It came the day before I left for New York, the middle of last month, and I read it during the train journey. It had so much substance to the story, so much atmosphere, and all written so convincingly and intelligently. I liked it *immensely* — and hope I may one day enjoy a leisurely visit in the Dalmatia... and perhaps I may be fortunate enough to have my own life companion with me. One would want to share with another all the satisfactions of that beautiful part of the world.

I was so interested in what you had to say about your visit at Milocer, the complete happiness you experienced there. I can understand so well the deep content... easy, independent, entire friendliness with those you love... absorbing all the beauty in the surrounding setting... I am so glad that you could have all those happy hours in the midst of your majesty's busy life.

Several times in New York I commenced a letter-talk with you, but each time destroyed the pages... All the hours were so crowded, and I do not like to write to you when I am obliged to be in haste.

Mr. Hays astonished me by turning over to me a quantity of really important material for my book. Some of the things he has given to me to use will have real news value, and thus be a great help to the sale of my book. There are some papers concerning the underlying reasons for the opposition to the ratification of the Peace Treaty by this government, and these give facts which have never before been published.

Of course, I had to make use of these papers in New York, and it kept me very busy making notes and copying some of the important material and photostating some documents.

In addition, I had interviews with a score of important people, and had amazing good luck.

For example, I had a very long visit with Mrs. Helen Rogers Reid who is the owner of the New York *Herald Tribune*. She is a very attractive, cosmopolitan, intelligent woman, and I was very interested in glimpsing the Hardings through her eyes. After he was nominated for the presidency she went to Ohio to discuss with him some of the proposed official appointments, and after he was President she was many times a luncheon or dinner guest at the White House. She suggested many interesting angles and gave me some very useful material.

But all this is too long a story to relate. It suffices to say that the month's stay was very successful in every way. I talked with the editor at Houghton Mifflin Company and they seem anxious for me to send in the manuscript as soon as possible. They said that as soon as I had completed even half of the final manuscript they hoped I would send it in.

I have written a few chapters and have sent them off to some people who were in official life at that time and are in a position to give me constructive criticism.

It is really going to be an interesting book, and I am more excited the nearer I come to finishing the manuscript. As you can imagine, there is real drama in the story of any man who, from such provincial beginnings, rose to one of the highest offices in the world. I do hope my finished book will be worthwhile. I have put in a great deal of study on my subject, but I suppose that newspaper critics who have not studied it at all but who are steeped in gossip and general impressions will be supercilious about the book when it appears. But if I feel that the book is a good piece of work, that will be some compensation.

Mr. Hays wanted me to do some further work for him, but I told him it seemed wisest for me to concentrate on finishing my book before tackling another project. And if the book is successful I shall have time for a little vacation and will also be in a stronger position to choose what I want to do next.

My last week in New York, I went out of the city and stayed for the weekd at the home of some friends. They have just built a charming house, furnished in beautiful taste, and it is on a hilltop overlooking a lovely little valley — about eight or ten miles out of New Haven, in Connecticut.

So for three days I experienced something of the same quality of complete happiness as your majesty enjoyed at Milocer. I am very fond of this girl. It is her aunt who has built the perfect house I just mentioned. She is very genuine and sweet, and it is wonderful to know someone like her when so many girls are *so* supercilious.

We climbed fences, tramped across damp fields, walked up country roads — in all the beautiful color of a New England Autumn. Our only company was a little white dog who bounced along ahead of us and obeyed our slightest inflection.

The hilltop house overlooks the entire valley, and you can see the little village, the white church steeple. Do you know the picturesqueness of a New England village? I doubt if there are any like them anywhere, with their white houses, simple architecture, old world gardens... The nearest hills were of course brilliant in many colors, and the further hills were in deepening shades of blue... It is all impossible of proper description, so I shall stop stumbling around for words.

I wished very much that in some way, your majesty could have come quickly and immediately from Roumania, and been there in that lovely place with us. I know, without any doubt, that you would have enjoyed it deeply.

It is, I think, a tribute to the quality of our spirit friendship that I always wish to share with you each genuine and beautiful moment... from all that satisfaction in the New England countryside during an entire weekend... to the briefest moment of joy which can come, for example, when one is stirred by hearing again some forgotten song.

Again I am stumbling! But I think you know. And although if I were to be presented to your majesty, I could never say these things again... our material lives are so far apart and so unlikely ever to cross, and because of your majesty's great kindness understanding and generosity I have the great privilege of "geistergesprache" wherein I feel no self-consciousness in attempting to express any feeling or thought.

By the way, I am enclosing a clipping — an article on Royalty in general and the Belgian house in particular. He makes some good points and with an intelligent understanding. However, I believe it has been my extraordinary privilege to know something of the spirit of a modern Queen who is greater than them all! I say this with complete sincerity. I have never known anyone whose spirit and philosophy I could so wholeheartedly admire as I do that of your majesty.

I had not thought about that: if Germany would want volume III of your *Story*. But now that I reflect on it, the bitterness of the volume was directed more to "the war" than to the Germans as a people. If they did not resent the frank references to Kaizer Wilhelm's character, in the earlier volumes, I imagine they could bear and even admire the spirit of independence and bravery of Roumania's Queen during those war days. Of course, censorship is more evident in Germany than we realize here in America, and I do not know how the German Government might feel about the third volume. But it would be interesting to see how the people would take it.

On the train from New York into Connecticut, I read some parts of the unexpurgated edition of T.E. Lawrence's *Seven Pillars of Wisdom* which has just been published here. I believe Cape has published it also in England.

I like his prose, the sharpness and clearness of it; but parts of the book seem excessively dull, and again there are intensely interesting passages. I found myself wondering if, even in his writing he was not "covering" and concealing real feelings... I liked the expressions of his devotion to Lord Allenby... Didn't Lord and Lady Astor know Colonel Lawrence rather well? It would be interesting to see him through the eyes of people who really knew him personally.

Robert Graves wrote a book about him, I never could get into it very far. I like the vigor of Graves' prose, but there is a quality of his own personality which is distinctly repelling at times. I also disliked the way in which Graves ridiculed Siegfried Sassoon several times in recent years.

Incidentally... this year America is observing the centennial of the birth of Mark Twain. Many tributes are being written about him, and it is beginning to appear as though Mark Twain was the least common denominator, literarily, for the taste of modern authors!

Have you read many of his books? I should be very interested to learn how you regard his work...

This reminds me: If you have not read Francis Stuart's new book, *In Search of Love* — I think you would be disappointed in it. He has written it, apparently, as a sort of novelty... it is a satirical farce. Some of it is quite clever, but it has none of the richness or depth or real feeling of his other books.

If you have still been unable to secure a copy of his earlier book, *The Coloured Dome*, I am sure I could find a copy here and would be delighted to send it.

I received a report that *Masks* would be published in London early this month, so I am expecting to receive my copy by each foreign post. I am very impatient to read it, and will take the liberty of sending my copy to your majesty after I have read it — asking if you would inscribe it for me.

Did the Julietta Studio portrait, which I sent last month, reach you safely? I wrote to the Studio to ask if they would send me proofs of some recent pictures. These came the other day, and there were two recent portraits that were extraordinarily beautiful. I have ordered finished prints... to add to my Roumanian portfolio.

This is the football season in America. I like the game, and there will be several important matches here in Washington; and then I shall probably get away for a day to see some of the games at the Naval Academy, and there are several important games at Philadelphia.

I like this time of the year — in spite of the colorful departure of Summer. I like the activity, the crispier, the tempo of Autumn. Usually I dread Spring... the thawing out process, and invariably I manage to fall heir to some Spring malady such as poison ivy — or am obliged to go to the dentist! But after a lazy, warm Summer the crisp Autumn air is really a stimulating tonic...

Will your majesty be in Bucharest during the Winter?

I can understand why your people are anxious to celebrate the occasion of your majesty's birthday. It is an opportunity to demonstrate their pleasure and their pride — and, at this great distance away, I shall share in their enthusiasm.

What name have you given to the new chestnut stallion? From the way you describe him he must be a beauty.

I have seen so little of Eleanor this year. Of course, I have been away from Washington frequently, but I know that earlier in the year we made several attempts to meet for dinner or the theatre and often one or the other of us would be obliged to postpone the meeting... We have gotten together only about three times this year! Each time, of course, Eleanor was entirely like herself and we had enjoyable visits... But my impression is that Mrs. Holton, head of the school, urged Eleanor early this year to concentrate all her energies into completing some special courses that would make her eligible to teach history at the school. I think Eleanor decided she wanted to have this teaching experience, and has worked very hard to successfully complete the work Mrs. Holton has mapped out for her.

When I saw her early in August, just before she left for a short vacation at home, she seemed tired but apparently encouraged by success. After she returned home she wrote me a very nice letter asking me to try to visit them at Little Falls, but I did not go to New York until the middle of last month — and Eleanor was due back at Holton at that time. As I have only just returned, I have not had an opportunity to get in touch with her; but I shall do so this week.

I shall be here in Washington for the rest of the year, unless something comes up that I do not now anticipate. But I have so much writing to do that I don't plan to go away for anything in the immediate future.

I do want to go to Connecticut again for a few days — next month if possible. It was complete happiness in that pleasant hilltop house, and my friend there is a wonderful girl — the best I know.

It seems as though I had not even commenced to say the things I started out to write when I began this letter, but it is growing so long that I had better stop now...

I do hope that the Italian program is not causing too much anxiety in Roumania. It is causing a great deal of excitement in America, and I think we have a confused idea of the principles and issues involved.

My life, at the moment, is full of activity and high hopes...

Devoted thoughts and wishes — always,

Ray Baker Harris

Her Majesty, MARIE
Queen of Roumania

XX

January 22, 1936

Your Majesty,

This is one of those times when it is difficult to begin, because so many thoughts are crowding forward at the same moment. As a matter of fact, I think this will be one of those letters which I do not often write — since tonight there are many feelings as well as thoughts.

But first of all... I shall of course be very eager to hear about the audience you have given to Beverley Nichols. If the years have changed him, I am sure they have at least made him no less charming and agreeable. He has deep sensibility and very keen intelligence, and he has of course seen and known a great deal — yet he has kept his enthusiasm and what most impresses me, the capacity for instinctive, thoughtful kindness.

It was just a year ago that he was in America for a short visit. I could not put aside the impulse to tell him something of my unusual spirit-friendship with your majesty, and I allowed him to read a portion of one or two of the letters. There are only three of four others who have ever seen the letters, though quite a few have of course seen the portfolio of pictures and the books in my small personal library. But I thought that Beverley would understand, where most others could not, the special spirit... And I think he did, though our visit together was short and there was no time to really discuss any subjects logically at length. He was in America only two weeks. We had dinner and an entire even together in New York, and then here in Washington we had lunch and a full afternoon's visit.

Beverley is about nine years older than myself, and when he first knew me I was *indeed* an infant — with all the courage and presumption of my youthful ignorance, not very sure nor at all wise... And Beverley gave me friendship and encouragement, and I shall all my life be grateful for it — because it was just the time I most needed an older brother and a friend.

I was his secretary and editorial assistant on the magazine all the time he was editing it in America, and so I saw him every day for many months — in all sorts of moods and under all sorts of circumstances... so I feel that I know him well. And that experience taught me a valuable lesson — never to form judgments about people from hearsay or gossip. I have heard things said of Beverley which I *know* are not only untrue but absurd. He has been ridiculed unfairly. It has taught me to keep an open mind about all people — especially famous ones — until or unless I can form a judg-, ment from personal experience. I mean this in the personal sense, of course, since one inevitably forms impressions, or agrees... disagrees with the things people write, say or do. But I try not to be influenced in any way by *second-hand* evidence. Newspaper accounts, I have found, are *invariably* obscure and deceptive.

So I shall be very much interested to hear about Beverley's visit...

I had to send a brief word by cable the moment I heard of King George's passing... because I know how many, many memories the sad hour will bring to your majesty, and my sincere and understanding thoughts go to you at this time. I took down your *Story* and read again your account of the "beloved Malta days," and I felt how your thoughts would come down through the years since then.

As you can imagine, there is great sentiment for the King here. Every formal and even informal social plan was immediately cancelled. Congress adjourned for the entire day... a thing done only once before — for Queen Victoria.

This world-wide regard for King George is a *cumulative* thing. The Prince of Wales, although greatly admired, cannot possess that tremendous regard his father possessed — until he has won it, year by year, through his own reign. He begins with overwhelming good will from everyone, but he has difficult years ahead. One cannot help but reflect that his task would seem less formidable if he had a Queen by his side. It must be a cruel task to rule alone, even with the members of his family standing by to help him.

Since practically all my life has been lived within the period of King George's reign, I find it difficult to accustom myself to the idea of a new King.

I *do* wonder what Fate holds for England under Edward!

Your wonderful letter was here when I arrived at home this evening. I open each new letter with as much anticipation and excitement as if it were the very first one! I was delighted to find the beautiful little picture — where you stand at the old cross on the hilltop, overlooking the sea. It seems a wonderful spot, and everything I have connected with Balcic has a very special appeal for me. I am very happy to have this nice addition for my Roumanian portfolio.

This reminds me: I secured the other day a copy of the Kurt Heilsher book of views of Roumania, and I have forwarded it by separate post several days ago. I feel greedy and inconsiderate to make so many of those requests, but would Your Majesty please write a few words of inscription in it — possibly a little sentiment of appreciation about Roumania, or a notation about some of the views — anything which may occur to you. The views in this book appeal to me very strongly. My little sister was especially taken in by the beautiful costumes. I find the odd crosses, the strange architecture, and the magnificent countryside immensely stirring.

I read with understanding what your majesty mentioned of the official, formal, and military sort of life in Bucharest just now. It recalled very vividly a different picture: the one which Mr. Hoppe described, after his visit to Sinaia and to Bran. He spoke of how the family and the guests assembled for luncheon, and how, after your majesty and the King had entered the room and greeted everyone kindly, the meal was wonderfully home-like and friendly. Mrs. Daggett, as I recall, wrote similarly... of the perfect hospitality. You express it perfectly when you say "the home-heartiness." What a contrast it must seem for those who remember those earlier days.

It was interesting to hear of Prince Michael. The pictures of him in the press show him grown up rather quickly.

About Eleanor: By now your majesty will have received my last letter in which I referred to my visit with Eleanor just before Christmas. I cannot understand it, and it is a situation which I cannot get hold of... It is all part of a strange isolation, which all her friends have experienced except those who are in the school. When we see Eleanor she is entirely disarming, and when I left her last time I definitely had the impression that she had written a note and was writing a long letter during her Christmas holidays. I have been inclined to lay the situation to Mrs. Holton, head of the school, who, so far as I could judge, likes to absorb the energies and interests of everyone around her. But perhaps a letter came to you after you sent this one to me. When I can discover a tangible explanation, I shall speak frankly... but now it is entirely puzzlement.

I'm glad you enjoyed the book *Victoria Regina*, and I think you would have liked the play even more — it had more human appeal and less of satire. It has only ten of the thirty scenes which are in the book, and they are the family scenes — done with real feeling and respect.

I would be much interested to hear of the things which you are painting. Has any of your work ever been reproduced? This really interests me very much, as it is another expression of your spirit — as is your literary work with which I am already well acquainted.

Speaking of your writing... after some difficulty I have finally located a copy of the English edition of *The Story of Naughty Kildeen*, which is quite scarce. It has not reached me yet, but I have word from the dealer that it is on its way. I shall send it on a little later, asking if you would inscribe it, as I want to assemble a full set of your published work. I now have all but two or three.

I am enthusiastic to hear that the fourth volume is actually begun. Will it be ready, do you think, by the end of the year? That goes into such an active, full period that I know it must be difficult to decide on the form the book will take. But it is a period that appeals to me — it is of the days that Mr. Hoppe, Mrs. Daggett, and others have written about — days and hours which are characterized, I am sure, by the wide horizon of your interests and filled with rich activity.

Yes, I see very clearly how hopeless is the burden placed on great men today. Men in high office know so well the situation "behind-the-scenes" that it must be a terrible experience for them to see the flood of insincerity, demagoguery, and deceit of their contemporaries in politics and public office.

I have learned a great deal about this sort of thing from my work on the biography... and much of it I could not undertake to even begin to discuss in my book. But it has been a depressing enlightenment for me!

It makes me think of my ambitions and view of life as a young boy, when I aspired to do great work that would take me to high places... and now I wonder if I want to battle up there... but what we know seems not the deciding factor, and mostly it depends upon our natures... so I'll not speak for my future.

I am delighted to hear that de Laszlo is to do another portrait of your majesty, and I should think he could do it beautifully. How long does it usually take for a portrait?

Thoughts seem to be crowding back in ahead of my feelings... I am just reminded that I read a book by General Mossolov the other day. Your Majesty mentions him in your *Story*. He sets down a very interesting portrait study of the Tsar and Tsarina. Although he does not reveal any important new facts, he does add the account of numerous episodes and incidents to his study. He also had personal dealings with Rasputin. It is almost entirely concerned with the period before the Tsar's abdication. Except for the anecdotes and stories it would give you no new facts, but I imagine you would find it interesting.

Did you ever hear about the part Lloyd George is supposed to have had in cancelling the arrangements to bring the Imperial Family to England? I suppose this is not a fair question for me to ask. The daughter of the British Ambassador to Russia wrote a book not long ago and said that her father had received orders from Lloyd George instructing him to cancel the arrangements the Ambassador had made for the family to be put on board a British cruiser. This was, I believe, before they were taken to Ekaterinburg. Others have made the same charge, and Lloyd George, apparently, has never denied it directly — always arguing away from the point. If this is true, it seems disgraceful.

People are certainly strange... and I am continually being stimulated or surprised or interested or depressed by the friends and acquaintances in my immediate world. It seems impossible to ever be quite sure of any of them, but I have been gratified to discover that the years each bring a saner perspective — so that the everyday assaults on one's emotions can be reined in and kept in hand. I do not think I observe or feel less deeply, but one acquires a faculty for standing a little above it. I say this badly, but I am certain you will understand.

But it is the greatest strength and satisfaction to have *one* sure, entirely friendly relationship — removed from daily, immediate things — to which it is possible to turn. It means more to me than I can ever say — and it will, all my life. I shall never need any material thing that cannot be supplied from within my material world; so that my friendship with your majesty is a thing apart — something that will endure *every year of my life*, which no material change can alter. I do mean this sincerely — with all my heart.

I particularly hope to visit in England and, aside from London, I am wondering what sections of the country especially appeal to you? I had a friend who lived for a year or more at a town called Campden, in Glocester, I think, and he thought it the most beautiful part of all England. But I have heard very similar descriptions of Devon and also Lancashire. The coast country appeals to me, although I have heard very little about it first hand. However, I think I shall stay away from Brighton which has always sounded to me as though it were like the American "Coney Island" — an awful place.

By the way, I have intended to enquire before if your majesty knew very much first hand about King Constantine and Queen Sophie of

Greece? It does seem that they were the hapless victims of a ruthless war politics. Some of the facts have been coming to light in recent years with the publication of certain diplomatic papers, revealing the absurdity of the charges made against them during the war. But even after the war they seem to have had a very disagreeable time of it. It is puzzling that they did not have the strength to strike back effectively at their critics, and defend themselves in some public way — but they seemed to have been smothered by abuse and criticism. I should be very interested in anything which your majesty might care to tell me about them.

This reminds me that for some strange reason the book by the Grand Duchess Marie, which was to be called *Family Portraits*, has never been published. It was announced by the publishers more than a year ago, and then no more about it. I had a glimpse of her at a dinner when I was in New York during last October. I was rather surprised by a certain hardness in her expression, but this was also oddly offset by a certain tiredness or weariness in her face too.

There seems much more to write about, but I must not permit my letters to become over-long... and other questions can wait for another letter, when perhaps I shall have more news of consequence to relate.

Meanwhile, with my devoted thoughts and wishes for your majesty — always,

Ray Baker Harris

Her Majesty, MARIE
Queen of Roumania

XXI

On the Overland Express
Enroute to San Francisco —
June 22, 1936

Your Majesty,

It has been more than a month since I left Washington and although I have many times wanted to speak with you about all that has been happening — this is my first opportunity to write a letter. If only the distance between us could in some way be dissolved, so that I might step into your sitting room at Tena Yuvah and, looking out of those large windows toward the sea, tell you reflectively of the people and places and the thoughts which have been my experience these past few weeks... But I shall relate as much as possible in this letter.

At the present moment the train is passing through the northern part of Nevada. We have just left a very little town called Elko, and by ten o'clock tonight we shall have passed Reno — and early in the morning I shall be in San Francisco... But I had better begin at the beginning of my travels:

When I left Washington I went directly to Cincinnati (in Ohio) and from there drove down to "Freelands," Mr. Howe's lovely place in Kentucky which I am sure I have spoken about before... It was a wonderful beginning for my journey, a full weekend of complete happiness and friendliness, entirely stimulating and enjoyable.

A serious-minded interior decorator would probably find much annoyance at "Freelands", since Mr. Howe has arranged everything to suit his own tastes and his comfort. It is a lovely, rambling sort of house which has literally "grown" with passing years. The gardens are particularly satisfying, and there is also many acres of farm land woods. The house itself is on a hilltop above the Ohio river, and the sunrise over the distant range was a sight which I willingly left my comfortable bed at five o'clock in the morning to see — a beautiful sight that would give you the greatest joy.

It is difficult to describe, but Mr. Howe maintains a very special atmosphere at "Freelands"... No one who visits there fails to respond to it. About the fireplace in the evening we talk of worldly things as though we were not in the world, but at a place apart. There would be so many small things to relate about Freelands, but it all comes down to this: I have never known even the most fleeting unhappy moment during any of all the hours I have visited there.

We made friends there with three small red foxes which came down to the edge of the woods after sundown... It was great fun to watch them, and they were quite friendly and would come for bones that were left nearby... but it was never very long before the mother fox would suddenly put in an appearance and hustle her trusting youngsters off to the safety of the woods.

There were several interesting guests there, and Mr. Howe had invited two people who could tell me quite a bit about President Harding.

Mr. Howe is president of the American Book Company, and he is a brilliant literary scholar. For years he has indulged his disposition to collect "association" pieces, so that today he has what is a priceless association library. For example, he has the original letters exchanges by Edgar Allan Poe and Charles Dickens, inscribed copy of a book presented by Poe to

Elizabeth Browning, inscribed Shelley, Keats, Hawthorne, Byron — an endless list of all the literary great, each item (whether it be letters, or manuscripts, or inscribed books) revealing a relationship between well-known contemporaries. You would be fascinated by the intense human interest of this collection...

But the weekend soon ended, and I was on to less peaceful and serene activity! I drove back to Cincinnati early in the morning, along the hilly, winding roads of Kentucky — everything fresh and just released from the mists.

In Cincinnati I was met by a college friend of mine who is now practicing law in Ohio, and he drove me up to his home. We arrived in time for lunch and then he took me to meet two people who had known President Harding. They did not give me any information of special consequence, but I was interested and somewhat amused by listening to their rambling recollection of Ohio politics.

I was interested in observing my friend, whom I had not seen since he graduated from college in Washington a few years ago, from the school. He is ambitious by nature, but a scrupulously honest person, and although he did not say as much I could see that he is restless and unhappy because his present work does not give measure of opportunity he would relish. He is trying to make himself believe that he is satisfied to be "a country lawyer," but an unguarded remark now and then during our visit told me quite another story. If he were not so completely honest, so unmovable in his principles, he could doubtless go far in politics. He has a fine mind, a good appearance, and the training and education for the law. But he would never compromise with those who control political futures in his State, and they would be afraid to encourage his success. If he goes forward politically it will be because he finds a strength somewhere else than among the "political bosses." I think he would prefer a strictly judicial career, on the Bench, but even the Courts are tied up with politics — especially in the beginning, among the lower Courts...

Next day I went on to Columbus (Ohio) and remained there for nearly ten days, working continuously upon various matters concerning the book.

First of all, I had long talks with the man who was the Attorney General for President Harding. You may know that he came under very heavy fire after President Harding's death — too long a story to tell here. Now he is old and more or less disgraced in spite of the fact that he was never convicted of the charges brought against him. He is lonely, and talked to me at very great length. He invited me to go down in the country to his "shack" for two days. The "shack" is in reality a very commodious and comfortable lodge, beautifully situated overlooking some of the most entrancing countryside I have ever seen anywhere. When he was Attorney General some of the most important and influential people in the world had visited that "shack", and I wondered at the echoes of countless conversations held there in the past.

It is fortunate that I had the time to visit with him leisurely. He was inclined to ramble a great deal, although he never failed to eventually give me a reasonably complete reply to my inquiries. When he was talking of President Harding, I had the feeling that I could rely completely upon what he told me; but when he spoke of himself and of matters with which he has concerned, I was a little more wary. He had qualities which appealed to me considerably, but I think I retained an objective feeling about him. I think I understand now why Harding liked him and trusted him, but writing about it will be quite difficult.

I went to see Harding's nephew, a young doctor, whom I had not met before. When I was in Ohio two years ago I had visited his father (Harding's brother) who has since died. The doctor and myself struck it off very well from the first moment, and when I left Columbus we were good friends. He is an extremely intelligent, modest, and capable young physician. He has taken over the management of his father's Sanitarium, has a large consulting practice, and also lectures at the University of Ohio.

We got on famously, and he ended our first visit by offering to take off an entire day from his work and drive me up to Marion (Ohio) where President Harding lived, and out to the farms where Harding had been born, where he lived as a boy, where his parents had lived, etc. We did this, and it was a remarkable experience. Of course I got a great deal more out of it by going with him, because he told me many things as we rode along... and explained many points which came up at the places we visited.

I must tell you one amusing incident, which even now makes me feel a trifle ill. We stopped at one old farm house, where descendants of the Harding family live. These people, as a matter of fact, own the crib (a huge, home-made, wooden one) in which Harding spent most of his first few months on this earth. They had some other mementos, and the farmer was a very garrulous individual, full to the brim with local history... While he was talking and showing these relics to us, his wife disappeared. Soon she reappeared with two large glasses of buttermilk for the doctor and myself! Well, a good many years ago I fought it out with my family that I *would not* drink buttermilk. I hate the stuff, and thought I would never be obliged to drink a glass of it again. But here was this farmer's wife, smiling and friendly, so obviously sure that I must like buttermilk, so kind to have gone to the churn and brought it in fresh... I could do no more than drink down the awful stuff with a smile. The doctor, it turned out later, disliked buttermilk as much as I did... but he behaved the same way I did, and I hope the farmer's wife never realized how stiff a price she was making us pay for our visit.

After the eventful day, we returned to Columbus and I had dinner at the doctor's home. His charming wife, two husky youngsters and a baby girl only six months old, made up his little family... I envied but certainly did not begrudge him that happy home, the absorbing professional work that keeps his hours filled with activity he enjoys, the fine work for others that he does at the Sanitarium... his is certainly a life that must seem GOOD...

It was such a complete stimulating, friendly day that when I returned to my hotel room it seemed very bleak and unbearable. As I had accomplished nearly all that I had intended to do there, I asked the former Attorney General for another interview in order to settle a few points... and as soon as that interview was ended, I packed my bags and left for Chicago.

That is the one difficulty for me when traveling. In the company of people I especially like, or with old friends of whom I have been fond for many years, I am so raised in spirits and stimulated that when we are obliged to part — and all I have to be with are the unfamiliar walls of a hotel room — the sense of unrest and indefinite longing are very hard to endure. Marriage, I think, would probably provide that sense of stability and balance which single people have difficulty in finding at such times as I have described...

My first day in *Chicago* I went out to lunch with a classmate and former roommate of mine, who has graduated in medicine and is serving his internship at the Cook County Hospital there. I had not seen him in a long time, but after a little bit we bridged the distance easily and parted finally the same good friends we had been at school, with a renewed and better understanding of each other...

The hospital (which is a charity hospital, operated by the State) is not in a very choice part of Chicago, so I returned to my hotel with a very depressing recollection of dirty streets, and more beggars and derelicts than I had ever seen in New York. It is wonderful experience for my friend, since the hospital handles every variety of case. I noticed that he was sympathetic and kind with these poor people. He has not yet become hardened or calloused to pain and suffering...

After I returned to the hotel, a friend of mine whom I have known all my life — and of whom I think I have previously spoken to you — came with her husband. They have been married just a year, and are very happy, very active... not at all self-centered, but mutually interested in so much of the best that life has to provide. It was a great joy to be with them. They took me driving around the lake shore drive, through the shopping and residential sections... and I saw more of Chicago than during all of my other visits. He is teaching at the University of Chicago, and they live almost on the University grounds — a charming little home.

I had a very busy day, talking at some length with General Dawes. He was Director of the Budget under President Harding and had many sidelights to tell me, and I found him genuinely interested in my project. The entire Dawes family is very unusual. I heard a good deal about them from young Doctor Harding. How did the General impress you when you met him in America?

After only two days in Chicago I was on my way again. I stopped off for a day at Quincy (in Illinois) to visit the graves of my mother's parents, and to visit an Aunt whom I like very much. She is quite odd, however, and I wished that your spirit could have been watching during the day I was there. It would have tickled your fancy... This aunt of mine has had a very odd life, too long a story to relate here... but she is very emphatic in her views, and has no hesitancy in stating them clearly and fully. The temperature was almost 110° the day I was there, so I did not feel like tangling with her on any of her pet theories.

The next day I arrived in Kansas City... I had planned to stay only through the weekend, three or four days at the most. I remained two weeks! I was completely taken in by all that I encountered there...

It is a very up-and-coming middle western city. I found people there very susceptible to cults of one sort or another, various religious beliefs out of the ordinary, the teachings of the Swamis, and the like.

There is a comparatively new religious group there called the I AM. It stresses the existence of a perfect body, into which it is possible to ascend after one has achieved complete harmony, spiritually, with that perfect body. It teaches the practicability of ascension *before* death... and is led by a group of "ascended masters."

I must confess that it did not mean very much to me. I understood what they claimed, but I could not respond to it in any way. At the same time, I could see that others were deriving real inspiration from this teaching... that it was providing them with a poise, with a stabilizing force for their energies.

Where religion is concerned, I quite am prepared to believe in the experience of another... even if I have not had that same experience myself.

But this is a digression, because I saw these things only very indirectly.

What really kept me in Kansas City, long after the time I had intended to depart, was my Uncle's family. I had visited them eleven years ago, when they lived is a very small town in Oklahoma. Aside from my Aunt and Uncle there are four cousins — two boys and two girls. The eldest boy is about my own age, the others form a scale downwards. Eleven years ago my eyes were sharp, but they were a boy's eyes and did not perceive very much beneath the surface.

These cousins have never had the opportunities which circumstance provided for my sister and for myself. They have always lived in a very small town, until they recently came to Kansas City. But they are wholesome, genuine, friendly, and generous and I was immensely attracted to them during this visit. I saw, as I had not seen before, the wonderful human qualities of my aunt (the wife of my mother's brother)... her unselfishness, her patience, her tolerance, her love... I felt the deepest admiration for her, and it was rather an overwhelming feeling. They have not much of this world's goods, but they have so much in admirable human qualities. I deeply enjoyed joining fully into their life.

In my life I have not had too much of comradeship. I have undertaken work sometimes beyond my years, and have devoted myself to it... and there have been intervals of acute aloneness. It meant a great deal to me to be among these young cousins — so entirely worthwhile in character, who were fond of me, and who took me into their lives in spite of all the things which distinguish my life from theirs...

Please forgive this vague digression, but the past ten days have been as happy, as completely happy, as any I have ever experienced.

Luckily I had a few extra days because I did not immediately hear from Mr. Hoover. It is important that I see and talk with him, and go over the material about the book. He is in a position to help me considerably in the matter of information. He finally wired on Saturday that he would see me on Thursday. This made it imperative to take the Overland Express straight through from Kansas City, so that I had no opportunity to stop over in Denver. This was a keen disappointment, because I wanted to go down to Colorado Springs for a visit with Miss Small. Instead, I have been traveling steadily since Sunday, and will reach San Francisco early tomorrow morning. I will write a note to Miss Small, and if any possibly should occur whereby I could see her on my way back to Washington, I shall surely do it. But my present plan, unless something changes it, is to go to New Orleans and take the boat to New York from there.

After I see Mr. Hoover, I go for a few days to visit my Grandfather at Santa Cruz — on the Pacific Coast. He is more than 90 years of age, and I had really never expected to see him again. It will be a strange meeting, as I have not seen him in many years.

Since leaving Kansas City, the train has been crossing miles and miles of that part of America which so amazes and confounds the European: the endless stretches of *totally unlived-in* land — vast prairies and brush land. This afternoon, however, we are getting into more mountainous country — the crests and peaks of which are all snow covered.

Traveling about this way, I am out of touch with newspaper reports, and sometimes have gone several days without news at all! As the Republican Party has nominated a candidate to oppose the reelection of President Roosevelt, the election-year is well under way. It is going to be an extremely bitter battle here, and there will be many scars, no matter who is the victor.

From my Grandfather's home I go on south to Los Angeles. Just how long I shall be there I cannot tell. Mary Pickford has asked me to call while I am there. I did some work in New York a number of years ago. She was on the committee... too long to tell about now, but when she heard that I would be in Los Angeles, she wrote to invite me to come to see her. I am looking forward to it, because she is one of the most admirable women in America — very fine, and very real. Age does not seem to touch her. I am curious to talk with her now...

By the time I reach Los Angeles, I hope I can write a more interesting and coherent letter. There are too many distractions both inside and outside of this Pullman train. I have had so much to think about and to feel during this journey that what I have written here seems only a casual skimming over the surface... I will do better when I can really concentrate, but I wanted to write a letter now... because it has been so many weeks since my last letter...

That reminds me... Just before I left Washington I posted a copy of the new book by the Princess of Pless. I had not time to read it before I left, so cannot say what sort of book it seemed to me... But she knew that it would be about persons probably known to your majesty, and that for that reason, if for no other, you might find it interesting or at least diverting.

I also received from de Laszlo a small print of the full-length portrait, now exhibited in Paris. He knows of my interest in his work, and my special interest in the Queen of Roumania, and he very courteously sent these copies without any request from me. He does not have the slightest knowledge, of course, about my very special privilege of conversing with your majesty. I was delighted with the portrait, and genuinely believe that it will endure as one of the really great portraits of any time. I am going to try to secure a larger print directly from Paris.

This has been a singularly self-centered letter, but I hope your majesty will forgive me all this "first person singular..."

There seems a great deal more to say, but I shall write another letter from Los Angeles. This one I shall mail in San Francisco in the morning.

With every affectionate thought and devoted wish,

Ray Baker Harris

XXII

June 25, 1936

Your Majesty,

Please forgive this hotel notepaper, but now I do not have my own with me and I want to add a brief postscript to the letter which I wrote on the train.

After rushing half way across the Continent without a stop between Kansas City and here, I find that Mr. Hoover has taken himself off into the mountains to rest and fish, and will not be back at Palo Alto until late Saturday. So my appointment is now for Sunday.

I am leaving here this afternoon and will go to visit my Grandfather at Santa Cruz, and will have to come back up to Palo Alto on Sunday — an awkward but a necessary arrangement. Then I shall leave Palo Alto late Sunday night and arrive at Los Angeles on Monday morning.

Mr. Hooover has always been erratic in the matter of seeing people. When he was President, I know that he would send for important men to come to Washington for a conference, keep them waiting most of the day, and then decide that the conference was not necessary!

I am glad, however, that I am going to have the opportunity to talk with him at some length. He was Secretary of Commerce in President Harding's cabinet, and went with Harding on that ill-fated journey to Alaska. There is a good deal that he can tell me, and he has indicated that he is willing to help me in any possible way.

I have been here in San Francisco since early yesterday morning, and am completely taken in by this city — the most interesting and unusual place I have ever visited. There are many high hills in the city, and some of them seem to go straight up into the air (and going down them is always a thrill, combined with anxiety about the health of the car's breaks!)... The air is crisp and fresh and the downtown section very clean, compared to New York. There is a good deal of the Orient here, and in fact I find San Francisco very much more cosmopolitan than any other American city. From the hills there are some wonderful views of the great bay. The colors are subdued but immensely impressive — the vast stretch of beautiful mountains, water, green shores... photos would do it less injustice than any description I could write. I wish I had a great deal more time just to wander about this city... there is so much to observe and absorb. I am completely fascinated by the tempo of the place.

Perhaps when I reach Los Angeles I may be fortunate enough to find a letter from your majesty. No mail has reached me en route, as I have had no certain address — and as a consequence everything has been sent on to Los Angeles and is waiting for me there.

All this traveling about has been a fine, stimulating experience for me... has stirred up so many new thoughts and ideas, given me a new appreciation of many things.

Beverley Nichols wants me to come to England next Spring, so that I may be there in London at the time of the Coronation. I don't know what may be happening to me between now and then, but if I can possibly manage it, I do want to go over.

I notice that King Edward is going to Cannes as usual, for a summer vacation. It seems odd for the King of England to be traveling outside of the Isle, because King George remained so close at home after the war... but it only emphasizes the fact that it is a new reign.

The newspapers carried a studio portrait of Queen Mary a few days ago, a study showing her with her grandchildren, and I was astonished that she appeared so much older than in any other portrait I have seen. It was her first picture taken since the King's death.

If I can possibly find some really good photos of San Francisco and the bay, I'll send them, but your imagination would have to fill in the wonderful coloring of the sky and water and the shore. It is a tribute, I think, to the quality of our spirit-friendship that every beautiful sight which I see always makes me wish that you could share my experience, and it is an exasperating sense of frustration not to be able to tell you properly, in words, about all the beauties of this extraordinary city.

I shall write again later, after I reach Los Angeles...

With devoted thoughts always,

Ray Baker Harris

XXIII

August 26, 1936

Your Majesty,

Today it is raining steadily, and I am taking advantage of a free morning to write once again — even though I posted a rather long letter only a week ago. But these opportunities for putting down thoughts in a leisurely way do not come very often...

I have just secured a copy of *Crowned Queens* for my set of your published work. It is not new to me, as I had read the book some time ago but did not have a copy of my own.

The other evening I was reading again certain parts of *Why?...* I do think it could be rewritten today with very fine results. As the original edition was privately printed in a limited number of copies, a revised edition, if published in the usual way, would be like a new book to the general public. If it could be edited and rewritten by you, giving it the same form and tempo as *Masks*, the result should be most satisfactory. In *Masks* you presented much deep feeling, many beautiful phrases and pictures, but at the same time you achieved a more concise and quick-moving tempo which kept the reader interested and alert. I think you could do this with *Why?* and at the same time retain the many fine word-pictures, the romantic feeling, and the very memorable thoughts which the people in the book speak... I am thinking particularly of Vaiavala's words: "It is the hours when we live beneath ourselves that darken our souls..." And there are numerous other quotations which come to mind — even the disillusioned philosophy of the old King.

Actually, it would not require a great deal of change. It would only mean putting aside some of the profusions in order that the "principal melody" of the book would become more distinct, and the form and direction of the story a little more apparent... just as you did so perfectly with *Masks*.

While I am speaking of your writings, this reminds me that the New York Public Library has a copy of a book published in the Romanian language — *Gânduri și icoane din vremea războiului* — which I understand contains a number of essays written by your majesty about thoughts and images in the time of the war. It includes two essays which I already have in manuscript form in English — "My Child" and "Czar Nicholas;" but there are other essays called "From My Love to Theirs," "In Thy Name," "Bucharest," "In the Winter War," "In the Spring," "Mother Pucci," "Tears," "Prisoners," "Resurrection," "All Souls Day," and "Silence." Have any of these been published in English in any form, do you recall? The titles I have given are translations of the titles of the essays in the Roumanian volume I mentioned.

Lately I have been rereading the two Siegfried Sassoon books *Memoirs of a Fox-Hunting Man* and *Memoirs of an Infantry Officer*, because he has written a third volume which will be published here in September. It is called *Sherston's Progress* and is a continuation of the other two volumes. Although published as novels, they are admittedly autobiographical. The second volume contained an account of *Sherston's* protest against "prolonging" the war, and how, because of his heroic record as an officer several times decorated, the War Board did not discipline him but sent him to a sanitarium as "temporarily insane." This, of course, was what happened to Sassoon himself. The second volume ended at the moment when he was sent to the sanitarium, so I assume this new volume will continue from there. I thought the first book had wonderful charm and sensitivity, and the second book was of course bitter about the war. If your majesty read these books, I wonder how you felt about them.

Robert Graves was his friend during the war, and was involved in the hospitalization incident, but after the war Graves and Sassoon broke apart; and Graves has written some supercilious things about Sassoon's work in recent years. But I never admired Graves very much, although I read both his autobiographical books. Sassoon is rather an obscure figure, and lives very much alone in Sussex, rather in keeping with the figure of the boy in *Memoirs of a Fox-Hunting Man*... I was wondering if you happen to know what is said of him in England.

Francis Stuart also has a new book to be published this Fall. I think I can secure an advance copy, and will forward it to you.

I am very eager to hear more about the recent English visit, and if England seemed at all "different" under the new reign. You have known England in four reigns. I had noticed in the press that Queen Mary is to leave Buckingham Palace and take up residence at famous old Marlboro House; and it has also been reported that King Edward plans to redecorate Buckingham Palace. This latter report may refer only to his private apartments. It seems odd to consider such changes, as Buckingham Palace I suppose has not really been altered a great deal from Queen Victoria's day, or Balmoral.

I have seen numerous pictures of "Cliveden" and was rather thrilled to receive a letter from your majesty which had been written there, since I know all the happy associations the place must have for you.

Several times I have reread that part of your *Story* which relates your early friendship with Lord Astor and his sister. It is good to read of a friendship so spontaneous, satisfactory, and to learn that it has been enduring through so many years.

My own years are few, and my early friendships go back only about ten years to college associations. With one exception, my childhood friends have been lost sight of... but there are two or three friendships which have endured through the past ten years and which I hope I may keep all my life. I value these few, because so many other friends have come and gone in the same period of time.

There is nothing more difficult than trying to sustain a friendship when the spontaneous desire for it has somehow been lost. People show themselves up very clearly sometimes, and friendships which have been alive and vital suddenly become quite dead — even if the outward relationship does not immediately change. It would be better if these "dead" relationships could be severed and cut off immediately, but often it cannot be done. I am speaking, of course, only of friendships... deeper relationships are even more of a complication, but at the moment I am singularly free from the latter.

For some years I have known a girl of whom I am especially fond. I have visited many times in her home. We get on perfectly and enjoy being together. We ride and swim, or merely walk in the New England country, enjoy the theatre, and our tastes are similar if not identical. I am always proud of her if we are with others, but we never remain apart from others but follow our own separate inclinations. There has never been anything openly sentimental in our relation. I have never written her what might be called a "love letter," nor has she to me. But we have apparently both enjoyed an unspoiled comradeship, which has its sentimental side even if it is not expressed.

I have thought of marriage, but have wondered if it could be successful in the absence of an overpowering sentimental feeling. Would that be necessary, or would the perfect comradeship and rational sentiment be sufficient. I try to tell myself that the "overpowering" sentimental feelings are usually short-lived and not to be trusted, but I am not sure of marriage without it. This sounds immature and silly, I suppose, and I have never expressed these feelings in words before. But I have no hesitancy in doing so here because, however badly expressed, I am sure you will not misunderstand. Being so completely in separate material worlds, I have no hesitancy in trying to say to you what I would not say to anyone I know personally.

Frank Buchman has just arrived in the United States, and if one can believe the reports of the interview he gave on his arrival, I must say he made some very fantastic and absurd statements. He said he had been in Germany for the Olympic games, and he was full of enthusiasm for Hitler and Fascism. He is quoted as saying he would like to see the entire world a fascist state, adding that in such a circumstance if Hitler could be turned to God it would save the world! It reminded me, grimly, of the way in which the name of Kaiser was so frequently linked with that of God... If he was quoted correctly, it certainly sounds like very foolish and irresponsible thinking. The idea is simply fantastic — first follow Hitler, and then Hitler will lead you to God! Of course I may be doing Mr. Buchman an injustice, as newspaper frequently scramble what one has really said!

It had been announced that Beverley Nichols would come over to America with Mr. Buchman this Autumn, but from reports Beverley is still ill and is taking a complete rest since leaving the hospital. Beverley has keen perception and judgment and it may be that he was not enchanted by the prospect of keeping company with Mr. Buchman in America, despite his genuine enthusiasm for the spirit of the Oxford Movement. But I do not think he would express himself on the subject. I have not heard from him directly since his illness.

I suppose you are now at Bran, and am wondering how long it will be before you go again to Balcic. I am interested to learn how the memory-garden and the meadow are coming on... I am sure you will develop it all most artistically, and some day I hope to see it.

I hope that conditions are not too troubled in Roumania. All of Europe seems overflowing with rumours and fears. I am really personally distressed by all that is happening in Spain. Whoever wins, the bitterness will endure for generations because there has been so much loss and bloodshed on both sides. It seems strange that it could happen in Spain. I have friends who have lived there and love the country and the people, and yet the people have turned vindictive and vicious on both sides. It is a terrible sight, and holds so much danger for the world.

This is a time when the strength and prestige of Britain is badly needed, and yet Britain itself seems uncertain and divided. King George, through the accumulated affection of three decades, could hold the Empire together in a single unit. If the new King can do the same!

I hope you safely receive the West Point book which I posted some days ago. It is a heavy volume and could not be sent by book post, but had to go by parcel post which is neither so fast or so safe as it cannot be registered or insured. But I hope it gets through all right, and that you may enjoy looking through the book. It is, of course, an undergraduate product — the cadets edit and publish the book themselves.

Have you read the Edith Sitwell biography of Queen Victoria? As yet I have not had an opportunity, but the book is being much discussed here.

For the present, I am steadily busy on my book and hope to have it done before the end of the year, meanwhile changes and plans for the future are brewing quietly...

With every devoted wish and affectionate thought, now and always,

Ray Baker Harris

Her Majesty, MARIE
Queen of Roumania

XXIV

Washington, D.C.
September 19, 1936

Your Majesty,

The interesting letter from Bran arrived quite safely, and the two photographs came the next morning. It is always a happy hour when the post brings a message from Romania — just as exciting as was the very first letter which came to me from your majesty. And I always offer renewed thanks for the wonderful good fortune that has given my life the richness of this friendship with a far-off Queen whom I profoundly admire.

In the same post I received from England a copy of the new book by Francis Stuart. I did not try to read it immediately, as I had one or two books which I am supposed to review for the paper next week. Late yesterday evening I put one of these aside, and thought that for a moment or two I would have a look into *The White Hare* book. It was hours before I could put it down, and then only because my eyes were extremely tired. I closed it very reluctantly, my mind filled with its pictures, and then this morning I reached for it the first thing after breakfast — and read it completely to the end.

I think you will find it fascinating. It has its wild and strange moments, with all that richness of feeling which he put into his earlier books. His characters, of course, are people apart.

You mentioned in your letter that you had seen an announcement of this book, and that you were getting it. If you do not already have a copy, please let me send mine to you.

I am enclosing a clipping of a most attractive picture of young King Peter's small brother. It is delightful, and I am going to try to find a good print of it. It is a happy and very mischievous expression!

No, the letter from Bran was the first one since the thoughtful message from Cliveden — so I will be very interested to hear about the visit at Nörter See, and the three days in Yugoslavia. Also I had not heard about Welbeck, the Duke of Portland's home.

This reminds me to ask if it is true that Buckingham Palace is to be redecorated by Elsie de Wolfe, as has been reported by the press. I suppose it was too early for you to sense any real changes in England this soon in the new reign? I read that you had gone to luncheon at Buckingham Palace with the new King and Queen Mary, shortly after your arrival in England, and I of course wondered how it must have seemed.

Everything you tell me about England interests me a great deal. I am looking forward to a visit there next year, though at the moment I am a little doubtful about going over for the May Coronation. It will be my first visit, and with the huge crowds, high prices for everything, and all the inconvenience, I am wondering if it would not be better to go when I can see things more satisfactorily. It would be exciting to go in May, but I am debating the idea.

I am pleased to hear that de Laszlo did another sketch. How many has he now done in all? I have photo copies of only two — the formal picture for the National Bank, and the sketch in the mourning veils. I am particularly anxious to see the one which is being reproduced by a special color process.

You mentioned that you have at Cotroceni another Bertram Park portrait, different from the one I sent but in the same dress; and also one in Roumanian costume made at the same time. Of course I would be very happy to receive these if they can conveniently be sent.

From a portrait by Bertram Park

Queen Marie in 1936

I am glad to learn that you are actually at work on the fourth volume, and I can appreciate all the difficulties it must present. It will require tremendous tact to tell those chapters, but I am sure you will do it instinctively and effectively.

As yet I have not seen Beverley's book, although he wrote that he was sending me a copy. It is not to be published in America until late next month, but my English copy should come any day. I am very impatient to read what he says about his Roumanian visit. I think I know about what he will say of the country, and it is impressive to contrast this with the impression which Mr. Hoppe had of Roumania after his visit in 1924. The contrast will speak for itself. It is distressing to realize that such a change could take place, and I can understand so well how your majesty must feel about it. And as you know the whole, true story — I hope you may find the way to make it impossible for others to distort that truth, even if circumstances make it impossible for your majesty to relate everything today.

Since I wrote the last paragraph I have taken down from the shelf my copy of Mr. Hoppe's book, and have read through some of it. Of course, Beverley visited Roumania only briefly and had not the same opportunity to know and see the country. But Mr. Hoppe in his Introduction specifically states that he saw no substantiation of the very things which Beverley apparently has commented upon. So I think their different impressions are significant — 1924 and 1935!

You have doubtless heard that the Queen of Spain is now in America. It is a very quiet visit, both because of her son's very serious illness — and because of the terrible conditions in Spain. I am enclosing two clippings — the only reports of her visit.

But to return to happier subjects...

For what publication is your majesty preparing the articles on Coronation? I shall want to subscribe for those issues. It must be rather a task to write six long articles on the subject, but you will have so much to tell from your own experience and also you have a special feeling for the significance of these English ceremonies, so that the articles should be most appropriate.

Eleanor telephoned me several days ago. She is back in the capital a week in advance of the time for the School to open. I saw her the night before last. We had a pleasant visit together, and then went to call on some mutual friends. It was a delightful evening, and Eleanor seems entirely like herself once again. We did not refer at all, except once or twice indirectly, to that strange year of 1935. I believe that she gave herself more or less completely to all of Miss Holton's wishes and plans during that year, and at the end of the year came to realize that this was a grave mistake. This Spring she seemed to have more or less asserted her independence, and was not too weighted by the School — and now, in starting this new year there, she said she had determined not to do too much there. She did say that 1935 had been a "terrible" year, and that she had returned to the school this year only after a definite understanding that she could return on her own terms, and have some free time. This seems wise, because, although the school has been good discipline for her — with all its responsibilities and tasks — there is such a thing as submitting to *too much* — to a stifling degree. I still do not quite understand about 1935 — it was strange and incomprehensible — but it was another's experience, not mine. I was glad to find her like herself again.

As it is now only a few weeks until the Presidential election in America, there is increasing excitement as each candidate begins his final campaign. President Roosevelt was elected four years ago and commenced his work with tremendous popular good will, and the cooperation of every able man in important fields. Today he has lost many of those who supported and believed in him most valiantly at the beginning. But it will be difficult to defeat him, because he has a large following — and as President he has much more power and prestige than his opponent.

In character and temperament, I think he is much like former President Wilson. Of course he is much more charming and humanly pleasant than was Mr. Wilson — but underneath his surface relationships, I think President Roosevelt has much the same sureness of his own superiority and excellence. If he were placed in the same position as was President Wilson, it is very likely he would behave in the same way — and would regard himself as the arbiter of how European countries should conduct their affairs. He has shown himself as very bitter toward any who disagree with his policies, which was a failing Mr. Wilson had also.

His ideals and instincts seemed of the best, but he does not seem to think clearly or have definite principles in achieving his objectives. He will try any scheme, or spend any amount of money, and, worst of all, he has made speeches which have antagonized one class against another. He has listened over-much to radical proposals, so that the head of the Communist Party in America — in making his report to Moscow — stated that although President Roosevelt was not giving them all they desired, he was giving them enough to warrant Communist support for his reelection.

Of course it is an endless discussion. I am opposed to his reelection, but all the same I cannot think so bitterly of him as a person — as many do. These extremes of feeling do no good, and leave scars between people.

Calvin Brown is at present working with the campaign of President Roosevelt's opponent, as he wants to see a more conservative Government — with trustworthy and experienced men in key positions. President Roosevelt has given many positions of high responsibility to men of little experience — with theories and not experience.

I have not yet met Mr. Brown, but I shall call upon him when I go to New York the next time. It will be interesting to meet him. He sounds like a stimulating person, and I was very much interested in his pamphlets.

This is rather a rambling letter, as there is not much to say about my own activities. Since returning here, I have had a great deal of work to do — work which accumulated in my absence, and my own personal work on the Harding book. My travels were a great stimulant, and there are a number of opportunities and changes brewing for the future — but at the moment I am so busy that I am only taking things as they come. A little later there will be more positive activities to deal with.

At the Library of Congress, it is fortunate I have work I like to do. It isn't "library work" at all — but editorial work on the various books and pamphlets which the Library publishes. I like to plan books and other publications, to work with the printer, and gradually to see a typewritten manuscript become an attractive printed page — according to the plan, with illustrations, different kinds of type, and the like. I could wish that the material I had to work with was less formal, but it is interesting work nevertheless and I like it.

I do not think I could work in the strictly Library field. I have seen those people too close at hand! They gradually become slaves to detail — attaching overwhelming importance to small things, because they haven't any really big responsibilities. Of course that is true of any work which involves routine and detail. But I don't get on with such people very easily. I prefer people whose horizons are not so limited, whose impulses are generous and not small. Those who make a fetish of small things invariably prove to be intolerant, or supercilious.

This topic takes my thoughts back to Francis Stuart's book... and I see very clearly the figure of the boy, Domonic, with his white, cold inner flame — the force of his spirit against the forces of the world. You will understand when you read the book — those three young spirits, so individual and far removed from the tempo of an urban life, and yet Francis Stuart makes them very memorable and beautiful and very real. It is a strange combination of pure romance and reality.

In reading *The White Hare* I quite lost sight of the Siegfried Sassoon book, which was the one I had partially read when I began Francis Stuart's book. Sassoon writes in a table-conversation tempo, and it is intellectually absorbing — but by no means the sweep or force, for me, of this other book. But a comparison is not fair. Francis Stuart has those qualities that come in the writings of the Irish — from a James Barrie or a James Stephens, or a Yeats.

I do not know if James Stephens has come to America this year. He usually comes in August or early September, and stays for two or three months at Mr. Howe's place — "Freelands". He is a strange little man, but when he puts his legs under himself, and is in friendly company, his talk is fascinating. I'll never forget a chilly October evening, several years ago, when we all sat about the evening fire at "Freelands" and listened to Stephens. He read his own poems, and talked of other poets, and of his experiences. He is of course terribly impractical, and even a little mad, but I was very much attracted to him — and grateful for the experience of meeting him. I understand his wife, whom I have never met, is quite the opposite: extremely practical, and domineering — a bit irritated by the literary reputation. I guess it makes it difficult for her to keep him "in hand..." But she almost never comes with him to America, although she did two years ago. Mr. Howe is fond of Mr. Stephens, and has helped him tremendously, and appreciates his art... but he has no illusions about Irish temperament! He knows them too well, and they also appreciate him. He gave a dinner, privately, in New York not long ago... and had only Irish people like Padraic Cullum, Dudley Digges, Stephens, and others. Of course you can imagine what the table discussions must have been like — with all the quick wit and nimble thinking, and their knowledge of the world...! Mr. Howe enjoyed it hugely, and described it to me not long afterward.

By the way (this *is* a rambling letter!) I wonder if you would mind sometime writing for me, on a separate piece of notepaper, those lines in the first volume — about Queen Victoria:

"Queen Victoria... She was a human, dear little old lady! She terrified everybody, spread an atmosphere of awe around her, but for all that

she was human, delightfully human. She did not expect you to be a hero
everyday of your life. Shut away in her regal abodes, surrounded by subjects who always lowered their voices when they addressed her, hedged in
by honors, by the ceremonious respect of those who served her as well by
her own desire of aloofness, there was all the same, beneath that outward
pomp and unapproachableness, a real human understanding of everyday
pain, fear of joy..."

I would like to place this quotation in my copy of Queen Victoria's
book which I have. This would give the book a direct connection with my
Roumanian collection.

I hope that conditions in Roumania are not as unsettled as some
recent press reports have indicated. All newspapers here gave a lot of attention to the dismissal of Foreign Minister Titulescu, and seem to think it
indicates an entirely new foreign policy by Roumania. But I don't think
Americans are ever very good at understanding the endless complexities of
European politics...

To a different topic entirely — Do you happen to know the poems of
Robert Frost? He is a new Englander, a very delightful man to know —
although my acquaintance with him is slight, though I know fairly well
some of his friends. He sent me an inscribed copy of his new volume —
and in it he wrote these amusing lines:

> The way a crow shook down on me
> The dust of show from a hemlock tree,
> Has given my heart a change of mood
> And saved some part of a day I had rued...

It is very slight as a poem, but the thought is pleasant. Days have
been partly reclaimed for me by little diversions too... Do you ever stay at
Sinaia? I have somehow received the impression that you have given it up
entirely for Bran and Balcic when you are away in Roumania from Bucharest. But I suppose Sinaia belongs mostly to the official past, whereas both
Bran and Balcic are intimately your own residences. I suppose you will go
to Balcic for part of October, and I shall be very interested to hear how the
Memory Orchard is developing. By the way, where do you plan to be this
year for your birthday anniversary?

I hope you have not been tired by so rambling a letter. But it has been a happy privilege to talk with you in this way, even though I had no very important news to relate this time.

        With devoted and affectionate thoughts, now and always,

                                        Ray Baker Harris

Her Majesty, MARIE
Queen of Roumania

XXV

                                        August 17, 1937

Your Majesty,

    You cannot imagine how greatly pleased I was to discover in the envelope from Roumania a letter entirely in your own handwriting once again! Of course I have kept a feeling each day that you were steadily becoming better, but it was wonderful to receive the fine letter as a tangible evidence of your returning strength. Please know that I feel immensely grateful to be one of those to whom your majesty should write so soon, and I have read and reread it many times since it came a few days ago. These messages always mean a very great deal to me.

    I'm delighted to learn that de Laszlo made a sketch of the young A.D.C., as I have felt a special interest in him because of what you have told me. I do not think he would have disappointed you, even if he could have lived much longer. I say that, remembering the remark he made at your table when your majesty's general "bonté" was being discussed: how he said that you were so genuinely kind that others who were not really so kind found it difficult to understand your kindness. This appealed to me as very true and penetrating, and, knowing that truth, I do not think he ever would have been swayed in his loyalty by critics or jealous ones. He would have seen through them, and would never have been taken in.

    It was also satisfactory to learn that your sister could be at Sinaia for a time, so that you could enjoy an intimate companionship with one of the family. Even surrounded by loyal and faithful ones, one can still feel lonely in the absence of one with whom there are no formal barriers of any sort.

    I have not been away from Washington even for a weekend since the beginning of the Summer, though I made one trip for a day down to the ocean shore. But I have been swimming at every opportunity. I usually go to the Wardman Park's outdoor pool at hours when it is crowded, and have done more swimming this year than all the other summers put together. I like it immensely. Yesterday morning, however, I nearly froze stiff when I went in at seven in the morning for a swim before breakfast. I go again tomorrow morning, unless it turns out to be a bad day. Lately we have been having many good ones for a change.

In the mornings I usually go alone, but I like to have someone with me in the afternoons or evenings — a perfect opportunity to visit and sit on the sidelines between swims!

There is a lot to say about swimming, but until this year I have been around the water only a little and never really realized how much I could enjoy it as a steady diet!

I liked the story about the old Turkish woman, Shefica. I suppose in these years she has not many joys, and it is pleasing to picture the joy which must come into her eyes when the Queen rewards her adoration with gentleness and kindness.

A long time ago I clipped from a newspaper the clipping of a picture of your majesty taken at Balcic, and in the background is the figure of an old woman. Could this, by any chance, be Shefica? I am enclosing it with this letter. I often mount clippings on a sheet of paper and add to a collection in a binder, when the picture is an interesting one. So perhaps you would return this to me later, and say if it is or is not Shefica. Perhaps I am making a horrible mistake, as I gather from your letter that there are members of your majesty's household who would be horrified if anyone mistook them for Shefica!

I can understand the anxiety of your Aides, since they probably know all too well that it is a great temptation to take advantage and misuse a Queen's friendship.

You spoke to me once about a young poet, a girl, whom you had tried to help. If only she could have held on to her great opportunity and privilege without trying to use it so as to advance herself with others. It was a wonderful chance for her to develop *herself*, by your friendly interest and attention, and she had to spoil it by bringing others into the picture and creating complications. I know it must cause you anguish when vanity spoils a promising relationship.

But once you also told me to remind you one day to tell about "Maruka" — a friendship which endured satisfactorily through many years.

I smile sometimes when I think back to days when I was a small boy — and how I observed the relations of my parents with their friends. In those days adults seemed to get along so smoothly and graciously with their friends and acquaintances — and I never guessed what thoughts lay behind those apparently calm relationships, what motives. In my parents' home the "grown-ups" always seemed so assured, so able to know what to do and say with each other — it all looked and sounded very easy and natural — *in those days.*

How much a small boy expects of people and of life! How confident he is of being able to take his place "when he grows up," how sure that he can become whatever he decides to become! It's a world one never finds, and it takes a little time to discover just what the world is when one is obliged to survive!

I expect less of others and more of myself today. But still, I do not like to have other people's faults pointed out to me. In a sort of subconscious way I am aware of the shortcomings of people of whom I am fond; but so long as they do not impose those qualities on me, I prefer to ignore their existence. It is irritating sometimes when my family believes that I do not see a person's faults and begin "warning" me about them.

I have a friend whom I like very much, and whose name you might recognize if I were to mention it. Well, mutual acquaintances have come to me (I suppose with the best of motives) to point out "things that people say" about him. I replied very emphatically that my friend had never shown me that side of his nature (if it really existed) and that so long as he did not, I didn't propose to credit what "others say."

In my last letter I think I mentioned that I had discovered a report published by the Royal Literary Fund which contains a full text of all that was said at your Literary Banquet in London two years ago. I was quite thrilled by it, as everything seemed so friendly and ended in a really sincere tribute to you.

I am enclosing an amusing little story — even though I do not know if it is actually authentic — about a small English boy who "flirted" with the two young Princesses at Balmoral. It is like one of your stories!

Also I am enclosing a page from the current issue of *Vogue* which my sister suggested you might care to see — a portrait of the Duchess of Kent, and another with Prince George. I noticed the other day that they were at Belgrade, and were to visit along the Delmatian coast — a place I one day hope to visit in a leisurely way.

My sister, by the way, and one or two of my close friends, are the only ones with whom I ever share a part of your letters. I have never felt that others would really understand the special quality of our "talks." Of course, the friends who know me well enough to come upstairs to my own rooms see the portrait and the signed prints and the original painting which I have framed, and they see the books. From these they know that there has been a contact of some sort, but I never explain or elaborate to satisfy their curiosity. I do try to interest people into reading your books, since this is the best way to give them the true picture of your personality as I know it.

Some days ago I wrote a note to say that I was immediately sending the latest Francis Stuart book, *The Bridge*. Something, however, seemed to tell me to read it first — and so I did... It is too bad to relate that the book is a disappointment after *The White Hare*, so I think I shall not send it, but wait until another really good book comes from him. I do not like to spoil the good impression from his last book. This new book is not actually bad, but it is not worth reading. I read for a hundred pages without a flicker of interest in the several people he was describing. I worked up a mild interest in the story and read on to the end. It was like a fairly good short-story that had been very unnecessarily prolonged into a book. And the story was not worth telling. If anyone other than Francis Stuart had written the same tale it would have been trash. He gave it a certain quality, but it would be very much of a disappointment to anyone who appreciated him at his best.

Instead I shall send a different book which I think may give you pleasure. Some time ago a British film company made a picture set in India, called "Elephant Boy" about a young native boy who dreamed about being a hunter. It made a most unusual motion picture — a beautiful thing. Now it seems that a woman has done a book describing experiences in making that picture, telling all about the boy and the great elephant and the adventures in creating the story. It seems very good, and so I shall send it by the next post.

Since I last wrote to you I have had interviews with several Senators — the most interesting of which was with young Senator Lodge. He is of my own generation, and so we looked back from the same perspective and had a most interesting discussion. He was very well informed about those days, since his grandfather was the Henry Cabot Lodge who was such a power in the Senate in President Wilson's day. I found this talk the most stimulating, the most productive of ideas.

The older Senators (who had actually been in the Senate when Harding was a Senator and later President) were inclined to project themselves into the picture a good deal — to tell me how they had brought this about, and how they had influenced this or that matter... all of which I am obliged to shake down very well before using! However, they gave me interesting leads.

This has been a very long session of Congress. President Roosevelt has been creating controversy after controversy, and just the other day appointed a very inferior man to the Supreme Court. President Roosevelt is an amazing paradox. As a person, he has great charm and warmth of spirit. But he has been given tremendous and unheard-of powers, so that today he is convinced (much as Wilson was) that he is absolutely right about everything, and that anyone who opposes him is a scoundrel. He also likes to do things which are more smart and clever than they are wise. There is such a thing as being *too* clever. I'm afraid there is serious trouble ahead here, as these tactics are creating more and more bitterness.

No, I do not have any pictures of Copăceni, the farm-place home, except the one exterior view of it which appears in the book by Kurt Hielscher, the German photographer. I would be greatly interested to see more of what it is like, as well as hear of the changes which were recently made over.

I will not write a longer letter this evening, as I do not want to send too long messages which might just now be tiresome to read. I am so very happy that you are steadily getting better!

With devoted thoughts and wishes always,

Ray Baker Harris

XXVI

September 10, 1937

Your Majesty,

All of last week I was visiting with my friends in Connecticut, and when I arrived home yesterday your wonderful letter from Bran was waiting for me. I was completely delighted by this evidence that your majesty is now feeling stronger and in more healthy spirits. Bran must be a great tonic at this time of the year, and I know with what real joy you will be starting for Autumn Balcic later this month. It is also good news that you now feel like returning again to the work on Volume IV. But I hope that the pleasure of returning to these tasks will not tempt you to do too much at first, because nothing is more important than conserving and restoring your own health and strength.

I was rather pleased to hear that you had never discovered the recording of Lekeu's "Sonata", because I shall be so happy to send it to you. Schirmer's, in New York, imported it for me from their agent on the Continent. I have asked Schirmer's to have their agent forward this recording directly to Bucharest, so that it should reach you quickly and safely. The recording consists of four records, two sides each, and is done by good pianist and violinist, but their work probably does not at all match Enescu's. Nevertheless, I think the music will give you pleasure. Please accept this recording from me as a birthday remembrance. I only hope it reaches you before October 29th, but such shipments seem to travel slowly. Unless there is a customs charge there would be no amount to pay, as it will have been prepaid.

It was very interesting to hear about General Zwiedineck, and I know it must make all the difference in the world to have someone who is absolutely loyal and resourceful and efficient to protect and manage the Household which is your own particular domain in Roumania. Countless people must come to a Queen's gate, and it must be a real assurance to you to have that gate guarded by one who is absolutely honest and devoted to your welfare. Even so, your tribulations are more than enough to be solved even by your patience and kindness and generous feeling. I am not saying this very well — but I see your majesty's world, and the crowd about your house, from a very great distance. And although I know that your immediate world is over-full with humans of all qualities, I always think of you as standing entirely alone in Roumania — giving, giving, abundantly to others — but entirely alone yourself. It is the price one must pay for having so much to give — in friendship, inspiration, and understanding. In your great spirit you are unlike most people whose spirits are smaller, and, judging you by their own limitations, they cannot comprehend. Even when they are good friends and loyal they cannot quite understand, so that it sets you definitely apart. And this aloneness in itself adds to your greatness.

My visit in New England was perfect in every respect. Two good friends of mine who had been in New Hampshire joined me in New York and we went to Connecticut together — after two very hot days in New York City. We took the train for a short run to Stamford, where the young girl I have spoken to you about met us with her car — and the four of us (Pat Harrison and his wife, my friend and myself) drove on from there. We had two hours' drive through wonderful New England country with its winding roads and rolling hills. The roads were lined by very tall trees which met overhead and made the passage almost a tunnel! The quaint New England houses with their stone and picket fences, gardens and huge old trees and green lawns — were a treat to the eye on every side.

We stopped for a late lunch at a most attractive tavern where the food was wonderfully good. Then we continued on our way to my friend's house, which is about eight miles from New Haven — in beautiful New England countryside — on a hilltop overlooking a small valley. We had not left the tavern far behind when it begun to pour! It rained and lightninged and thundered at a great rate. The lightning seemed to bounce off the top of our car, so close did it come several times. We lit cigarettes and pretended to be much more nonchalant than was actually the case! It continued to rain the rest of that day and night, and all the next day and night. But nothing could spoil my country holiday, and I enjoyed the rainy days as much as the fine cool and clear ones which followed.

My friend's aunt, at whose house we stayed, is a delightful woman. She is today not so wealthy a woman as she once was, but her house is filled with really beautiful things which are in perfect taste. It is a real home of beauty and comfort. On the cold, wet evenings we remained indoors — to a delicious dinner, coffee before a blazing fire, and a pleasant evening is pleasant company.

They have a Japanese houseboy who manages the kitchen — Hama. He is amazing and amusing and exasperating! He is wonderful in many ways, but he has some funny prejudices and is somewhat set in his beliefs. For example, my hostess wanted to serve sliced peaches on ice cream for desert — and he protested violently, saying that peaches on top of the ice cream "wouldn't look nice!..."

The hills and ranges were still green, and colorful flowers were still about. I want to go up again a little later when the leaves are turning and the whole countryside is one riot of the most wonderful colors imaginable. I like the crisp, cool, clear weather of Autumn in New England. You would love that part of America if you could visit in its old, comfortable homes in a leisurely way.

I was surprised to learn that you had not heard from Eleanor Horton. When I saw her in late April she asked me particularly if I had any direct news, saying that she had written a long letter just before your illness became known. Then last month she sent me a note from Little Falls, asking if I had news of you. This note said she had sent a letter to you when she first came home (in August) but that it probably had not yet reached you. Perhaps this last letter reached you after the letter to me was posted. I have seen little of Eleanor this year, mostly my own fault because it has been one long year of unexpected visitors and other distractions in addition to my daily work; but the few times I saw Eleanor she seemed to be much more herself, and seemed to have worked out her relation to the school on a more satisfactory basis. Mrs. Holton herself left in July for some sort of Mediterranean tour.

Yes, I was glad when the over-stimulating friend left town! He is an amazing person, exhausting by the intensity and scope of his enthusiasms, but he has qualities which one really admires. You would have smiled: Just before I went to Connecticut this friend came back through Washington. He had been in New York and New England. Well, he asked me to join him for supper at a very fine sea-food restaurant here — a balcony place overlooking the river wharves. It is the truth that all through this dinner I did not speak more than a dozen words. Such a torrent of an account of his experiences! The sea food and all the task made me very sleepy indeed before the evening was over! He goes everywhere and does everything and nothing escapes him... He lived in New York at the Hotel Pierre, visited immensely wealthy people and stepped with the Du Ponts in Delaware on his way back South. That is a world which I know very little about... as I have neither the money nor the time nor the inclination for "society" as such, and it was mildly entertaining to hear his vivid descriptions. But I was relieved when he had left — feeling that I could be in my office without the danger of his crashing in with some overwhelming enthusiasm to take me to see some statue or building he had just "discovered". He is kindly and thoughtful and likes to give people pleasure. But I enjoy him more at a distance, by way of the post, than when he is actually here in person!

I can well imagine how people have crowded into your life, intensifying their own enjoyment of things by the stimulation of your appreciation. I expressed that poorly, but I think I understand how people have continually drawn from your vitality to enrich their own lives... the desire to possess one who most nearly satisfies their ideal, feeling that their own deep emotion somehow gave them the right to expect to be "the only one" in your special regard. And I can understand how distressing it must have been for you, all your life, to try patiently to give joy to such people and yet, for their own good hold them at a distance so that the relationship would not spoil.

Also I can understand how your majesty would be unaware of the strong tide, the sort of growing hunger in these people, until it came to the surface and was hard to ideal with or to appease... everyone wanting more and more, never being satisfied with the share that their good fortune had made possible for them. I think I can understand the anguish with which your majesty again and again encountered these human complications. This would have been the same if you had not been born to royalty and the limelight of a throne... but how much more difficult for you with a thousand watchful, sometimes unsympathetic eyes... with considerations of State policy... politicians... and all the rest that is a part with royal lives.

No one seemed to give me much encouragement about going to England in the late part of the year. Everyone always said — "Oh, yes, you will enjoy it, *but* the Spring is the time of year to see England first — at its best..." So I gradually dropped the plans for this year, and if it is at all possible — and now I see no difficulties — I shall go over next April or May. I am looking forward to it with deep anticipation.

England today has its hands over-full with the troubles of the world. One can admire men like Mussolini and Hitler for bringing their countries out of chaos and corruption, establishing order and giving the people pride in country again... but when men have such tremendous power it seems they eventually slip into the idea that they must reform the world in their own way. Germany, Italy, and Japan is a strangely disturbing alliance. Russia and France are not so much better it seems when it comes to sense of honorable dealing and common sense... Poor England has difficult hours trying to keep the world applecart from overturning. Our newspaper headlines scream war news every day. People here are rapidly taking sides... "Incidents" are provoking the patience of Governments... Where and when will it end? I was joking the other day about "bring in the Oriental trenches by Christmas...", but actually it is not such a joke and the war-spirit can sweep the country like a forest fire.

I know that Prince Michael must have made a fine impression in London. He seems tall and good-looking and well-poised from his pictures. What sort of activities interest him?

It was delightful to hear that Princess Ileana had named her son Dominic. The little boy in *The White Hare* had sensitiveness and bravery and the spirit which could say "Yea" to life. I don't think Francis Stuart ever created a more appealing figure. I return to that book frequently.

It will be fine if Princess Ileana and family can come to you at Balcic for a happy Autumn reunion. I hope that these plans will work out satisfactorily.

I am enclosing three Balcic pictures which I would like to add to my portfolio of signed prints. These I think are unusually attractive portraits.

Lately I have not heard from Beverley who is in France for a short holiday, although he is probably back in London by now. I had an article about him in one of our American magazines. I do not care very much about the magazine, but it has a large national circulation and they gave my article a nice layout.

I'm sorry that my brief holiday in the country is ended; but here I am back amongst the every-day contacts with many people and all the usual ups and downs of the daily mill. I have not much news to tell about myself today... There is much work to do, certain friends to enjoy — but there is no *one* relationship, no special occurrence to upset my ways just now!

I must get *Strange Glory* and *The Root and the Flower*, as from what you tell me I am sure I shall find these books appealing. Since you told me about him, I have read up a good deal on Frederich II of Hohenstaufen. I would like to read about him in the German, as one finds in English mostly uninspired accounts of all his endless activities — out of which it is not possible to see the figure himself very clearly. I must improve my German so that I can enjoy reading it — as my present slow translative powers take all the pleasure out of it!

Sometime when you feel like it, I hope you may tell me something of the artists who have performed in your white-domed room at Cotroceni and how you remember them? Especially I would like to hear something of Enescu.

I sometimes think that of all musical artistes the *great* singers are the most fortunate. To pour all that emotion into an aria or a song, to feel the response, the thrill of the audience — the whole power of it must be overwhelming — a complete satisfaction that other forms of artistic talent (painters, writers, composers, etc.) receive in only modified forms.

I never heard Melba, but Beverley once played for me a gramophone record made, I think, when she was nearly 60 — and it was the voice of a young girl, Geraldine Farrar and Maria Jeritza have impressed me most of the modern women singers I have heard... there being force and substance of tone in their voices.

Ray Baker Harris

XXVII

January 11, 1938

Your Majesty,

Yesterday evening I had come up to my rooms after dinner, and turned on the radio so as to catch the regular early evening news broadcast. Suddenly came the astonishing and shocking words that your majesty's illness had taken a critical turn and that "all hope has been now abandoned by members of the Royal Family..."

This was too profoundly distressing to even contemplate, but not until your reassuring radiogram arrived this afternoon was there any hopeful report. The newspapers only confirmed the broadcast report, as you will see by the clipping enclosed. I talked with Eleanor Horton on the telephone and she, like myself, was very deeply disturbed... You can then imagine the overwhelming relief when your radiogram arrived this afternoon. I was happy to be able to call Eleanor and give her this encouraging news. The newspapers, even yet, have not corrected the earlier reports — so I am more than ever grateful for the direct word, as otherwise there would still be horrible doubts.

I remember that Princess Ileana was hoping to take you out of the atmosphere of sickness, to Vienna and Meran, even before the Christmas holidays; so I can imagine the disappointment of this latest delay. It is the delay most of all which must be exasperating, because of course it must only be a matter of time before those red globules shall be disciplined and properly returned to full duty! I had never before even heard of red globules, or even guessed what important sort of service they perform.

I do pray with all my heart that you will be enabled to have a Winter with loving, intelligent care that will bring you to the beginning of Spring with renewed strength and the joy of strong good health. For there should be much happiness for you this year, a hundred compensations for each of the denials of 1937...

There are so many personal tasks that I know it would give you joy to turn to — the completion of Volume IV, the book on flowers which you once mentioned, one of your children's stories with the Sulamuth Wulfing illustrations, and other happy undertakings of The Queen-Artist, which have in the past, and will in the future, enrich the world.

You will be interested to hear that George Enescu is being enthusiastically applauded. He conducted a symphony (Beethoven) two weeks ago and it was broadcast. He did a violin solo which was intensely moving. He has a very heavy concert schedule, but there is not to be another New York appearance until March. I would love to hear him play the Lekeu "Sonata" as, having already heard him, I can imagine how beautifully he must do it. Ordinarily I am not very partial to violin music, but Enescu really thrilled me and moved me deeply in a way that I have experienced only a very few times before.

I was interested the other day to read of the engagement of your niece to Emperor William's grandson; and we read of Prince Michael's going to Athens, after the bad experience at sea, for the marriage of Prince Paul.

There seems to be no end of active events in your world... it being reported that the King goes for a State visit to England quite soon, and in the midst of momentous changes in Roumania. There has been a great deal in the press about the recent political changes in Roumania, and it has excited all sorts of editorial comment and endless speculation. I am enclosing an article about the King which appeared in The New York *Times* two days ago, as well as a news story. I have no idea as to the accuracy of these stories, but think I you may be interested to see what is being reported in America.

By the way, I have meant to enquire if the cross on your notepaper was designed by you? I have always admired it, and noticed in the picture of General Zwiedineck that he wore this cross as one of his decorations. Is this the Regina Maria Cross?

Speaking of crosses, I think the Roumanian holy crosses are particularly intriguing. When I turn the pages of the book of Kurt Hielscher pictures of Roumania I am always pausing at the pictures of wayside crosses — so distinctive and attractive in conception and design. Some day, when I come to Roumania, these crosses will not seem strange to me — but full of interest, and familiar to me.

At the present time I am full of enthusiasm at the thought of my coming visit to England in the Spring. I want to go down to Cambridge and Oxford, and to one or two other places, but for most of the time of my visit I shall be in London. It seems quite definite now that I shall go, and I expect to sail in the Aquitania about the middle or latter part of May and remain a month. I look forward to sending to you my impressions and experiences, and I will write an "installment letter" on board ship, as well as from London.

I have never crossed the Atlantic, though I have been in the Orient and across the Pacific. The Orient is not an attractive scene these days. Friends of the family who are there (not in the zones of war) write very pessimistically, as they are convinced that Japan has embarked upon a war of conquest that has only begun.

America and England *must* work together to keep Peace in the world. I think England alone could maintain world stability, once her present plans are nearer completion — but I am a great and firm believer in working, practical friendship between America and Great Britain.

These are busy, full days with me. I regret to say that most of my business is with matters that do not too greatly concern me (at the office) and I have too little time for those interests I personally value. Even so, I like my full days.

As I have told you, lately I have been taking my degrees in Masonry. I received a first initiation, a beautiful and memorable experience, and have since then been going through a course of study, and now I am ready for my second degree. This will be followed by more study, and then I get my final initiation into the Third Degree and become a Master Mason.

Masonry, in America at least, is a subject for joking among non-Masons. I confess that some phases of Masonry do not appeal to me, but to the sincerely interested I have found that it can offer much in wise teaching. I have no desire to venture into the Masonic playgrounds (like the Shriners), but the teachings of the degrees appeal to me immensely. Its religious principles impress me as all that could be asked as a guide to a decent life, with that quality of brotherly friendliness which, so strangely, seems lacking in Churches today.

Also, Masonry gives one a sort of common denominator for friendly relations with many people who otherwise would not touch one's life. It depends, I suppose, upon how deeply one seeks out the things which Masonry has to bestow.

Have you heard much of Masonry in England?

I shall be eager to learn what you heard from England concerning the first thirteen chapters of Volume IV... In a way this Volume will also be a History of the first years of Greater Roumania, the Roumania which your majesty made possible.

I will not write a longer letter this time. I only want to say again how vastly relieved I am to know that it was a slight relapse and that you are quickly regaining the lost ground. I feel much easier tonight than I did at this same hour last evening!

With affectionate, devoted thoughts now and always,

Ray Baker Harris

Her Majesty, MARIE
Queen of Roumania

XXVIII

Washington, D.C.,
March 10, 1938

Your Majesty,

It was wonderful to see the postmark of "Merano" and to know, even before I opened the envelope, that at last it had been possible to carry out the plan of going to the Italian Tyrol.

The note came during the day while I was at my office, and my sister, seeing the postmark, telephoned to tell me the good news that an envelope had arrived addressed in the loved handwriting "...and postmarked at Merano!" Later, when I arrived home and opened it, my sister was delighted that your majesty had also remembered her with the attractive hand-colored card.

I am intensely pleased by the news of your sure and continuing improvement; and in this complete change of surroundings, with those whom you love near to you, and for a time now relieved of Cotroceni cares, I feel confident that the convalescence will be sure and also increasingly strong. It will be a temptation at first, as strength returns, to overtax your energy — but I am sure that you realize this and will be careful to take things easily.

Merano must be a wonderful spot. The picture on the card is breathtaking — and I know how you will be stimulated by these scenes and sun and air.

The time for my visit to England is rapidly approaching. If I can carry out my plan, I shall sail in the S.S. Berengaria from New York on May 18th — not much more than two months from today. I will have nearly three weeks for my first visit in England, and then I return from Southampton in the S.S. Aquitania on June 11th. It is a short visit, but I am sure it will not be my last. I know that London will not be a disappointment — everything I have heard about it appeals to me. I will be there most of the time, but going down to Oxford for a day or more, and to Cambridge — and perhaps to Dover and some other points in South England. But I want to take my time and do as I please, as "tours" never appeal to me.

Unfortunately, a few doubts have come up. Last year I could not go, partly because I had spent so much money the year before in going to California, and partly because the Coronation crowds would have added difficulties to the visit. This year I can afford it — but there is some danger I might not be able to leave my work for a month in the Spring. The new annex building of the Library of Congress has just been completed and the whole establishment is to be reorganized. The Publication Section over which I have charge is even more involved than most of the offices, because the shifting and new arrangement of the stock will need careful planning and supervision. We have been so badly overcrowded for space, and this is the opportunity to expand and put things in order. I must be on hand when this work is going on, and it is believed that the new building will be ready some time in June. As I will be able to get back by June 18th, I hope I can go ahead to England in May as I have planned. But at the moment things are a little uncertain.

I refuse to entertain the thought that the visit may again be postponed, and have even gone ahead and bought my accomodations.

Beverley has asked me to keep the first evening open, so that he can show me my first views of the sights of London. A friend of mine at Oxford has asked me to come down there for a few days, and if I can go over I know it will be a full and memorable visit. I hope that soon I may be able to write you that the plan has turned into a certainty. I will know by early next month.

Two nights ago I received my third degree in Masonry, and so now I am a "Master Mason." It was a very impressive experience. Four of us took our degrees at the same time, and as one of them is in the military service — the degree was conducted by a group of Army officers.

I am enjoying this Masonic work. In Lodge one meets with men of all walks in life — Bank presidents, army officers, sit side by side with policeman, clerks... and material wealth, social position, official prominence, even talents, count for just exactly nothing. All meet on the level of being just men, and in the Masonic work we get to know each other for human qualities.

I have met several men to whose personal qualities I have been much attracted, but these have been revealed to me as would never have been quite possible in the event we had met outside of Lodge. Of course, you understand I do not mean this in any snobbish sense... but, after all, we are all more or less oriented to our own personal worlds — and in our contacts with strangers there is seldom a real opportunity to "break the ice" unless the acquaintance is somehow prolonged, which is seldom.

But as we sit in the Lodge discussing the work, or together in small groups in the various Masonic studies, the barriers gradually come down and we discover many mutual interests and feelings. Of course, men are still individuals — and one likes some and cares less for others, but there is something about Masonic principles and work that is especially inspiring.

It offers more enrichment of spirit than one finds in the merely social fraternities. Here are many opportunities for doing good and helping others.

Also, there are many paths in Masonry. Some lead merely to playgrounds. One has to watch one's step.

Do you recall the friend I have mentioned several times in recent letters — the "new friend" of last Autumn? Today he told me that he is to be married next month, and he has asked me to be Best Man. I am much gratified that he should ask me, and glad to stand up beside him on this special day. In one sense, though, it is a little depressing! I am beginning to feel like a masculine edition of the girl who "was always a bridesmaid, but never a bride!" This is the third time in recent years that I have been Best Man at the weddings of friends of mine. I shall be glad if one day I can manage to be the bridegroom myself!

And speaking of weddings, I notice that your niece is soon to marry Emperor Wilhelm's grandson.

Have you heard from England regarding the first chapters of Volume Four? I am eagerly looking forward to it. I suppose it may first appear in the *Saturday Evening Post*? It will be so absorbing to read of those years of your majesty's most intense activity — the first years of Greater Roumania.

Incidentally, will you by any chance refer to Mr. Hoover — the episode involving his attitude toward Roumania after the War? Having met and talked with him, I can well understand how he could take a position and absolutely refuse to consider any deviation. It is a great pity that somehow he got off on an unfair attitude toward Roumania. I suppose many were jealous of giving Roumania her just dues (as they were at first in Paris until you appeared on the scene)... and other interests must have gotten to Mr. Hoover first, and prejudiced him. Historically, it is a very interesting circumstance, and not much known.

When you can conveniently write, I shall be so interested to hear all about your surroundings at Merano.

I will not make this a longer letter, but will write again next week.

Meanwhile, with all affectionate thoughts and wishes,

Ray Baker Harris

Her Majesty, MARIE
Queen of Roumania

XXIX

March 22, 1938

Your Majesty,

It was a great joy to find your letter on my desk when I arrived home earlier this evening, and it had come very quickly through the post — only eight days! I have just read it again, after coming up to my rooms from dinner — and I want to answer right away.

This has been one of those wonderful Spring days — warm, but with enough crispness in the air to make one feel really stimulated. Many trees are in bloom, and I only hope that a Spring blizzard does not arrive... one of the most severe snow storms ever experienced here came, a few years ago, in April! Already we have had freak changes. Early this month we had a warm spell, and things began to bloom. I'm enclosing a clipping of two pictures made in the White House grounds: one, the crocuses on the front lawn; the other, the same scene *the next day*! I know how much you will be enjoying the Spring scene where you are, and hope that the seasons in your part of the world are not as mixed up as ours!

I am happy that your health is improving, and only wish that I had ten million sturdy globules to put completely at your disposal to speed the exasperatingly slow convalescence. I keep having the feeling that this strange illness may depart as suddenly and as unexpectedly as it arrived. It seems logical that this might happen. I like the idea that the many doctors are being sent off... One good man who knew his business and was sympathetic would be worth a room full of "specialists". And I can imagine that they probably tripled their fees just because they were attending a Queen.

Both Eleanor Horton and I were so gratified when we learned that you had succeeded in getting away to Merano, because we felt that there you would have matters more in your own hands, away from Cotroceni cares and with an entire change of scene.

What staggering events have occurred during the past ten days since my last letter. I cannot imagine Vienna under a completely German regime — everything regimented and made super-efficient, with all its cultural, artistic life "regulated" by decrees. I was relieved to notice in the New York *Times* dispatch from Vienna that Archduke Anton had not been directly effected, as was the case with so many others. The dispatch quoted him as saying tactfully that "...We are much too busy with our children and occupied with our gardens to be involved in these political events..."

The military precision of the anschluss was immediately evident
even here in Washington — so far away from the scene. The Austrian flag
on the Legation was brought down the same day, and the German flag
raised!

No one here seems to feel that there will be a war, but at the same
time there is a pessimistic feeling that this episode is by no means the end
of the series of "surprises".

After the horrible example in Spain, I cannot see how any Government could allow itself to be drawn into a war. In the last war German cities were relatively undamaged — because the Armistice was signed before
the Allies really penetrated into German territory. But this could never be
the case in a war today, with air fleets being what they are. Aggressor and
defender alike would be sure to have their cities cruelly damaged; and it
does seem that Governments realize this, and do not want to be drawn
into war. Even relatively impotent China was recently able to bomb the
Japanese island of Formosa.

It seems that the German "surprises" have all been amazingly
planned and organized so as to be so sudden and complete as to avoid
actual war.

Well, enough of this subject — but it is so much in everyone's
thoughts.

It is an interesting contrast which you mention in connection with
President Harding. Harding, of course, was essentially a *provincial* personality — a nature that was rather alien to subtleties and sophistication. A
very sophisticated person would have described him as "dumb"— and he
was, of course, to their world. But I have read so many of his personal letters and writings, and talked with so many who knew him, that my conception of him differs from most of the *general* impressions. This is the
difficulty in writing a biography which will be read by the general public!

It is amusing about Mr. Bolitho. I have other friends who know him,
although I never mentioned their names in the two times I wrote to him.
The first time I wrote him was to send him the Prince Albert letter (a pho-
tostat copy) which was unique and which I thought would interest him
because of its family association, referring to Prince Leopold's birth, etc.
Then, the second time I was impelled to write him a short note because
his Edward VIII book was being violently criticized, and I wanted to say
that I understood something of the difficulties he faced in writing that
book. He must have received countless such letters, so it is natural that he
would never remember mine — which were really only notes.

If he is in England when I am there in May it is likely I shall meet him. What is he like? Easy to talk with?

My plans are still unchanged — that is, I am still determined to go over in May — but there have been changes, just in the past three days.

As I wrote you, I planned to sail in the S.S. Berengaria on May 18th from New York. Well, suddenly the Berengaria has been taken out service. During the last three voyages there were mysterious fires in the ship. It is possible you may have read about them. The last fire started in a state-room while in dock at Southampton. So the Cunard Line has decided to discard the ship. This changes all the schedules.

Tentatively, I have changed my sailing to the S.S. Brittanic which sails from New York in May 14th and is a slower boat — 8 days. The S.S. Aquitania which I had planned to take home from Southampton on June 11th, now sails from Southampton on June 8th under the new schedule.

This leaves me only 15 days in England, but these are the only sailings which fit in with my plans, as I must be back here by the middle of June.

If I went over later I could stay in England longer, but I want to go in May. So I think I shall go on the 14th, even though it means a shorter visit. "First visits" are supposed to be brief anyway, aren't they? It will make me all the more anxious to return there soon again.

I will probably be in London a week, go down to Oxford and to Cambridge and one or two other places during the second week. I would love to meet and talk with Miss Marr, and when my plans are definite I will write, or telephone to her house from London and arrange a convenient time to call. This will be a great treat for me.

I read with deepest interest all which you wrote concerning Free Masons. Except for the symbolism, I do not think American Masonry resembles the European groups. I know that it is cut off *completely* from the French Masonic groups. French Masonry is regarded here as clandestined and entirely foreign in spirit and conception to American Free Masonry.

Of course, there are many paths to Masonry, and I have gone only a little way. So far, I have been told or taught nothing which in any way conflicts with my religion, and political subjects are not even discussed.

One must go through the first three "degrees" before becoming a Master Mason. There are some thirty degrees after that, but they are merely elective and need not to be taken.

Each degree has a symbolic meaning. The actual words and forms are supposed to be kept secret, but there is no secret about the symbolic aspects. The first degree symbolizes birth and infancy. The second degree symbolizes growth and manhood. The third degree symbolizes death, resurrection, and everlasting life.

I have been told that in many European countries this symbolism (which is regarded as purely symbolic in America) is treated *very* literally, and is carried out to all sorts of absurd, fanatical extremes. Also, abroad, admission to Masonry is closely restricted, and I suppose such groups might very well indulge in secret undertakings and purposes.

But here it is more essentially a fraternal organization. In this city alone (where the entire population of men, women, and children is 350,000) there are some 25,000 Masons — so you can see that this is "secrecy" on a *very* large scale! — unlike small groups in separate European countries.

The work is almost entirely devoted to charitable undertakings, done quietly, effectively, and without ostentation.

The thing which has appealed so strongly to me is the opportunity to meet with all manner of men — under conditions where all barriers of wealth, position, talents worldly consequence, are removed, for the hours when they meet together.

Englishmen and Americans are much too strongly imbued with love of fair play and independence to relish any secret plotting, or to put themselves under any yoke where they would be obliged to take action against their will; but I do not think the same is true of many European groups — where secret societies and plottings are an age-old practice!

If Masonry ever conflicted with my conscience, I should withdraw immediately.

But I can well understand your feeling, and because of General Zwiedineck's very special place in your household, it is proper that his entire loyalty should be centered there — and that he should not be identified with any individual group — because, after all, the Royal House is above all separate groups.

I enjoy talking with you frankly about this, and hope you will not mind if I speak of it from time to time again as thoughts may arise.

Of course, it *is* much different here in America. There are several million American Masons — of all religious faiths except the Catholic, and of *all* political beliefs and affiliations. So it is not the same situation as abroad.

But enough about Masonry.

Thank you so much for writing in my copy of *Albert the Good*. It will be so nice to add this to my collection.

Lately I have been especially interested in locating copies of your books. My own set of your writings is nearly complete, and of course is very special as all the copies are inscribed to me. But I like to find other copies of your books, and give them to different public libraries in this country. Already, most of your books are difficult to secure — and I want to put copies in libraries where they will be kept safely and many people will be able to borrow them, now and later.

I always like to interest people in your books, because there they come in direct contact with your spirit. If they are capable of comprehending, these books will open the door to them — much more effectively than anything one could say. For I am so completely an admirer of your majesty that it is like the times when you speak of London — people smile tolerantly, recognizing overwhelming enthusiasm. But when I can get them to read your books — particularly the life *Story* — it is my turn to smile, because usually *they* become enthused, taken by surprise at having found a quality which they did not anticipate — and which is strongly winning.

I am trying to get together a complete set of your writings for the Library of Congress here; and to other libraries, I give separate books — as sets of the *Life Story, Crowned Queens, The Country That I Love, Masks,* and one or two of the children's books.

My large portfolio of pictures I shall one day have mounted and bound into several volumes. As long as I live I will keep them with my collection, but arranging that after me they will be placed in the Library of Congress (the National Library of America) for others to enjoy. Arranged chronologically, these pictures are almost a biography in themselves. My collection of your books will also, after my day, be placed in the Rare Book Collection of the National Library, with the stipulation that these volumes may never be taken out of the Library, but that anyone may be allowed to see them and read them there. The Library will already have a set for ordinary borrowing purposes, but my inscribed copies will be a special collection which ought to be faithfully preserved.

Of course this is looking rather far ahead, as all during my own lifetime I shall keep the collection, and add to it other items which have an "association" interest — things about Roumania in the days when you were reigning sovereign, English and Russian associations, and the like.

Incidentally, this reminds me to sent you a clipping which may give you a smile if you have not already seen it. It is a picture of King George VI riding in the 1899 an auto once owned by King Edward VII.

Did you ever read the various books of the *Whiteoaks of Jalna* series? Part of it was done into a play which I saw a few evenings ago. Ethel Barrymore appeared as "Old Gram" and a young English actor, named Haggard, did the role of Finch. In this play version Finch is nearly the central character, along with Gram. If you never read the books these names will mean nothing, but very probably you "know" the Whiteoaks family — with all their virtues and vices.

I have had two very pleasant visits with Eleanor Horton recently. She is much more herself this year than before, and has worked out her relations at school so that she feels more independent and less *obliged* to accept dictation from Miss Holton, and so Miss Holton does not presume to take as much advantage as before.

The young lieutenant is returning soon, and I was glad to see that Eleanor is working out this problem — and not allowing Miss Horton to "manage" the matter, by trying to persuade Eleanor not to be here when he arrives. Eleanor told me she had discussed these things with you, and that your understanding made it so easier to face the situation with more assurance.

"Little Eleanor" (my sister) likes Eleanor, and we have several times had pleasant evenings here.

Francis Stuart's new book will soon be published, and I will forward a copy immediately. I hope it is another of his really good ones.

Things have been going very well and happily with me these days. I hope it did not creep into my letters, but somehow during January and February — and even to the first of this month — nothing seemed to go really right for long. It was rather inexplicable, and all the more exasperating because it was *little* things that were continually going wrong. I have been working so steadily and hard during the Winter — are then the erratic, sudden changes in climate, I felt defeated and couldn't seem to get a hold on things. Do you ever experience "periods" or interludes like that? But gradually this month everything seem to straighten out, and now I am feeling very fit and entirely optimistic. I am glad for the good weather lately, and the opportunity to be more out of doors in spare hours. I went riding last Saturday, for the first time this year. If this good weather keeps up, I plan to play some golf later this week — or next.

I am rather amused to find myself enthusiastic about golf, because for a long time, although I played occasionally, I made fun of it as "an old man's game." I still do not like it as well as some other things (I am eager to be swimming regularly again), but I find myself playing golf more and more — and actually played very often last Summer.

About a year ago I sent a few installments which had appeared in a newspapers — the letters between Tzar Nicholas II and His Mother, Empress Marie. The series was suddenly discontinued, but now the complete letters have been published in book form. I would send a copy immediately, but feel sure You must already have seen a copy. If not, however, I will be more than glad to send a copy. Of course, these letters will interest you immensely, so revealing in every way of two contrasting, yet related temperaments.

From your letter I assume that you will be at Merano until after Easter. I hope the Easter Day will be very happy for you, and that some of those you love best will be also at Merano. I will think of you especially on that day.

As this is becoming so long a letter, I will end it here and write soon again.

Meanwhile, every devoted thought and wish,

Ray Baker Harris

Her Majesty, MARIE
Queen of Roumania

XXX

June 28, 1938,

Your Majesty,

The post arrived just as I was leaving the house this morning, and it was a *great* joy to receive your note. Somehow, I had felt sure that at Keisse-Hirsch you would not be disappointed but would discover the right road for a sure return to health, and so I was especially happy to hear that you had found an energetic young doctor in whom you had complete confidence. The recovery will never seem speedy enough, but the important thing is what it will be certain and sure.

I have sent a copy of Beverley's book, *News of England*; and also I shall send a very small book of only 40 pages called *The White Way*, which you can read in less than an hour. It may amuse you. Only a few copies were printed some years ago and I came across it by accident. It is very attractively written — a story of George Washington coming home from the war on Christmas eve to Mount Vernon. You may appreciate it more as you have visited Mount Vernon and know the setting, but there are certain passages which I think will appeal to you as they did to me. As you have probably read elsewhere, Sally Fairfax was an early love of Washington — and one that had to be denied.

When you feel like writing, I will be very interested to hear what you think of Beverley's book. It is stimulating for anyone, but for one who intimately knows and loves England it will have even deeper significance. It is the most vigorous thing he has written since *Cry Havoc!*

This letter is being written in my small study room, high in the attic of the Library of Congress. It is a perfect place for working — all my material conveniently at hand, isolated from any possible interruption. There is only one difficulty — I must keep my back to the window! The view is so breath-taking that unless I turn my book on it I should never get any work done. I can see all over the city of Washington, and it is really a marvellous sight. Yesterday evening I *had* to drop my work for a bit and watch a bad story creeping over the city — brilliant lightning, blackest clouds, patterns where the light of the setting sun still showed through — all sorts of varying patterns... And the wind howling around my attic window like the worst March gale you ever heard. This must be somewhat like one of the tower rooms in Castle Bran!

I have ended my work for this evening and am writing this before going home, so that I can post it on the way.

As I get into this work of writing the final draft for my book, it becomes more and more interesting, and I begrudge all hours during the day when I am busy with my "regular" work; so that, once or twice a week, I take "a day off" and really get a good deal accomplished. Usually I just work a few hours in the evening, get ready to write the next "part" on which I am working, assembling everything which has to do with it, reading, making notes, writing letters to people who can clear up certain points or give me additional information; and then, when the weekend comes, I can write steadily. It is rather a stiff schedule, but I do not mind it. Several mornings a week I play some early golf, and Sunday mornings I take a boat down the river for a few hours or go riding. So I keep feeling fit, and really feel much better in every way than at any time during the past Winter.

This evening as I was going over some of my material I came across these sentences written by the man who was President Harding's Attorney-General. He is a political pirate of the old school, but from our first meeting I was rather attracted to him. He has his points, and has been rather roughly maligned. Anyway, here are the sentences which amused me:

Senator Penrose always told the truth, sometimes more brutally than I thought necessary, but we understood each other. He was a stand-patter. So was I. Still am; always will be; proud of it. A stand-patter knows where he is, where he came from, and most of the time where he is going and what he is doing or trying to do. The Progressive-fly-by-nights were never dependable, were all for themselves, using the political party as a vehicle for their own advancement and personal popularity, excitable, irritable, spectacular, hardly ever standing on both feet at the same time, resting one foot so that they might jump quickly at the first flash in the pan that would give them publicity and impress the public that the world rested on their shoulders...

Well, that is enough to quote; and perhaps to your majesty it may not seem as apposite an observation as it seems to me. On the other hand, I suppose politicians the world over, conservative and "progressive" ones, are much the same. I have a good deal of sympathy with the viewpoint he expressed, although at the same time I am exasperated by reactionary attitudes; but I have come across a number of these so-called "progressive" politicians in this country and also had the impression that they were extremely self-centered, selfish, playing to the crowd and not very reliable.

There is a good bit of political history which necessarily comes into the biography of any President; but, on the personal side, I have become very much interested in doing a good portrait of Mrs. Harding in my book. She was of course a great influence in her husband's life, and their relation to each other is an interesting job for the biographer. She had a character and personality full of contradictions. She could be a Tartar and again could be *very* feminine; she could be blunt and tactless, and again could be full of thoughtful consideration and kindness; she could be shrewd and practical, and also amazingly superstitious. She was never in really good health and lived on nerves and on her adoration for her husband. On his part he had the greatest patience with her, and had respect for her judgment; but he could also firmly turn her down. He never embarrassed her when he might differ with her before others, but had a tactful way of making it *seem* as though he were deferring to her. That spontaneous kindness of heart made it easy for Harding to be always gracious and tactful, and it was also the one weakness in an otherwise strong character; but I do not feel that was to *his* discredit — the shame is on those who value so little and betrayed the friendship he gave them.

Of course, these are sentiments I do not express in my book. I am telling the story, and each reader will form his own judgments and conclusions according to their own charity and perception. I am not writing "a defense," I am writing the truth as I have found it — as if no other books had been written and there were no need for "defense". I do not argue with anyone, I only tell the story — and will also show at the end of the book the evidence for all my statements of fact.

It amazes me to consider how, (not only with Harding but with others as well) genuinely fine and honorable people can have their reputation torn to shreds by those who are neither fine nor honorable; and now the general public accepts without question all the "scandal" that it related (no matter by whom), but demands the most incontrovertible proofs before it will believe anything creditable about public figures who have been maligned. It is one of the unlovely aspects of life which has its explanation, I suppose, deep down in human nature and rooted in the dim and far distant past.

I have had the feeling sometimes that the genuinely good things in this world inevitably attract a counter-force of evil, and that those who are genuinely good *must* sooner or later experience this. It seems to me a matter of spirit more than of humans — as though good and evil forces merely *used* people in this warfare. When I speak of genuinely good people, I do not use the phrase in any narrow or conventional sense. In fact, I think the most moral-living deacon *can* have the very least in real goodness of spirit.

But how did I get on to this endless and vague subject?

Two friends of mine are bound for Guatamala for a Summer holiday. To me, Guatamala seems the most profoundly uninteresting place in the world, but my friends are full of enthusiasm and eager to be leaving. The equatorial countries, paradoxically enough, leave me quite cold. I would like to go again for a visit to Manila, where I was born; but mostly I want to visit in England, and on the Continent in Germany, Austria, Delmatia — and, of course, one day on the shores of the Black Sea. Also, lately, I have had an increasing interest in the Scandinavian countries, since a friend of mine, who is with one of the large steamship lines, went to live in Stockholm. He has been traveling around both in Norway and Sweden sending me the most glowing accounts and some amazingly beautiful pictures which give me an entirely new conception of that part of the world. I like also what I have heard of the modern progressiveness of the Scandinavian countries.

Francis Stuart's book has finally arrived. I have not quite finished it, but it is another disappointment. Much of his unusual touch is in it, but the people in this story are by no means as attractive or as worth writing about as the people in *The White Hare* — quite the contrary! All the same, I think I will send you a copy of this book — and if, when you have begun it, it seems too disappointing you can put it aside.

Have you ever read any books by Graham Greene, the English author? I rather liked his first book, some years ago, called *The Man Within* — and so for some time I followed his later books. But he seems to be obsessed by the world's misfits, and in no recent book has he presented even *one* admirable or attractive figure.

I am not drawing a parallel with Francis Stuart, because I have enjoyed most of Stuart's books — and have been disappointed in very few of them.

Will you be returning to Roumania after you leave Dresden, or perhaps visit at Sonnberg or Belgrade? I imagine you are eager to be again at Balcic and at Bran.

The time is growing late, and this letter endless — so I had better bring it to an end be on my way home.

I will write again; and meanwhile — my every devoted thought and wish,

Ray Baker Harris

Her Majesty, MARIE
Queen of Roumania

XXXI

July 15, 1938

Your Majesty,

Just today in the New York papers there is a news dispatch that your majesty has so much recovered at Dresden that you are leaving immediately for Sinaia. I am greatly delighted, and shall be even more pleased when you can go later this year to enjoy the satisfactions at Bran and Balcic.

I wrote to you as soon as I received your note earlier this month, and the very next day I received a more than kind letter from Princess Ileana. She gave me the happy news that you had been responding wonderfully to the treatments at Dresden, feeling more and more like your old self again. Your complete and entire recovery can come none too soon for all of us who have been so distressed by the prolonged burden upon all your patience and courage.

Summer has really arrived here, and the temperatures go higher and higher each day. I have had to slacken my stiff writing schedule and go swimming a little oftener! And tomorrow, Saturday, I am taking a boat down the river for all of the afternoon.

I seem to be yielding to temptation right and left, because also I have tentatively accepted an invitation for several days with my friends in New England at the end of the month. If only you could see their hilltop place... it is perfect, and the days are so easy and friendly and agreeable there!

Have you read about the round-the-world fliers who left New York only four days ago, and are now back there! Hughes and his three companions are the heroes of the day and being wildly feted everywhere. One hopes that Hughes will not suffer from *too-much* acclaim, as Lindbergh did, and have no privacy or life of his own any more. He told of one experience after leaving Moscow. It seems they were saved only because they were flying in the day time and in good weather. Certain Siberian mountains which on their charts were indicated as only 5,000 feet high loomed up suddenly ahead of them almost 9,000 feet. If they had been "flying blindly" or at night, by instruments, they surely would have crashed into the peaks; but as it was they were able to see them ahead and to "climb" over them. It was certainly a thrilling flight.

Lately I received and finished reading the new Francis Stuart book, and am uncertain whether to send it to you or not. Definitely it is not up to his other books. The story's imperfections are somewhat glaring, and the people are neither appealing nor attractive. One feels only pity and some distress for "Julie", who comes to England from South Africa as a girl of 13 with her older sister. Julie has been a sort of invalid, and is being brought to England for an operation by a famous brain surgeon. On the boat they meet a young Jew named Goldberg. To everybody Goldberg is cheap, unscrupulous, ambitious — yet Julie, who has lived a life so much apart, has no conventional standards by which to judge him. He has a vital force, and to this she responds. When later he is arrested and sent to jail (most justly!) for arson, Julie is only rebellious. Much of this, concerning their relationship, is sordid and unattractive. When he is in jail, Julie becomes friendly with an Irish boy and goes with him to his home in Ireland; but the good, simple life there does not attract her sufficiently to prevent her ultimate return to Goldberg in the end.

Francis Stuart's prose is still the same in quality. It has that force which makes one care about, and remember what he says; but this is a book one does not particularly want to remember. One is rather fascinated by Julie's strange and unique character, but does not enjoy seeing her life turn out as it does. And, as I say, many of the passages are decidedly sordid. The prose is the same, but this time Francis Stuart is looking at people who are by no means so unusual and attractive as those who were in *The White Hare*.

If you think you would be interested to read it nevertheless, I will gladly post a copy to you.

This reminds me to say that I posted yesterday a rather beautiful enlargement of the photograph of de Laszlo's portrait — the one for the Roumanian State Bank. It is such a special picture. I wonder if your majesty would be willing to inscribe it to be with my name and a few words, on the mounting? I would deeply appreciate your kindness, and be very proud to possess it. I packed it heavily, and hope it reaches you safely and undamaged. It is really a very "royal" portrait. What are the colors in the original?

Did Beverley Nichols' book interest you? Parts of it seemed disconnected to me, but there was apparently much truth in his observations. I was much in agreement with many of his observations — for example, that "the modern intellectual does not debate, he denounces." We see so much of that in this country now. Little legitimate argument, and many tirades! I liked his description of the *Daily Worker* newspaper which, he said, would ignore the event if a "working man" should run over a child accidently with his car, but would make many headlines about it if "a gentleman" did the same thing — and the impression would be conveyed that he did it on purpose!

I suppose this is the first of a number of books which will be written by those who are dissatisfied with conditions in modern England. I understand that Winston Churchill has already written a most controversial book.

We also read a good bit of Lloyd George's criticism of the British Government's course, but I cannot work up much enthusiasm for this particular former Prim Minister. I have been prejudiced against him ever since I read of his actions in connection with the proposed escape of the Tzar and his family from Russia, which was blocked by Lloyd George. It was a disgraceful business, and purely politics — and showed him as lacking the courage to stand up against a difficult situation, sacrificing lives in order to make things easier for himself. It is harsh judgment, but from the facts — which he has never denied in any of his writings — it is all too plain.

I am enclosing a little clipping about the Duchess of Kent on Princess Mary which may amuse you, if you have not already seen it.

There is much interest in the coming visit of the King and Queen of France. Everyone hopes they will have a safe journey, and certainly it seems that every effort is being made to receive them under every precaution.

I was very amused when talking with a small boy about 10 years old, at the Wardman Pack swimming pool the other day. His mother is Spanish and his father is Irish, and he has certainly an attractive combination of qualities. His name is Patrick Moran and his father is a distinguished and interesting man... But what I started to say was that we got to talking as we sat by the side of the pool, and he was telling me about living for several years in Mexico City. He mentioned some of the subjects he had in school there, and I was surprised they taught such advanced subjects in the early grades. He promptly explained that in Mexico they taught all the hard subjects while the boys were young, because when they grew older they became two dumb to learn anything...!" I thought this was a unique explanation, but have learned that it is not entirely an exaggeration!

When this reaches Your Majesty I hope you will be feeling wonderfully well, and more and more "on your own."

With every devoted thought and wish,

Ray Baker Harris

Her Majesty, MARIE
Queen of Roumania

Index of Names and Places

Alexander I, King of Yugoslavia "Sandro" (1888-1934) — married Mignon (Mărioara), Princess of Romania. Marie's son-in-law: 104, 116, 192.

Alexandra, Czarina of Russia, "Alix" (1872-1918) — born Princess of Hesse. Married Nicholas II, Czar of Russia. Marie's first cousin: 38, 39, 102.

Alfred, Prince of England, "Affie" (1844-1900) — The Duke of Edinburgh, later Duke of Coburg-Gotha. Second son of Queen Victoria and Prince Albert. Married Marie Alexandrovna, Grand Duchess of Russia. Marie's father: 22, 30.

Averescu Alexandru (1859-1938) — Romanian politician and marshal, leader of the People's League, founded in 1918 (People's Party, beginning in 1920). Military studies in Italy and Germany. War Minister in 1907, Chief of the General Staff, Commander of the Second Army Corps in the First World War, Prime Minister in 1918, 1920-1921 and 1926-1927, Crown Councillor in 1938: 87.

Angelescu Constantin (1869-1948) — Romanian politician, doctor in medical sciences, professor, academician, Ph.D. in Paris (1897). Minister of Public Works in 1914 and of Education and Religion. Prime Minister (1933-1934), Crown Councillor in 1938: 35, 38, 70, 78.

Anderson Henry — Lt. Colonel from the American Red Cross, the Commission for the Balkans: 32, 87.

Augusta, Kaiserin of Germany, "Donna" (1858-1921) — born Princess of Schleswig-Holstein. Married Wilhelm II, Kaiser of Germany. Marie's cousin: 202, 203.

Balcic — Queen Marie's private residence, built between 1925-1926; it included 63 estates bought by the Queen herself. Although according to Marie's will the property was left to Ileana, Balcic came to be owned by Carol II: 94-96, 98, 103, 117, 125, 126, 132, 133, 137, 138, 142, 148, 151, 153, 155, 161, 162, 178, 203, 225, 241, 248, 250, 253, 254, 257, 275.

Boyle Joseph Whiteside, "Joe" (1867-1923) — married Mildred Raynor (1), Elma Humphries (2), gold prospector in the Klondike and Colonel in the First World War in Russia and Romania. King Ferdinand conferred him the Grand Cross of the Order of Romania: 87, 88, 124.

Bran — A castle, private property of Queen Marie. The town hall of Braşov gave it to the Queen in 1920. It is divided in two wings and has 57 rooms. According to Marie's will, the castle went to Princess Ileana. In 1948 it was taken over by the Ministry of Art and Information (see *Monitorul Oficial*, IB, #140, 19 June 1948). Today it is a museum. In 1990 it was visited by mother Alexandra (Princess Ileana): 125, 133, 148, 158, 169, 181, 190, 196, 203, 209, 217, 225, 241, 243, 248.

Brătianu Ion I.C. (1864-1927) — Romanian politician, president of the National Liberal Party, minister and Prime Minister several times. He took part in the major political events during the reign of Ferdinand I: Romania's entry into the First World War, the land reform, the universal vote, the new constitution in 1923: 29, 35, 51.

Minister of Justice, of Public Works, Foreign Minister, of Internal Affairs, and of Finance. During the First World War he was a supporter of the Triple Alliance. As Prime Minister, he negotiated peace with Germany in 1918, which brought about misfortunes and the loss of political prestige: 26, 46.

Marie, Queen of Romania (1875-1938) — born Princess of Edinburgh. Eldest daughter of the Duke and Duchess of Edinburgh. Married Ferdinand, King of Romania: passim.

Mignon (Marie or Mărioara), Queen of Yugoslavia (1900-1961) — born Princess of Romania. Married Alexander, King of Yugoslavia. Marie's daughter: 25, 85, 92, 104-106, 108, 116, 125, 126, 132, 191.

Mary, Queen of England (1867-1953) — born Victoria Mary, Princess of Teck. Married George V, King of England. Marie's cousin: 97, 110, 118, 126, 127, 130, 135, 188, 211, 237, 239, 243, 277.

Mihai, King of Romania between 1927-1930 and 1940-1947 (1921-) — married Anne, Princess of Bourbon-Parma. Queen Marie's grandson: 28, 29, 63, 108, 117, 135, 140, 225, 257, 259.

Nicholas II, Czar of Russia "Nicky" (1868-1918) — married Alexandra, Princess of Hesse. Queen Marie's cousin: 24, 38, 39, 42, 68, 102, 145, 148, 270.

Nicolae, Prince of Romania, "Nicky" (1903-1977) — married Ioana Doletti (1), Theresa Figueira de Mello (2). Marie's second son. He was regent between 1927-1930, and in 1937 he was forced by King Carol II to renounce his royal prerogatives: 25, 92, 131.

Rădescu Nicolae (1876-1953) — Romanian politician, Colonel, later General, he opposed the authoritarian personal regime of Carol II and the Romanian-German alliance. Prime